Ideology and Spatial Voting in American Elections

Ideology and Spatial Voting in American Elections addresses two core issues related to the foundations of democratic governance: how the political views of Americans are structured and how citizens' voting decisions relate to their ideological proximity to the candidates in a given election. Focusing on testing the assumptions and implications of spatial voting, this book connects the theory with empirical analysis of voter preferences and behavior, showing that Americans cast their ballots largely in accordance with spatial voting theory. By carefully deriving the empirical implications of spatial voting theory and through the use of novel survey techniques and statistical methods, Stephen A. Jessee's research shows that voters possess meaningful ideologies that structure their policy beliefs, and powerfully affect their voting decision moderated by partisanship and differing levels of political information. Jessee finds that while voters with lower levels of political information are more influenced by partisanship, independents and better-informed partisans are able to form reasonably accurate perceptions of candidates' ideologies. His findings should reaffirm citizens' faith in the broad functioning of democratic elections.

Stephen A. Jessee is Assistant Professor of Government at the University of Texas at Austin.

T0384711

Ideology and Spatial Voting in American Elections

STEPHEN A. JESSEE

University of Texas at Austin

CAMBRIDGE
UNIVERSITY PRESS

CAMBRIDGE UNIVERSITY PRESS
Cambridge, New York, Melbourne, Madrid, Cape Town,
Singapore, São Paulo, Delhi, Mexico City

Cambridge University Press
32 Avenue of the Americas, New York, NY 10013-2473, USA

www.cambridge.org
Information on this title: www.cambridge.org/9781107638389

© Stephen A. Jessee 2012

First published 2012

Printed in the United States of America

A catalog record for this publication is available from the British Library.

Library of Congress Cataloging in Publication Data

Jessee, Stephen A., 1980–
Ideology and spatial voting in American elections / Stephen A. Jessee.
    p. cm.
Includes bibliographical references and index.
ISBN 978-1-107-02570-7 (hardback)
1. Voting – United States.   2. Ideology – United States.   I. Title.
JK1967.J43   2012
324.973–dc23   2012010126

ISBN 978-1-107-02570-7 Hardback
ISBN 978-1-107-63838-9 Paperback

Contents

List of Figures

List of Tables

Preface

This book is about the policy views of ordinary Americans and how these views relate to the choices they make in elections. More fundamentally, it is about how well the political behavior of voters can be described by a simple formalized theory called spatial voting.

Early on in my political science training, I was struck by what I viewed as a large disconnect in the way political scientists thought about voters. On the one hand, many theories dealing with the behavior of candidates, members of Congress, or others abstracted away voter behavior, either explicitly or implicitly, as conforming to some simple decision-making rule. Most commonly, it was assumed or implied that voters cast their ballots for the candidate who was closest to them in some ideological space. By contrast, the empirical political behavior literature spent much of its time chronicling the idiosyncrasies and overall lack of political competence among the vast majority of voters, often concluding that the electorate was incapable of making reasoned choices based on ideological concerns. The stark contrast between these two views struck me as fundamentally problematic. Either most of mainstream political behavior was ignoring a simple, direct, and elegant explanation of voting or much of the existing theory about the behavior of candidates and elected officials rested on unsound foundations.

My initial efforts to investigate these ideas came up against a significant stumbling block. Testing spatial theories of voting would require knowing the ideological positions of voters and candidates for office on the same ideological scale. But to the extent that useful measures of voter ideology and candidate positions existed, they were generally not comparable in any meaningful way. My discovery of a solution to this problem can be traced back to a raffle I won during a reception at the annual meeting of the Midwest Political Science Association years ago. The victory entitled me to a conduct a free survey of 1,000 respondents with the Internet survey company Polimetrix (now YouGov). The company was founded and run by Douglas Rivers, who had taught me introductory statistics and for whom I had later served as a teaching assistant. After talking with Doug about how exactly I would use my winnings, I came to realize that we had both been thinking about similar issues in the measurement of ideology. Doug generously offered to work together on a survey to investigate some of the questions we had both been asking, and the survey that resulted from this collaboration now serves as the first half of the data analyzed in this book.

Because of this and because of the huge impact he has had on my thinking about political science, statistics, and other areas, Doug deserves special thanks not only for his influence on this project, but for making it possible in the first place. Opportunities to learn from Doug in classes, in informal discussions, and through research collaborations have been some of the most valuable experiences of my academic career. Many other people also had a strong influence both on this project and on my scholarly development during my graduate training at Stanford University. Simon Jackman introduced me to many of the techniques I have applied to this project including latent traits modeling and Bayesian statistics and has offered useful advice on research and political science in general. Paul Sniderman also offered an important perspective on my work and has given me a great deal of valuable advice on being a scholar. Dave Brady and John Ferejohn, both individually and through the "pizza and politics" seminar series they ran, gave me some of my first introductions into what it meant to make the transition from reading political science to doing political science. Both Keith Krehbiel and Ken Shotts in the Graduate School of Business were instrumental in shaping my thinking about theory and theory testing in political science through their teaching, and both have given very helpful comments on this project.

I also benefited greatly from having such excellent graduate school colleagues. Talking with and learning from these people was one of the most valuable parts of my graduate education. Thanks go to Robert Anderson, John Bullock, Alex Kuo, Matt Levendusky, Neil Malhotra, Laura Miller, Alex Tahk, and many others.

Many individual scholars offered valuable feedback on earlier drafts of the book or on related projects. These include Paul Goren, Tim Groseclose, Jeff Lewis, Boris Shor, Walt Stone, Lynn Vavreck, and John Zaller.

Very special thanks go to Jim Adams, who has been unbelievably helpful and generous from the time when I started being put on conference panels with him as a graduate student through the completion of this project. This book is surely much better because of his comments and ideas (to say nothing of the foundational work he has done on testing theories of voting that has strongly influenced my thinking in this area). I also thank audiences at UC-Davis, UCLA, The University of North Texas, and Southern Methodist University for insightful comments.

My colleagues at the University of Texas have been tremendously helpful in nurturing my development as a scholar. Gary Freeman has been the best department chair anyone could ask for and has been extremely supportive of junior faculty, myself included. I have also received great feedback on both my research and on the book publishing process from Bethany Albertson, Zoltan Barany, Terry Chapman, Tse-min Lin, Eric McDaniel, Patrick McDonald, Scott Moser, Tasha Philpot, James Scott, Daron Shaw, Sean Theriault, Nick Valentino, and Kurt Weyland. I benefited greatly from receiving a College Research Fellowship during which I wrote much of the first draft of this book. I also received assistance from the College of Liberal Arts through a Special Funding Request that was used to pay for the second survey analyzed in this book and from a University of Texas at Austin Subvention Grant awarded by President William C. Powers, Jr., which provided support for the publication of this book. I also thank my editor Robert Dreesen for being amazingly helpful, thorough, and fast.

Finally, I thank my family for being incredibly supportive throughout my life including during my education and my wife Nalinda for always being there and for putting up with the many complications that graduate training, the academic job market, and the process of writing a book can bring about.

1

Introduction

The central feature of democracy is that the will of the people determines the policies enacted by the government. In representative democracies such as the United States, citizens influence the government primarily through voting in elections. The success of democratic governance, therefore, rests in large part on the ability of citizens to select leaders who will act in accordance with their policy preferences. In the end, a government lives up to this democratic ideal (or does not) through the enactment of specific policies. How, then, do citizens' votes relate to their preferences over government policy outputs? What intervening factors either assist or interfere with voters' selection of candidates who espouse views closest to their own? Understanding the relationship between citizens' policy views and their voting behavior is central to the evaluation of elections and of democratic governance more generally.

This book studies the opinions of ordinary citizens on specific policies and the relationships between those policy views and people's vote choices in presidential elections. Specifically, it focuses on testing the empirical implications of spatial theories of voting, which, in their simplest form, assume that each citizen's policy views can be represented by a location on some liberal–conservative policy spectrum, with each candidate in a given election each taking a position on this same dimension. Each voter then casts his or her ballot for the candidate whose position is closest to the voter's own ideological location.

The allure of such an approach is that it provides a model of decision making that is extremely simple and easy to work with: voters' choices are dictated solely by their ideological proximity to candidate positions. Furthermore, it is relatively straightforward to derive analytical results about things such as the optimal positions that office-seeking candidates should take. As a consequence, spatial representations of elections and politics more generally have become ubiquitous in the modern political science literature. The simple spatial voting framework has spawned a multitude of theories, arguments, and more elaborate models (statistical as well as formal) to describe and account for voting behavior not only in elections but also within institutions such as Congress and the courts.

Despite the large impact that spatial theory has had across the discipline, however, there remains a strong, perhaps even pervasive, sentiment that ordinary voters do not possess the tools necessary to engage in anything resembling spatial voting. Political science therefore finds itself in a situation in which a huge body of theory and knowledge in the field is based, whether explicitly or implicitly, on some form of spatial voting theory – a theory of which many political scientists are fundamentally skeptical. This unfortunate situation calls out for some measure of resolution. Does spatial voting theory provide a reasonable account of the decision making of ordinary voters? Or does a significant portion of political science theory need to be revised or even abandoned because of the implausibility of its basic foundations?

The goal of this book is to resolve this tension by directly testing the observable implications of spatial voting theory. I accomplish this goal through a combination of novel survey design and statistical applications, which allows for the most direct estimates to date of the ideological positions of ordinary voters relative to the positions taken by candidates in presidential elections. The findings are, for the most part, encouraging. On average, the actual behavior of voters conforms quite closely to the predictions of spatial voting theory – much better, in fact, than most of the extant political behavior literature would seem to suggest. On closer examination, however, it becomes apparent that the basic spatial model can provide a more accurate account of voter behavior when modified to allow for the effects of other factors. Specifically, both party identification and political information exert strong moderating forces on voters' use of spatial decision making. These results suggest that spatial voting theory, particularly when modified to account for partisan and informational differences, provides a very accurate depiction of the behavior of voters in American elections. Perhaps more importantly, the results suggest a way in which the fundamental tension between some of the most prominent approaches to the study of voting can be reconciled or, at the least, compared in terms of their ability to explain the choices of voters in recent presidential elections.

Unlike most other work in this area, this book focuses on understanding the nature of ideology in the American public and the relationship between voters' ideological positions and their choices in elections. While much of the existing work on spatial voting deals with the theoretical consequences of assuming spatial decision making by voters, this book is centrally concerned with testing the microfoundations of these theories. Accordingly, I focus on testing, rather than assuming individual-level models of spatial voting, and on the policy views and vote choices of ordinary citizens rather than on the predicted behavior of strategic political parties or candidates for office. The work presented in this book also represents a key advance in the measurement of citizen ideology and of the comparison of the ideological positions taken by voters and candidates. While much of the existing work relies on either rough proxies for ideology or strong assumptions about the nature of people's perceptions or preferences (often going so far as to assume some some variant of spatial voting or preferences in order to generate these estimates), the methods employed here produce direct estimates of the ideological positions of voters and candidates on the same scale without the need for heroic assumptions.

The Political Behavior Tradition

In order to gain a full perspective on spatial voting theory, it is important to place it in the context of the field of voting behavior more broadly. Traditional approaches to the study of voting generally fall into what has been termed the *political behavior* research tradition.[1] This approach primarily emphasizes an attitude-driven model in which many factors work together to determine which candidate a citizen supports. The relevance of a given factor within the behavioral tradition is usually established by showing that it has a strong relationship with vote choice, either in terms of the magnitude of an effect or the amount of variance explained. The political behavior tradition has largely been characterized by different "schools" of study, each emphasizing the importance and centrality of one type of variable in affecting the political views and actions of ordinary citizens.

---

[1] The term "political behavior" also is used to refer to the study of the opinions and political actions of ordinary citizens. As such, it could be argued that spatial voting falls within the political behavior subfield. I use the term here, however, to refer to more traditional approaches to the study of public opinion, voting, and other topics.

The sociological approach, often referred to as the Columbia school of political behavior research, studies political actors primarily in terms of their social group memberships. Exemplified by Berelson, Lazarsfeld, and McPhee's (1954) classic study of voters in Elmira, New York, during the 1948 presidential campaign, this approach emphasizes how social groupings, such as race, religion, or union membership, affect people's political beliefs and decisions (see also Lazarsfeld et al. 1944). According to this view of politics, people typically associate with others who tend to be from similar economic, racial, and religious groups as themselves. As a consequence of this, the Columbia school argues that political views are strongly related to one's sociological characteristics.

Reaching prominence shortly after the sociological approach, the so-called Michigan school is arguably the best-known school of thought within political behavior. This approach emphasizes party identification as an "affective orientation" that powerfully shapes people's political beliefs and perceptions. Also sometimes called the "psychological approach," this school of thought is often identified with the classic text *The American Voter* (Campbell et al. 1960). According to this school, party identification is a highly stable attitude that is developed through socialization, most strongly parental socialization. It is argued that these partisan loyalties profoundly affect how people perceive political stimuli and interact with the political world. This "affective orientation" toward the major political parties provides the primary basis by which voters decide how to cast their ballots. A central argument of many works in the Michigan school is that the vast majority of voters do not hold any sort of meaningful ideology, but instead have their political actions guided primarily by partisanship.

By contrast, theories of issue voting or policy voting, broadly construed, emphasize that the specific policy views held by citizens have an important impact on their vote choices. More forcefully, issue voting often argues that people's policy views are the main factor influencing their votes. Issue voting generally is confirmed by showing that voters' policy positions have some strong relationship with vote choice, in terms of either the magnitude of an effect or the amount of variance explained, and often after controlling for other factors such as partisanship, income, or other demographics.

Under the general umbrella of issue voting fall several different lines of argument, each posing a different mechanism for how issues affect voting. Single-issue voting (e.g., Levitin and Miller 1979; Hurley and Hill 1980; Conover et al. 1982; Erikson et al. 1993) argues that voters, or at least some class of voters, decide which candidate to vote for based only on one particular issue. References to this sort of behavior are often found in journalistic accounts of elections and campaigns. For example, it is often said that "gun rights voters" or "pro-life voters" were key to a certain candidate's victory, implying that there exist groups of voters whose choices were caused solely, or at least predominantly, by the candidates' positions on one of these individual issues. Ideological voting, which can be seen as a special case of issue voting, states that people have policy-based political ideologies that affect vote choices . Ideological voting thus argues not only that voters have their choices shaped by policy views, but that these policy views are held together by a meaningful ideological structure rather than being a collection of separate, unrelated beliefs.

The political behavior tradition, as I have defined it here, has arguably served as the dominant paradigm for studying voting in elections for the better part of the past century.[2] While this general approach has clearly generated a wealth of important findings, its basic template often seems to be to put forth some variable X as a (perhaps *the*) central determinant of vote choice and to support this assertion by demonstrating a relationship between X and voter behavior in some regression model. To be fair, many of the works in the political behavior tradition, including some of the flag-ship works discussed previously, do much more than demonstrate a basic relationship between some variable and vote choice. Furthermore, several scholars specify and test general theoretical models of various political behaviors (see, e.g., Fiorina 1981; Zaller 1992; Lupia and McCubbins 1998). Within the broader political behavior tradition, however, there remains some sense of skepticism of most attempts to understand vote choice or other political actions with simple, clear, formalized theory.

Spatial Voting Theory

Spatial voting theory represents arguably the most direct and concise framework through which to study the choices made by voters in elections. Although the basic concepts behind spatial voting theory were first articulated by Hotelling (1929), the theory was most prominently

---

[2] This brief review of political behavior literature clearly omits many important works. The central objective of this discussion, however, has been to illustrate the basic approach in this tradition rather than to catalog the many important works falling under this broad umbrella. Accordingly, the works included have been chosen both for their centrality to the political behavior literature and for their relevance to later questions addressed in this book.

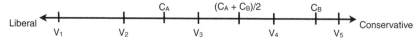

FIGURE 1.1. Simple spatial voting example

expanded on in the context of two-party elections by Downs (1957) and in more general theoretical terms by Enelow and Hinich (1984).[3] Spatial voting theory posits that the policy views of voters can be represented as points in some ideological space, most commonly a single liberal–conservative spectrum, with candidates also taking positions in this same space. The key assumption of spatial voting, or proximity voting, as it is sometimes called, is that voters will cast their ballots for the candidate whose position is closest to the voter's own ideological location, often called the voter's *ideal point* because it is the location to which the voter would ideally like policy to be moved. Spatial voting therefore conceptualizes voter decision making as solely the result of the voter's ideological proximity to the positions of the candidates in a given election.

As a simple example, consider a hypothetical election with five voters, having positions V_1, V_2, V_3, V_4, and V_5, respectively, each deciding between two candidates: candidate A and candidate B, who take positions at C_A and C_B, respectively. If the voters and candidates are located on a liberal–conservative spectrum as shown in Figure 1.1, we can examine how each voter would cast his or her ballot under simple spatial voting. If each voter were to choose the candidate closest to his or her own ideal point, we could simply measure the distance from each voter to each of the candidates to determine the decision of each voter. An even easier solution is to simply divide the voters at the midpoint between the two candidates' positions, labeled $(C_A + C_B)/2$. All voters to the left of this point will be closer to candidate A than to candidate B and hence will choose A. Conversely, all voters to the right of this midpoint will cast their ballots for candidate B.

The simplicity of the spatial approach has served as both a tremendous advantage and a fundamental criticism of the theory. Because the spatial voting model is extremely simple to work with, its basic assumptions have been used in countless other theories and arguments to provide assumptions about the behavior of voters. Furthermore, because spatial voting leads to direct predictions about voter behavior, it is easy to derive useful results and produce strong, testable hypotheses. This stands in

---

[3] See also Black (1948) for an application to voting in committees and legislatures.

contrast to the political behavior tradition, in which theories are often less precisely and formally stated and therefore result in weaker hypotheses (or sometimes few testable hypotheses at all).

The simplicity of the spatial theory of voting, however, also has led to many of the strongest criticisms of the approach. Objections to the basic spatial voting framework have generally taken two main forms. First, scholars have questioned the basic premises of the theory. A common objection is that most voters do not hold "real" ideologies, but at best possess some haphazard, unstructured set of separate policy beliefs. According to this view, representing voter ideologies spatially is fundamentally misguided. Even if voters did hold spatial ideologies, it is often argued, the task of estimating the ideological positions of the candidates in an election and comparing the distance between each of these candidates and the voter's own position is far beyond the attention span, if not the ability, of the vast majority of voters.

This line of objections was most famously articulated by Converse (1964), but still has broad support in the field today. According to this general strain of argument, most voters are not equipped with the basic tools necessary for engaging in spatial reasoning; hence, the use of any sort of spatial voting is well beyond their capacity:

[L]arge portions of an electorate do not have meaningful beliefs even on the issues that have formed the basis for intense political controversy among elites for substantial periods of time. Where any single dimension is concerned, very substantial portions of the public simply do not belong on the dimension at all. (245)

With regard to the ability of voters to understand the electoral landscape, others, including Kinder and Sears (1985), have offered similarly pessimistic opinions:

Often thought of as essential to [the democratic] process is an electorate capable of distinguishing the package of policies promoted by one candidate from the package promoted by competitors. In this respect (as in others), the public often seems confused and ill-informed. (663)

If these accounts were accurate – if the general public was largely devoid of any meaningful form of ideology and could not differentiate the positions taken by the various candidates or parties in elections – the basic assumptions of spatial voting theory would seem to be untenable.

The second type of objection to spatial voting theory deals with what might be termed second-level implications of the theory. One of the most well-known results to stem from the spatial voting model is the so-called median voter theorem (Hotelling 1929; Black 1948; Downs 1957). This result states that if voters act according to the simple spatial model described previously, having ideologies on a single dimension and choosing the candidate whose position is closest to their own, then strategic candidates in a two-candidate majority-rule election will have an incentive to converge to the position of the median voter. In fact, a candidate who takes the same position as the median voter can never be defeated.

To see why the median voter theorem holds, imagine that one candidate positions him- or herself at the median voter's ideal point. The second candidate's position must fall either (i) to the left of the median, (ii) to the right of the median, or (iii) at the median. If the second candidate takes a position to the left of the median voter, then the median and all voters to his or her right (and possibly some voters between the median and the second candidate's position) will clearly be closer to the first candidate and hence will cast their ballots for him or her. Therefore, because these voters necessarily constitute a majority by the definition of a median, the first candidate will win the election. Similarly, if the second candidate positions him- or herself to the right of the median voter, the median and all voters to his or her left will vote for the first candidate, giving him a majority. The best the second candidate can do in this situation, in fact, is to set his position at the median, taking the same position as the first candidate and thus tying him.[4] Furthermore, imagine that the first candidate takes a position different from that of the median voter. The second candidate then can simply position himself anywhere between the first candidate and the median and will be guaranteed to win the election. This is because he will be closer to the median and hence win the votes of at least the median and all voters on the opposite side of the median from the first candidate. Therefore, any candidate positioned at the median voter's location cannot be defeated, and any candidate who does not position himself at the median voter's ideal point can be beaten by a strategic opponent.

The median voter theorem is therefore often seen as predicting that all candidates should move directly to the position of the median voter. It is sometimes further argued that candidate convergence to the position

---

[4] There are several possible assumptions for how a voter, the median voter in this case, should cast his or her ballot if two candidates are the same exact distance from the voter's ideal point. The most common of these is that the voter will "flip a coin," having an equal chance of voting for either candidate. Therefore, the two candidates will not necessarily tie, but would have the same probability of winning in this situation.

of the median voter is an implication of spatial voting theory, presumably due to the fact that the median voter theorem employs the basic assumptions of spatial voting. Critics of the spatial model, or of the rational choice approach to the study of politics more generally, often point to the divergent positions taken by candidates in real-world elections as evidence that the spatial model is fundamentally flawed (see Green and Shapiro 1994 for a particularly prominent example). According to these arguments, the tendency of Republican candidates to be more conservative than Democratic candidates in American elections constitutes strong evidence against the spatial model of voting.

Candidate convergence, however, is not a direct implication of the spatial model's assumptions about voter behavior, but rather results from the addition of several further assumptions. The median voter theorem assumes not only that voters will choose the candidate closest to them, which also is an assumption of basic spatial voting models, but also that candidates are motivated solely by winning elections, that elections consist only of a one-stage contest, that all citizens turn out to vote, and that there are only two candidates in an election, among other relatively strong assumptions.[5] Therefore, any observed violation of the predictions of the median voter theorem in actual elections does not, on its own, disprove the spatial model's assumptions about voter behavior. Instead, such findings simply demonstrate that the exact situation described by the assumptions of the median voter theorem are not met in actual elections. In other words, if the median voter theorem's predictions of candidate convergence are violated in actual elections, this merely implies that at least one of the assumptions on which the median voter theorem is based must be false. This, however, is trivially true given, for example, that candidates must generally go through a two-stage (primary and general) election process to win office and that turnout rates typically fall far below 100 percent of registered voters.

All of these things call out for a more direct examination of the implications of spatial voting theory, most importantly of the prediction that voters cast their ballots for the candidate who is ideologically closest to their own position. These direct tests have not been conducted in large part because of the difficulty of obtaining the necessary measurements of voter ideology and candidate positions on the same scale. In the absence of such estimates, scholars have been forced to rely on indirect tests, leaving the validity of the fundamental assumptions made by the spatial

---

[5] See Grofman (2004) for a discussion of candidate convergence under spatial voting theory.

model about voter behavior an open question. More rigorous and direct examinations of these assumptions are necessary in order to accurately assess the plausibility of the spatial voting model.

Theory, Rigor, and Parsimony in the Study of Politics

Spatial voting theory, at least in its simplest form, is built completely upon a very small number of assumptions. This can be both a blessing and a curse. The benefits of a parsimonious theory are that it is generally easy to understand, simple to work with, and more likely to yield broad and important results. The main drawback of such simple theories is that they often make strong, sometimes unrealistic or even implausible assumptions. To the extent that the assumptions of a theory are unreasonable, the results yielded by the theory may be less believable and ultimately less useful for understanding the real-world processes under study.

Any theory, particularly one in the social sciences, must strike some balance between parsimony and plausibility. A theory that is too simple will be unlikely to have much relation to the actual social process being studied. A theory that attempts to take into account all of the complexities inherent in a given situation, however, will prove unwieldy and thus unlikely to generate any meaningful insights. The actual balance chosen between these two, usually competing, goals is in some way arbitrary. In a sense, one's preferred balance between parsimony and realism in political science research is a statement about how scientific one believes the study of politics should be and of how much one values knowledge of specific cases as opposed to understanding of general underlying processes.

One side of this argument is exemplified by the position of Kramer (1986, 16), who argues that the goal of science "is to demystify experience, and simplify it, not to extol its complexities." Spatial voting theory certainly falls into this category of science. For this reason, many political behavior scholars may object to the serious consideration of the spatial model as an accurate representation of voter behavior in real-world elections. For instance, simple spatial voting theory posits no direct role for sociological factors or for the party identification described by the Michigan school.[6] Accordingly, two voters with the same ideological

---

[6] Spatial theory typically treats the ideology of voters as given. Whereas the political behavior tradition often focuses on the determinants, whether sociological, psychological, or otherwise, of these views, spatial theory tends to abstract them away. One way of looking at this difference, then, is less a matter of a fundamentally different view of how science should proceed so much as a focus on explaining a different level of phenomena.

position will be predicted to behave in the same way in any election regardless of how they may differ on other characteristics. This, on its face, is likely to arouse immediate opposition from a large segment of political behavior scholars.

The other side of this argument asserts that social processes, by their very nature, do not submit well to formalized, simplified theoretical explanation. Political processes, it would follow, cannot be understood as the result of some set of basic equations or formally stated assumptions. In one sense, this is almost certainly true. There is clearly a great deal more randomness (or at least randomness from the perspective of an outside observer) inherent in political processes than, for example, in the basic behavior of physical objects. It seems implausible, for example, that an equation as simple as Newton's law of universal gravitation could explain voting or any other important political behavior as effectively as Newton's law explains the falling of objects to the earth. A somewhat common reaction to such realizations among political scholars seems to be that students of voting behavior and of other political phenomena should abandon efforts to reduce political behavior to simple theories. But virtually all scientific theory begins with basic setups and elaborates to take into account other relevant factors. The dismissal of theoretical rigor as being useful in the study of voting behavior would be somewhat akin to deeming Newton's original theory useless because it could not explain why feathers fall to the ground more slowly than stones. Scientific progress, particularly in theory building, typically builds up from simple but incomplete theories to broader ones that are able to explain more and more phenomena. This strategy is even more essential when constructing social scientific theory because of the open-ended and complex nature of most social phenomena.

The aim of this book is not to demonstrate that spatial voting theory is "true" in any literal sense. In fact, any reasonable person should agree that the theory, along with virtually every other theory in the social sciences, is far from exactly true. The aim here is instead to assess how meaningfully the behavior of voters in real-world elections can be explained by the relatively simple set of axioms assumed in spatial voting theory. In the chapters that follow, I argue that the spatial model, albeit with some important modifications, provides a useful depiction of voter behavior in actual elections. In particular, I hope to convince readers that spatial theory represents a profitable approach to the study of voting and of politics more generally despite, and in many ways because of, its simplicity. By focusing on the role of the ideological proximity of voters to candidates in determining voters' choices, we can develop important insights and understandings that would have been impossible to glean from looking at the full set of all conceivable influences on voting behavior. In fact, given the large body of research in which some form of spatial voting is assumed, whether explicitly or implicitly, the proceeding arguments serve largely as an effort to shore up the theoretical foundation on which a significant portion of the study of American politics is based.

Plan of the Book

Chapter 2 discusses the basic concept of ideology, including how it has been defined within the political science literature. The prevailing views and controversies dealing with ideology are outlined, and an overview of the political science literature on ideology is presented. Chapter 3 moves on to the measurement of the ideological positions of citizens. In particular, a novel survey design and statistical applications are used to produce measures of voter and candidate ideology on the same scale – a key requirement for the testing of theories of spatial voting.

Chapters 4 through 6 focus on the direct testing of spatial voting theory, including more elaborate spatial models. Chapter 4 presents spatial voting theory in its conventional utility-based framework. The theory is then generalized to accommodate random errors on the part of voters and the possibility of biased voting decisions according to the spatial standard. An important correspondence between the basic spatial model and relatively simple statistical models is derived and used in order to conduct tests of the empirical implications of spatial voting theory. It is shown that, on average, the decisions of ordinary voters correspond fairly well with the predictions of simple spatial voting theory.

Chapter 5 generalizes the spatial voting model in order to allow for the possible effects of party identification, a variable that has played a central role in the political behavior literature for decades. It is demonstrated that partisanship induces significant biases in choices of voters relative to the spatial baseline. Although the behavior of independent voters is shown to be largely compatible with spatial voting predictions, partisans exhibit large deviations from what might be termed unbiased spatial voting. Democrats and Republicans, even at identical ideological positions, have dramatically different vote probabilities, with those for independents falling somewhere in between. Issues of valence politics are also discussed, and the relative size of the effects of ideology, partisanship, and valence are assessed.

Chapter 6 explores the role of political information as both a mediator and a moderator of spatial voting. It is shown that more informed voters have a higher ability to discriminate ideologically between candidates, resulting in more precise voting decisions. Furthermore, political information appears to offset the impact of partisanship, shrinking the gap between the behavior of Democrats, independents, and Republicans with similar ideological positions as information levels rise. Even at the highest levels of political information, however, significant gaps between the behavior of Democrats and Republicans remain, with independents acting largely in accordance with the prescriptions of spatial voting theory.

In Chapter 7, I examine voters' perceptions of the ideological positions of candidates. In order to engage in spatial voting, voters must presumably be able to assess their ideological proximity to each of the candidates in a given election. To do this, voters must have at least some basic sense of where each candidate stands. Whereas previous work has often argued that most voters are incapable of understanding the ideological positions of candidates, I demonstrate that, at least on average, voters are able to form relatively accurate pictures of the ideologies of candidates and elected officials. Furthermore, voters' perceptions of their ideological proximity to candidates are quite accurate and differ little by party identification.

Chapter 8 concludes by discussing broader implications of the findings presented in the book. Implications for citizen competence and for the functioning of democratic governance are discussed. More specific suggestions also are made about the direction of future voting research, and the status of spatial voting within the field of political behavior more generally and the need for clarification of certain areas of interest are highlighted.

2

Political Ideology

> An "ideology" may be seen as a particularly elaborate, close-woven, and far-ranging structure of attitudes.
>
> (Campbell, Converse, Miller, and Stokes 1960, 192)

The concept of ideology plays a central role in a wide range of political science research. In the fields of public opinion and voting behavior, the study of ideology has charted a somewhat controversial and contentious history. In addition to difficulties with providing even a basic definition for the concept, there has been extensive debate regarding, among other things, what fraction of the public can be said to possess a true ideology, how ideologies are structured, how stable ideologies are over time, and whether ideology has a meaningful effect on various political behaviors. Because of the importance of the concept of ideology to a large body of both theoretical and empirical research, the answers to these questions should be of central interest to American politics scholars. The resolution of these issues is particularly important to the study of spatial voting because this approach sees ideology as the central determinant of vote choice.

This chapter discusses the basic characteristics of the study of political ideology. I begin by describing the various ways in which the term has been defined in the political science literature. Next, I discuss some of the ways that scholars have sought to measure ideology. I then move on to examine the question of how ideological American politics is. Finally, I discuss the suitability of various definitions and measurement strategies for ideology for the investigation of spatial voting theory.

Defining Ideology

In the most general terms, an ideology is a way of conceptualizing the world around us. In order to form perceptions or make decisions, people must rely on simplified models of how the world works. Making all but the most basic choices in everyday life would involve unbelievably complex calculations if every possible factor were considered. Even decision makers at the highest level must rely on conceptual versions of reality rather than a full understanding of the world when making choices. For example, in a recent congressional hearing, Alan Greenspan acknowledged that the model he perceived for how financial systems operated, which implied, among other things, that markets would have incentives to police themselves even in the absence of strong government regulation, had been called into question by recent events. Greenspan, responding to a question from Rep. Henry Waxman (D-CA) about whether he was guided by his "ideology" in making decisions in his position as chairman of the Federal Reserve Bank, stated that ideology "is a conceptual framework [involving] the way people deal with reality. Everyone has one. To exist, you need an ideology."[1]

In politics, ideology has a somewhat similar meaning. A political ideology can be said to be a cognitive model structuring one's understanding of and interaction with the political world. Beyond this basic definition, however, there is little agreement on the specific meaning of the term despite the widespread references to ideology across many different political science literatures. Definitions of ideology have, for the most part, fallen into one of three categories: ideological sophistication, ideological identification, and policy ideology.[2]

The concept of ideological sophistication, most famously discussed by Campbell et al. (1960) and Converse (1964), deals with the degree to which people organize their political views around abstract, often philosophical, principles and concepts. "Ideologues," who hold the highest level of ideological sophistication, "rely in some active way on a relatively abstract and far-reaching conceptual dimension as a yardstick against which political objects and their shifting policy significance over time [are] evaluated" (Converse 1964, 215–16). Research in the area of

---

[1] House Committee on Oversight and Government Reform hearing, October 23, 2008. Transcript: http://oversight.house.gov/images/stories/documents/20081024163819.pdf (accessed June 8, 2010).

[2] Here, I follow the terminology used by Knight (1985).

ideological sophistication has often focused on estimating the proportion of the population falling into various categories, from true ideologues to those whose political beliefs are devoid of any ideological content. Accordingly, ideological sophistication does not directly relate to citizens' political beliefs themselves, but rather pertains to how citizens describe their reasons for having those particular beliefs.

The second prominent definition of ideology in the political science literature can be termed ideological identification. This concept, which also has been called symbolic ideology (Free and Cantril 1967; Cantril 1999; Ellis and Stimson 2007), generally refers to citizens' personal identifications with the ideological labels "liberal" and "conservative." In other words, ideological identification deals with how a person thinks of him or herself and his or her political beliefs relative to these commonly used political categorizations. Symbolic ideology is thus not directly tied to any specific policy or issue beliefs but is somewhat analogous to the classic "Michigan school" concept of party identification. Much like party identification is often defined as an affective orientation to a political party, ideological identification represents how a person feels about and identifies with terms such as "liberal" and "conservative."

The third major approach to defining ideology is policy ideology. Policy ideology, which also has been called operational (as opposed to symbolic) ideology, deals with the specific policy views held by citizens. In particular, most accounts of policy ideology are defined in terms of some form of *constraint*. Constraint is a set of relationships that bind together a person's beliefs across a range of different political issues into some sort of systematic structure. For example, if someone were to tell you that he supports gun control, is pro-choice, and favors increasing regulations on big businesses, you would likely feel somewhat confident in predicting his views on unrelated topics such as gay rights or the war in Iraq. Because the person has expressed several opinions that, in common political parlance, would be considered liberal, it would stand to reason that he would be likely to hold the liberal positions of favoring increased rights for homosexuals and opposing the U.S. invasion of Iraq in 2003.[3] Clearly, this will not always be the case – there will be individuals who support liberal policies on guns, abortion, and regulation but tend

---

[3] Obviously, the meaning of the term "liberal" varies considerably across different contexts. Here and, unless otherwise stated, throughout the rest of the book, I follow its general meaning in contemporary American political discourse rather than referencing ideas of "classical liberalism" or other terminology. I similarly refer to the contemporary American definition of the term "conservative" unless otherwise noted.

to be more conservative on taxes, crime, and trade. On the whole, though, it would be expected that a person holding liberal views on several different issues would be more likely than not to take the liberal position on any other given issue. By contrast, in the absence of ideology – the absence of any form of constraint relating views on different issues together – we would gain little or no information about a person's likely views on one issue by asking his or her opinion on several other issues.

The constraint that binds together citizens' political views could come from several possible sources. Perhaps the strongest form of constraint that has been proposed in the political science literature is that of an underlying philosophy on which all specific political views are based. Under this definition, citizens believe in a core set of principles that serve as foundational axioms from which their political views are logically derived. Any new issue that a citizen encounters is evaluated against these philosophical standards in order to determine what views the citizen should have on that particular policy. This notion of constraint implies deep thought about basic philosophical issues and a coherent logical system of values on which one's political beliefs can be based and that falls close to the definition of the far-ranging political values held by politically sophisticated "ideologues."

Some other possible sources for constraint exist in a somewhat weaker form, which could involve basic views about the role of government providing an underlying structure for specific policy views. In contemporary American politics, we may think of different basic beliefs about the role of government that correspond to traditional ideological "types" within the electorate. Liberals, for example, could be said to believe that while the government should be involved in ensuring the basic economic needs of all of its citizens, it should not intrude into their personal or moral lives. Conservatives, by contrast, generally believe that while it is not the government's role to impose its will on the country's economy, it should take action to enforce certain moral views on the population. While other ideologies, such as libertarianism, which generally argues that the government should keep its involvement in both the economic and moral lives of its citizens to a minimum, also could be said to exist, the central ideological concepts of liberalism and conservatism have permeated much of the common parlance as well as the theoretical analysis of American politics.

In addition to these causes, Converse (1964) outlines several possible mechanisms by which citizens might develop ideological constraint. The first is through logical relationships between different policy views.

For example, a person who thinks that spending should be increased across a wide range of areas and that the government should not run a deficit may logically conclude that taxes must be increased in order to accomplish these things. A second source of constraint could be psychological. In this case, a person's general values or other views could imply certain relationships between different issues. This sort of constraint, while less formal than logical constraint, would still, according to Converse, satisfy a relatively strong definition of ideology. Other possible types of constraint that may imply weaker forms of ideology include personal interest – people supporting issues that benefit themselves – or socially constructed constraint in which ordinary citizens associate certain policy views with each other because political elites or others have "packaged" these issues together and created an impression among the public that they are somehow linked.

On the whole, policy ideology, as characterized by constraint between individuals' views across different issues, deals with the specific policy beliefs held by citizens and the relationships between these different beliefs. Policy ideology is therefore not centrally concerned with citizens' values or motivations for holding specific beliefs, but rather is focused on the relationships between the beliefs themselves. As such, it emphasizes actual opinions on specific policies instead of sophisticated justifications for political beliefs or feelings of identification with ideological labels.

Previous Approaches to Measuring Ideology

Just as multiple definitions have been posited for ideology, several different strategies also have been employed by political scientists for measuring the concept. These approaches have ranged from open-ended interviews about people's views and their reasons for holding them to simple questions asking respondents to summarize their political views with a single number. In most cases, these measurement strategies have been closely tied to the particular definition for ideology that is being employed.

To measure ideological sophistication, scholars have typically used open-ended questions asking respondents to explain their political views and their reasons for holding them. According to Converse (1964) and others, true ideologues should be able to express ideological motivations for holding their policy positions when asked by researchers to explain these views. Therefore, the detection of ideological sophistication depends not on the particular beliefs held by a person, but rather on their stated motivations for holding these beliefs.

While this measurement strategy holds some promise in revealing the underpinnings of the ideology of respondents, it also suffers from several problems. In particular, it is possible for an individual to have relatively strong core values or attitudes that structure his or her opinions on different issues, but not be able to (or have the desire to) explain these things. In this case, researchers may conclude that an individual does not have any sort of ideology when, in reality, he or she does have some meaningful structure to his or her political attitudes, but simply does not have the ability or the desire to clearly explain it to an interviewer. Perhaps more seriously, respondents who do provide some explanation for their views are likely to do so in vastly different ways. It then becomes a largely subjective task to divide them into categories based on the degree of ideology they exhibit, let alone to devise any such categorization system to begin with.

By far the most commonly used measure of ideology is the "seven-point scale" question from the American National Election Studies (ANES) – the most widely analyzed source of data for researchers studying American political behavior. This item has been included, with minor wording variations, in every ANES survey conducted since 1972 and therefore provides an excellent time series of the ideology of Americans. The standard question reads:

Here is a 7-point scale on which the political views that people might hold are arranged from extremely liberal to extremely conservative. Where would you place yourself on this scale or haven't you thought much about this?

This question may be thought to provide a measure of people's ideological identification in the sense that respondents choose the ideological label that they think fits them best. This approach offers several clear benefits. It is very straightforward to implement and takes up very little survey time, making it very attractive, particularly to researchers who may not be centrally interested in ideology but seek a simple measure of it, perhaps as a control variable in their studies of other phenomena. The question also has a long history, making over-time comparisons fairly straightforward.

But there also are important disadvantages to consider when using ordinal scale self-placement questions as a measure of citizen ideology. In particular, this question becomes problematic when researchers use it to measure actual ideological positions of citizens relative to each other or to candidates on any objective scale. First, the question assumes a single given ideological dimension for respondents rather than allowing the researcher to uncover the specific form of ideological structure that may underlie citizens' policy views. The dimension referenced in such self-placement questions is explicitly defined as being between liberalism and conservatism. While much of the modern discourse about politics is framed in these terms, it is still possible that many respondents actually have their political beliefs held together in a framework that is significantly different from this one or that respondents do not understand these terms to have the same meaning intended by the researcher. Again, the standard question wording provides no immediate way to examine such possibilities. Furthermore, if respondents held ideologies structured over multiple dimensions, they would be forced to somehow collapse their ideological positions into one value. The question thus provides little information with which scholars can investigate the actual structure of citizen ideology, including how positions on political issues are related to each other and how many ideological dimensions citizens tend to exhibit. Instead, the self-placement question assumes a particular ideological dimension, defined by the survey author, and forces respondents to place themselves on it.

Perhaps more seriously, though, the seven-point ideological scale is in a fundamental way undefined. Even if the political views of Americans were structured on a single liberal–conservative dimension, there would be little if anything preventing different respondents from interpreting the scale in dramatically different ways. If respondents think of the scale differently, then their responses may not be directly comparable. As a best-case scenario, if such scale use differences were simply random, not systematically related to respondents' individual characteristics, these variations would only result in a reduction in the precision of measurement. If, on the other hand, how respondents use these scales is systematically related to their demographics, political views, or other factors, results could be misleading.

It is not difficult to imagine possible factors that could affect respondents' conceptualizations of these ordinal scales. For example, citizens living in a very conservative environment may hold political beliefs similar to those around them and therefore believe that they are a "moderate" on the seven-point scale. In a more liberal environment, however, citizens holding those same views may be more conservative than the majority of people they know, causing them to think of themselves as "conservative" on the standard scale. In this way, a citizen's political surroundings could affect the way such scales are used. The standard ANES ideological scale question, then, is likely to be more of a measure of how respondents think of their own ideology and their relative ideological position to others than it is a direct measure of their actual ideology.

Finally, aside from the issues mentioned in the previous paragraphs, the actual results of measuring citizen ideology with ordinal scales is a fairly lumpy classification in which there is only limited ability to differentiate between various respondents. The ANES ideology question has seven response options (aside from "don't know"), and some other versions of the question have even fewer possible answers. While ideology is generally thought of as a continuum with many possible values, standard questions force respondents to choose from a relatively small number of categories to describe their ideological position. Consequently, inferences will be significantly more difficult to make because of the granularity of the data. Overall, ideological self-placement scales provide reasonable measures of the affective orientations that citizens have toward the ideological labels of "liberal" and "conservative." Therefore, they represent a useful measure of ideological identification. These measures become problematic, however, when used as measures of actual policy views.

A final approach to the measurement of ideology is to attempt to tie the measurement process to the specific beliefs that ideologies are said to structure. This strategy corresponds closely with the concept of policy ideology, which defines ideology as a set of relationships structuring people's policy views across different issues. Under this approach, researchers measure the beliefs of citizens on several different policies. If these views are ideological – that is, related to each other through some form of constraint – we should be able to observe associations between people's opinions across different views. For example, those who support some policy A may be more likely to support some policy B and also to oppose some policy C. In the absence of ideology, a person's views on one issue would tell us little or nothing about their views on any other policy. Therefore, by measuring citizens' policy views across different issue areas, researchers can formally and objectively test whether there exist any relationships between people's views on different policies. To the extent that these relationships exist and strongly structure people's political beliefs, this will provide strong evidence that people do possess true ideologies.

There are, however, drawbacks to such an approach. First, the measure requires significantly more work to produce than do simpler ideology measures. For example, self-placement scales require asking survey respondents only one question to produce an ideological placement for them. Measuring ideological constraint based on individual policy views, by contrast, is likely to take several questions – one for each specific policy view that is to be measured. Furthermore, measures of ideology based on specific policy questions are unlikely to be comparable with previous surveys unless the policy questions asked are very similar to those in the current survey. This would make it difficult for researchers to study time trends in ideology, for example.

For these reasons, some researchers, particularly those who have only a peripheral interest in ideology and want to focus most of their studies (and most of their survey time) on other areas, may find the requirements of this policy-based ideology measurement undesirable. These scholars may prefer to use simpler, more traditional measures, such as the ANES seven-point scale, even given the limitations of these measures discussed previously. Scholars who seek a more in-depth understanding of ideology in the American public, however, will find several important benefits in a policy-based ideology measurement strategy.

First, this method does not make any *ex ante* assumptions about the specific form of constraint that should be present if people's views are in fact ideological. Unlike traditional ANES ideological self-placement questions, for example, this issue-based approach does not specify one particular ideological dimension and seek to measure people's ideology by that specific metric. Instead, people's individual policy views are measured, and these are used to uncover the nature of the ideological dimension or dimensions (if any) that underlie these beliefs. It is then straightforward to produce estimates of each person's ideological position on these dimensions. This approach allows survey respondents, rather than survey authors, to define the ideological dimension(s) underlying their political beliefs. Rather than a researcher anchoring a scale with terms such as "very liberal" or "moderate," measuring ideology based on individual policy views allows for the exploration of relationships between people's policy views across different issues and, therefore, for the understanding of which if any, dimensions, provide the main underlying structure for citizens' political beliefs. Second, measurements of ideology that uncover latent ideological dimensions based on associations between different policy views produce ideology estimates that fall on an ideological continuum rather than in a set of five or seven possible categories.[4] Therefore,

---

[4] Technically, the number of different ideological positions that can actually be estimated from a given set of policy questions will be determined by the total number of possible response patterns. For example, for seven policy questions, each with "support" or

a policy-based ideology measurement strategy produces a much richer set of estimates for citizen ideology, allowing researchers to observe more nuanced variation than would simple seven-point scales. Finally, by measuring people's views on specific policies, giving response options such as "support," "oppose," "agree," or "disagree" for various policy proposals, the ambiguity of both the questions and response options is significantly reduced. For example, asking someone whether he or she agrees or disagrees that the minimum wage should be increased is a fairly objective question. It is unlikely that most respondents will perceive these options in dramatically different ways. This stands in sharp contrast to liberal–conservative self-placement questions in which different people could have very different perceptions of what it means to be "extremely conservative" or "moderate," for example. If two different respondents both say that they support immediately bringing all troops home from Iraq, it seems safe to say that they are expressing the same view, or at least something very close. Similarly, two respondents who are asked whether they would support or oppose a national ban on handguns are very likely to think about this question in the same way.

Are American Politics Ideological?

One of the central questions in the study of ideology in American politics is whether most American citizens can be said to be ideological in the first place. In large part, answers to this question have depended on the definition of ideology employed and the specific methods used to measure ideology. Here, I focus on four particular features that have been examined in order to investigate whether citizens hold meaningful ideologies: explanations for policy views, observable constraint between issue positions, intertemporal stability of ideology, and impact of ideology on political actions.

The earliest and most prominent investigations of the level of ideology in the American public focused on assessing the ideological sophistication of citizens. As discussed in the previous section, this approach emphasizes that people who hold real ideologies should be able to justify their policy views in terms of overarching principles and values. Early studies by

---

"oppose" response options, there are $2^7 = 128$ possible ideological positions that could be estimated. For ten questions, there are $2^{10} = 1,024$ possible positions. Therefore, for even a moderate number of policy questions, these ideology estimates will, in practice, be closer to a continuum of values than the small set of possibilities typically used in ideological self-placement scales.

Converse (1964) and others asked people to explain the motivations behind their political beliefs, evaluating their responses in terms of their level of ideological thought. Based on this approach, Converse concludes that only a small fraction of the population (2.5 percent of his sample and 3.5 percent of voters) can be said to be true ideologues, defined as "respondents who did indeed rely in some active way on a relatively abstract and far-reaching conceptual dimension as a yardstick against which political objects and their shifting policy significance over time were evaluated" (215–16). A second group of respondents, who expressed some abstract ideology, but did not seem to hold it as a central part of their political beliefs, were classified as "near-ideologues." This second group comprised 9 percent of the sample and 12 percent of voters. The largest group of respondents, according to Converse, did not express any sort of ideological thinking, but instead seemed to base their political beliefs and feelings toward parties and candidates primarily on the expected outcomes for different social groups. For example, a union worker might have favorable feelings toward the Democratic party because he views the party as being pro-union. This group made up 42 percent of the sample and 45 percent of voters. The final two classifications used by Converse were "nature of the times," which included voters who evaluated parties and candidates largely on the basis of current national conditions (24 percent of the sample and 22 percent of voters) and those whose views had no issue content whatsoever (24.5 percent of the sample and 17.5 percent of voters). Similarly, some more recent work has argued that only a fraction of the American public has the capacity for ideological thought (see, e.g., Stimson 1975; Knight 1985; Jacoby 1991).

Converse's findings, often described as the "nonattitudes" thesis, have had a profound impact on the course of research in political behavior.[5] His argument that only a small fraction of Americans could be said to be ideological, even by a broad definition of the term, provided a stark baseline by which to evaluate both the competence of the electorate and the general functioning of American democracy. This line of reasoning, combined with much of the work from the Michigan school of political behavior research (e.g., Campbell et al. 1960), suggested that most Americans relied little on actual ideologies or policy views in making political decisions, but were primarily influenced by party identification

---

[5] In fact, by some interpretations, the "nonattitudes" thesis goes beyond the argument that most citizens do not hold meaningful ideologies to say that members of the electorate rarely hold meaningful views even on individual issues.

(also referred to as partisanship), which was defined as an affective orientation toward (or personal attachment to) one of the major political parties. According to this school, party identification dominated the political thoughts and actions of most Americans, with true ideologies or any sort of deep political thought being rare.

Later research sought to revise these findings, emphasizing the weakening of partisan bonds during decades following Converse's work (e.g., Nie et al. 1979). In addition, some scholars have argued that Americans have become more ideological in recent years, suggesting that the classic Michigan school view of voters may no longer apply as well as it did in the middle of the twentieth century (Abramowitz and Saunders 1998; Bafumi and Shapiro 2009). But the "nonattitudes" findings still resonate powerfully with many students of political behavior. There remains a strong sentiment across much of the subfield that ordinary citizens do not possess any sort of principled, coherent ideological thinking.

Another method for assessing the level of ideology in the American electorate is through the ideological self-placement questions such as the ANES seven-point scale item discussed in the previous section. Rather than requiring an extensive explanation for one's policy views, these questions instead ask respondents to indicate how they identify with the traditional labels for the American ideological spectrum. Accordingly, this approach provides an assessment of the degree to which citizens think of themselves as ideological.

Table 2.1 shows the percentage of respondents giving each response to the ANES ideology question over time, from 1972 until 2008. Overall, these responses show at most minor changes in the distribution of respondents' ideological self-identification. There is some evidence that the percentage of moderates and of "don't know" respondents have declined slightly in recent years, but evidence of any significant shift is somewhat speculative.[6] In each year of the ANES, large portions of the electorate classified themselves as some type of liberal or conservative, and roughly a quarter of respondents in most years considered themselves to be ideological moderates. A significant percentage of respondents, however,

---

[6] A simple linear regression predicting the percentage of "don't know" or "haven't thought about it" responses by the year of the study gives a negative and significant coefficient ($p < .01$), estimating a decrease of .26 percentage points each year. Results for a similar linear regression predicting the percentage of "moderate" responses does not produce significant results, but the total percent placing themselves as moderates or answering "don't know" shows a significantly negative time trend ($p < .01$) using this method, estimating a .30 percentage point decrease each year. Clearly, more sophisticated analyses would be needed to determine the actual nature of any such trends.

TABLE 2.1. *ANES Self-Reported Ideology by Year*

	'72	'74	'76	'78	'80	'82	'84	'86	'88
Extremely Liberal	1	2	1	2	2	1	2	1	2
Liberal	7	11	7	8	6	6	7	6	6
Slightly Liberal	10	8	8	10	9	8	9	11	9
Moderate, Middle of Road	27	26	25	27	20	22	23	28	22
Slightly Conservative	15	12	12	14	13	13	14	15	15
Conservative	10	12	11	11	13	12	13	13	14
Extremely Conservative	1	2	2	2	2	2	2	2	3
DK, Haven't Thought	28	27	33	27	36	36	30	25	30
N	2,155	2,478	2,839	2,284	1,565	1,400	2,229	2,170	2,035

	'90	'92	'94	'96	'98	'00	'02	'04	'08
Extremely Liberal	1	2	1	1	2	2	2	2	3
Liberal	7	8	6	7	7	9	12	9	10
Slightly Liberal	8	10	7	10	9	9	9	8	9
Moderate, Middle of Road	24	23	26	24	28	23	22	25	22
Slightly Conservative	14	15	14	15	15	12	10	12	12
Conservative	10	13	19	15	13	15	21	16	17
Extremely Conservative	2	3	3	3	2	3	4	3	3
DK, Haven't Thought	33	27	24	25	23	27	22	25	25
N	1,967	2,483	1,783	1,712	1,280	849	1,490	1,211	2,319

Weighted percentages from American National Election Studies. *Note:* There was no ANES conducted in 2006. Ideology measured using variable VCF0803 in ANES Cumulative Data File, weighted using variable VCF0009A.

declined to place themselves on this scale, answering "don't know" or that they haven't thought much about this.

These results suggest that although the vast majority of Americans may not satisfy the criteria defined by some political scientists for holding truly ideological political beliefs, this has not prevented them from describing themselves in ideological terms. In fact, in each of the last four ANES studies as well as seven of the last eight, at least half of ANES respondents have used some sort of association to the terms "liberal" or "conservative" to describe themselves, with roughly a quarter of respondents describing themselves as ideologically moderate.[7] This suggests that the level of ideological identification is significantly higher than that of ideological sophistication, at least as measured by Converse (1964). Many Americans think of themselves in ideological terms, even if some scholars do not classify most people as ideological.

A second method of assessing the level of ideology in the American public has been to analyze the level of constraint between the political views of citizens across different policies. In the most widely cited of such analyses, Converse (1964) argues that citizens' attitudes across different issues show little relationship with one another, indicating at most a minimal amount of ideological constraint in the American public. Other studies, however, have argued that these findings are misleading, coming as a result of suboptimal measurement methods, or that the level of constraint in the public has increased in the time since Converse's original study (see, e.g., Nie and Andersen 1974; Stimson 1975; Bafumi and Shapiro 2009). The most common form discussed for this constraint is a unidimensional ideological structure. Multidimensional organization also is possible, although it typically introduces additional complications for theoretical models. The dimensionality of ideology is discussed in more detail in the next chapter.

Researchers also have studied the stability of citizens' ideological self-identifications over time. According to this approach, respondents who provide similar answers about their ideology in repeated surveys are likely to hold more meaningful ideologies than those who give different answers

---

[7] Whether people who self-identify as moderates can be said to think of themselves as ideological is somewhat unclear. Although they have placed themselves on the ideological scale, not saying, for example, that they haven't thought about this, they do not align themselves with either the liberal or conservative ideological label. Therefore, it could be said that they do not identify with either of these ideological labels, but do think of themselves in ideological terms, albeit as moderates. See Treier and Hillygus (2009) for a related discussion.

at different times. It is argued that while stable responses indicate deeply held feelings, unstable responses are likely to be indicative of weakly held attitudes or respondents who do not understand or care about the question being answered. In studies involving repeated surveys, respondents have shown some degree of response stability to ideological identification questions, but responses are generally less stable than party identification (Converse and Markus 1979; Levitin and Miller 1979). The finding that ideological identification shows some degree of persistence lends credence to the idea that such responses represent meaningful affective orientations toward ideological labels.

Research has generally found less stability, however, in responses to specific issue questions over time than in ideological self-placement questions, which has led scholars to conclude that these views on individual policies may be less centrally held than are overall ideological predispositions. Converse (1964), for example, finds that correlations between individual responses in the first and third waves of his survey are nearly identical to those between either the first and second or second and third waves. Findings of general instability, however, have been questioned by several researchers. Achen (1975) points out that the very correlations that Converse cites as evidence of opinion instability are actually consistent with completely stable opinions measured with random error in each time period. Achen then shows that accounting for the measurement error inherent in individual survey questions produces estimates of issue opinions that are much more stable than previously thought (see also Jacoby 1995; Erikson 2009). Similarly, Ansolabehere et al. (2006) find that while responses to individual survey items display a high degree of variation over time, averaging together responses to multiple items produces issue scales that are much more stable and show stronger relationships to vote choice and other variables.

A final standard for assessing ideology American politics is the relation it has with important political actions, most notably voting behavior. Much of the conventional wisdom in political behavior suggests that the vote choices of many (perhaps most) Americans are generally devoid of any issue content, instead depending primarily on partisan loyalties, simple retrospective evaluations of the economy, or other major factors. But difficulties in measuring ideology, including the aforementioned issues with measurement error, as well as changes in the general nature of American politics have raised important questions about whether conventional wisdom should be revised.

The degree to which ordinary American can be said to be ideological in their political thinking remains a controversial subject. While much of the debate centers around differing definitions for ideology or different methods for assessing its presence, a basic division still remains between those who see American politics as predominantly ideological and others who believe that ordinary voters are far more primitive in their political thinking. On the whole, the fact that such a fundamental question in the study of American politics remains undecided stands as an unfortunate situation and calls out for resolution.

Ideology and Spatial Voting Theory

Strategies for measuring ideology, just like definitions for the term, can take many forms. The important question for scholars in choosing a definition for ideology or a method for obtaining estimates of the ideology of individual citizens is not which definition or measurement strategy is objectively "best," but rather which is best suited for the study of the specific theory or the investigation of the particular hypothesis in which the researcher is interested. In my case, I wish to focus my study on spatial theories of voting in American elections. Therefore, the key questions are which definition of ideology and which method for measuring it are best suited to this pursuit.

As previously discussed, spatial voting theory assumes that both voters and candidates for office hold ideological positions in some finite dimensional (typically low-dimensional and often one-dimensional) space. This theory, often expanded through the addition of random utility disturbances or other factors, predicts that voters will cast their ballots for the candidate who is ideologically closest to their position. Because spatial voting theory assumes an ideological continuum or, in more than one dimension, an ideological space, we should seek to define ideology in a way that, at the least, allows for the possibility that ideology will be spatially structured. Furthermore, one of the most attractive aspects of spatial voting is its potential to provide a unifying theoretical framework that ties together citizen preferences on specific policies, voting decisions, candidate behavior, and, ultimately, the policy outputs of government. To do this, however, the ideological foundations of spatial voting theory must be built on concrete policy positions rather than on vague appeals to abstract concepts such as "liberalness" or "conservatism."

The distinction between self-placed ideology (as in the ANES seven-point scale question) and more policy-based measures is closely related to the distinction between *symbolic* and *operational* ideology. Symbolic ideology refers to citizens' identifications with ideological labels such as "liberal" and "conservative," while operational ideology involves people's specific views about actual policy decisions. Although it may seem at first that the distinction is trivial, it is well-known that while the American public tends to be more symbolically conservative, with larger numbers of the public identifying as conservatives than as liberals, most Americans voice fairly broad support for classically liberal programs such as government intervention to solve social problems (Free and Cantril 1967; Cantril 1999; Ellis and Stimson 2007). Measures of ideology such as the ANES ideological self-placement question are essentially measures of symbolic ideology – how citizens think of themselves in ideological terms. By contrast, policy-based measurement strategies will produce measures of operational ideology, which are a spatial representation of the specific views people have of different policies.

In addition to these basic differences between symbolic and operational ideology, we can ask which of these two types of ideology is most appropriate to serve as the basis for spatial voting theories. First, spatial voting generally assumes that there exists some objective ideological space. Symbolic ideology, however, can be perceived in vastly different ways by different voters. What one voter sees as "slightly liberal," for example, may be thought of as "extremely liberal" by someone else. Symbolic ideology, then, is in a basic sense undefined. There is no way of objectively determining, for example, whether John McCain is moderate, slightly conservative, conservative, or extremely conservative. Similarly, there is no way of objectively arbitrating between someone who thinks that the health care reform bill passed in 2010 was very liberal and someone else who views it as fairly moderate. It is interesting to consider what ideological labels citizens associate with themselves, candidates or elected officials, and specific policy proposals, but there is no objective ideological space that underlies these symbolic terms. Even if someone said, for example, that he was "slightly liberal," but his friend claimed that this was incorrect and the person was actually "very liberal," there would be no way to determine objectively which was true. Symbolic ideology is, in a fundamental way, in the eye of the beholder. This quality directly contradicts the idea inherent in spatial voting that there exists some objectively defined ideological space in which each voter and each candidate takes some position.

It is possible, however, that there exists some underlying ideological dimension that structures the specific policy views of voters. If spatial theory can be built on this sort of ideological foundation, it will result in a stronger theoretical framework for several reasons. First, detecting ideological structure through the examination of citizens' specific policy views has the potential to empirically establish, rather than simply assume, that ordinary Americans hold political views that are related in meaningful ways to some underlying political dimension. Second, tying ideology to concrete policy proposals results in an ideological dimension that has some objective definition rather than simply referencing vague terminology. Finally, by defining ideology with regard to actual policy positions, the spatial theory of voting has the potential to provide a theoretical link between the views of ordinary voters, the strategies of candidates for office, and the policies enacted through the legislative process.

Although the benefits of defining and measuring ideology in relation to specific policy positions may seem obvious, this has proved more challenging in practice. In particular, political scientists have generally relied on rough proxies for ideology, measures of symbolic ideology (i.e., ideological identification rather than actual policy ideology), or have been forced to employ heroic assumptions in order to formulate measures of citizen ideology. This problem has been particularly challenging for those seeking to analyze spatial theories of voting because testing such theories requires measures of ideology that place both citizen and candidate ideology on the same scale. The following chapter moves on to present a method for obtaining such ideological estimates, which are directly tied to concrete policies, without relying on such strong assumptions.

3

Measuring Political Ideology

Belief systems have never surrendered easily to empirical study or quantification. Indeed, they have often served as primary exhibits for the doctrine that what is important to study cannot be measured and that what can be measured is not important to study.

(Converse, "Nature of Belief Systems in Mass Publics," 206)

Despite the prominence of ideology in both the political science literature and everyday discourse about politics, the measurement of ideology remains a relatively underdeveloped area of research. Political scientists have agonized over finding the best methods to measure things such as political sophistication (Luskin 1987; Delli Carpini and Keeter 1993) and racial resentment (Kinder and Sears 1981; Sniderman and Carmines 1997), but more often than not they seem content to use a simple, seven-point self-placement questionaire to measure the entirety of people's political ideology. This seems particularly odd given the status of ideology as a central variable in many political science theories.

The detection and measurement of ideology are important for the study of spatial voting because the theory assumes that ideology, or, more specifically, a voter's ideological proximity to the positions of candidates, is the central determinant of their vote choice. Therefore, empirically testing spatial theory requires accurate measurements of the ideology of voters on the same scale as the positions of candidates in a given election. This requirement has not been easily met in past studies, which have often relied on less-than-ideal data sources accompanied by strong assumptions in order to produce the ideology measures required for such investigations.

Spatial voting theory argues that voters base their choices on their ideological proximity to candidates in a given election. What is implicit within this general framework is that the policy views of voters can be realistically depicted as ideological locations in some low-dimensional (usually one-dimensional) space. This implies not only that the policy views of voters are related to each other by some underlying structure, typically called constraint, but also that the structure underpinning these political beliefs is the same for all citizens and can be represented spatially. In most studies of spatial voting, these requirements are simply assumed away, often as a result of measuring ideology with ANES-style self-placement questions, which assume a single liberal–conservative dimension and ask respondents to place themselves somewhere on this scale. Finally, theories of spatial voting are built on predictions about the relative positions of voters and candidates. Therefore, testing the implications of these theories requires measurements of the ideology of voters and candidates on a common scale. Previous studies have generally struggled to produce such estimates, often relying on heroic assumptions and unrealistic simplifications.

This chapter describes the results of a different strategy for the measurement of ideology. It begins by investigating whether the individual issue beliefs of citizens are organized into some coherent and meaningful structure – what has been termed *constraint* by previous authors – and whether that structure is consistent with a spatial representation of ideology. Using a novel survey design along with the technique of ideal point estimation, principled measures of the ideological positions of voters on the same scale as the positions of candidates in the 2004 and 2008 presidential election are produced. These comparable measures of voter and candidate ideology will provide the tools necessary for the most direct examination of spatial voting theory to date.

Previous Approaches to the Measurement of Spatial Ideology

Most of the work on spatial voting has dealt with deriving theoretical predictions, usually for candidate positioning, under the assumption that voters hold ideological positions in one or more spatial dimensions and cast their ballots for the candidate whose positions are closest to their own. The simplest models involving two candidates competing for office in a unidimensional policy space have generally led to predictions of candidate convergence. More elaborate models, however, have explored the theoretical consequences of things such as valence dimensions, in which one candidate has a nonspatial advantage over the other (Ansolabehere and Snyder 2000; Groseclose 2001). Others have derived equilibria for candidate strategy under spatial voting that includes random error (Schofield et al. 1998; Adams 1999; Lin et al. 1999). Scholars also have elaborated on the basic spatial framework to include the effects of nonspatial factors that may differ across voters and push them toward one candidate or the other independent of the voters' ideological proximity to each candidate (Adams 2001; Adams and Merrill 2008).

Empirically testing even the simplest versions of spatial voting theory, however, has proven challenging. The primary difficulty has stemmed from the need to measure the ideological positions of voters on the same scale as the positions taken by candidates in a given election. While several approaches have been used to generate these estimates, each has important shortcomings. The most common method for comparing the ideological positions of voters and candidates relies on five- or seven-point ideological scales. Researchers often measure voter positions using survey respondents' placements of their own ideologies. But it is not obvious where candidates should fall on these scales. The most common solution has been to assume that candidate positions are equal to the average of respondents' perceptions of the candidate's ideology on the same ordinal liberal–conservative scale (see, e.g., Brady and Sniderman 1985; Alvarez and Nagler 1995; Adams et al. 2005). This represents a very strong assumption, particularly given that a key question related to spatial voting is whether voters can form accurate perceptions of the ideological positions of candidates.

Some researchers have attempted to obtain more accurate measures of candidate positions by relying on the perceptions of district "experts" about candidate locations (e.g., Stone and Simas 2010). While this approach may result in somewhat more plausible estimates of the true positions of candidates, it is unclear whether the five- or seven-point ideological scales presented to respondents adequately capture the central ideological dimension of American political discourse. In other words, these standard questions tend to define ideology as researchers see fit, rather than to analyze the actual political views of citizens in order to discover possible ideological dimensions that may underpin these views.

Other scholars have used scaling techniques to place candidates into the same ideological space as voters. One method that has been used is to assume that respondents' preferences between candidates are dictated by their ideological proximity to them. Using scaling techniques, it is then possible to estimate an ideological space including voters and candidates together (Weisberg and Rusk 1970; Cahoon and Ordeshook 1978). This approach, however, *assumes* that voters' preferences over candidates are determined by spatial proximity. Therefore, the resulting estimates are clearly not ideal for testing spatial theory because they assume that the key hypothesis being tested is true. Somewhat less problematic are the ideology estimates of Aldrich and McKelvey (1977), who assume that respondents perceive the ideological positions of candidates with some error and use scaling methods to estimate an ideological space that includes both candidates and voters.

In all of these cases, however, very strong assumptions are used in order to produce estimates of the ideology of voters and candidates on the same scale. Furthermore, none of these techniques is grounded in specific policy positions. One of the key virtues of a spatial representation of politics is that it provides a connection between actual policy proposals, the views of ordinary voters, and the candidates elected to office. Ultimately, the general logic of spatial politics can provide a unifying framework within which to study voter decision making, candidate behavior, legislative voting, and the policy outputs of democratic governments. Therefore, the ideal tests of spatial voting would rely on measures of voter ideology that were tied to concrete policies rather than vague references to subjective terms such as "liberal" or "conservative."

Grounding Ideology in Policy

It is certainly a simpler task for citizens to express approval or disapproval of a specific policy proposal than to take an inventory of all their political views and predispositions and combine this information into one specific number that represents their place on a political spectrum that is defined by survey writers. Perhaps more importantly, different people are likely to use different methods for summarizing their ideology, resulting in problems with the comparability of such ideology measures. Still, political scientists rely primarily on a simple ordered scale on which survey respondents place themselves as the primary measure of political ideology. As a comparison, career advisers do not simply ask people what jobs they would be best suited for; psychiatry does not consist solely of asking patients what mental issues they are afflicted with; and standardized tests certainly consist of more than just a single question asking test takers how intelligent they are. Yet the favored method for measuring ideology in survey research consists, more or less, of asking people, "What is your ideology?"

When seeking to measure political ideology, it is important to note that while citizens' policy views are observable by simply asking them survey questions on these subjects, their ideologies cannot be measured directly. Just as we cannot weigh a person on a scale or scan him or her with a machine in order to reveal traits such as intelligence, happiness, or sense of humor, there is no way to detect a citizen's ideology through direct measurement. Therefore, bridging the gap between citizens' observable policy views and the unobservable ideologies that provide the structure for these views represents the critical step in producing useful measures of ideology.

If, as here, a political ideology is defined as a meaningful structure that ties together one's positions across a wide range of policy areas, we should seek a measure of ideology that is firmly grounded in citizens' actual policy beliefs. Accordingly, the measurement of ideology presented here is based not on people's perceptions of their own ideology or on their feelings toward political figures, but instead on the actual positions they hold on specific political issues. In particular, by looking at the associations between people's views on these different policies, we can determine what form of constraint, if any, systematically links together people's opinions across different, often seemingly unrelated issues. We can then move on to estimating the ideology of individual voters based on these stated views.

Like many latent traits, ideology does not lend itself well to direct measurement. We can, however, measure policy views, which may be thought to be affected by an individual's ideology. In this way, an individual's ideology, much like other latent traits, can be learned about by posing specific questions of that person and then considering what underlying ideology would be likely to have produced the answers given. If ideology is a cognitive structure that organizes one's policy views, then the investigation and measurement of ideology should begin by looking at citizens' actual views on specific policies.

Assume, for example, that we have a survey indicating respondents' views on a series of policies. In the absence of any meaningful ideology, these responses should have no strong associations with each other. A respondent's views on abortion, for example, should be unrelated to his or her views on welfare or tax policy, which should be largely independent of his or her opinions on foreign affairs. His or her views on defense spending should be unrelated to his or her views on civil liberties, which should be essentially separate from his or her thoughts about the environment. In short, policy views in the absence of any form of ideology should not show strong associations with each other. An individual's opinions on one issue should be independent of his or her views on a different issue.

If, alternatively, citizens have their views structured by some sort of ideology, we should be able to observe associations between policy views on different subjects. People who tend to support a given policy should be significantly more likely to support some different, perhaps seemingly unrelated, policies and less likely to support others. In order to measure policy ideology rather than, for example, ideological sophistication or ideological identification, attention must be focused on the views of citizens on specific policy issues. By grounding the measurement of ideology in actual policy views, it will then be possible to investigate the degree to which these views are bound together by some underlying structure or whether they instead consist of completely separate opinions.

This policy-based foundation for political ideology also is more compatible with a spatial view of politics more generally. According to the spatial view, many aspects of the political system, whether they are citizens' opinions, their vote choices, the positions advocated by candidates, or the policies ultimately implemented by a government, can all be thought of in spatial terms. In fact, a spatial conception of policy provides arguably the most useful (and the most parsimonious) basis for theoretically linking all of these things together. Voters have policy views that can be represented by positions on a single liberal–conservative dimension, which they use to decide for whom they will cast their votes. Candidates, recognizing how voters make decisions, choose ideological positions for themselves that give them the best chance of winning or maintaining office. Legislators and other elected officials will then make decisions that are most likely to result in policies that are as close as possible to their own positions (which are most often the positions that will result in the highest probabilities of their reelection).

While the spatial view of policy ideology provides, in many ways, a unified framework with which to explain much of political action, it remains a fairly controversial approach. At the most basic level, skeptics contend that the policy views of most ordinary citizens, to the extent that they have any meaningful policy views in the first place, are not organized into any coherent structure. The central objective of this chapter is to refute these claims and to show that a spatial view of ideology, firmly grounded in actual policy positions, provides a realistic depiction of the opinions of the American public.

I make this argument in a series of steps. First, I describe two national surveys that ask citizens to state their views across a wide range of different policies. I demonstrate that these views show strong associations with one another, indicating some sort of underlying ideological constraint, and that, furthermore, the structure of this constraint can be accounted for quite well by a single liberal–conservative ideological dimension. A general framework for the measurement of ideology is then presented within which the ideological views of ordinary citizens can be estimated alongside the positions taken by candidates in presidential elections. This critical advancement in measurement will allow in subsequent chapters for the most direct testing to date of spatial theories of voting behavior. Finally, some of the most common criticisms of spatial voting theory – those based on predictions for candidate positions in simple single-stage elections – are discussed. It is shown that, consistent with conventional wisdom, candidates in recent presidential elections did take dramatically divergent positions. These findings, however, which have often been cited as a basic failure of spatial voting theory in general, are shown to be the result of combining the basic axioms of spatial voting theory with several different assumptions, many of which are objectively false in real-world elections. Therefore, the empirical falsification of these predictions does not speak directly to the validity of spatial theory itself.

Measuring the Policy Views of American Voters

If our ultimate goal is to test the empirical implications of spatial voting theory, the data we seek should have two properties. First, because spatial voting theory generally deals with ideologies that are assumed to structure people's views on specific policies, we should seek measures of citizens' policy positions on a variety of different proposals. Second, because spatial voting theory makes predictions about the voting decisions of citizens based on their proximity to the candidates in a given election, testing spatial voting theory requires data capable of producing measures of the ideology of ordinary voters on the same scale as the positions taken by candidates. With the aim of satisfying both of these requirements, two large-scale surveys were fielded to national samples of respondents. In addition to asking a set of basic political questions on topics including partisanship, vote choice, and other matters, each survey asked respondents to state whether they supported or opposed a series of policy proposals dealing with a wide range of different issue areas. These stated policy positions will form the foundation for the examination of political ideology, and later of spatial voting, in the American public. A key advantage of these two surveys is that they measure the views of citizens on policies for which we also know the positions taken by candidates in the 2004 and 2008 presidential elections. This will ultimately allow for the direct estimation of the positions of both citizen and candidate ideology on the same scale, overcoming the comparability gap that has in the past represented the single greatest challenge in the testing of spatial voting theory in real-world elections.

The first of these two surveys, conducted during December 2005 and January 2006, was administered to 5,871 Americans from the Polimetrix PollingPoint Internet panel.[1] The survey asked respondents to state their position on specific policy proposals that had actually been voted on in the U.S. Senate. A list of twenty-seven significant and important Senate votes was compiled by examining all Senate roll calls from 2004 through 2005.[2] These votes were chosen from a variety of issue areas, including taxes, the environment, gun control, and trade. They were selected because of their relation to what might be expected to be important political issues that citizens would care about. Consideration also was given to the ease with which information about the proposals could be summarized on a questionnaire. Accordingly, votes on things such as complex appropriations bills or regulatory rules, while arguably important, were omitted from this survey. The policy proposals chosen consisted of twenty amendments and seven bills. A list of the votes, along with the percentage of respondents expressing support, opposition, or no opinion on each of them, is presented in Table 3.1.

Each survey respondent was shown a random sample of fifteen of these policy proposals and asked about his or her views on each one. The survey, as seen by respondents, showed a relatively concise bullet point summary of the important features of each proposal. Respondents were then asked how they personally would vote on the policy and could choose response options of "yes," "no," or "don't know." Respondents

---

[1] This survey was designed in collaboration with Douglas Rivers of Stanford University.

[2] Respondents also were asked to state their positions on the Senate confirmation votes for Supreme Court Justices John Roberts and Samuel Alito, but these items are not used in the proceeding analyses because they do not deal directly with policy measures and, as a consequence, could be influenced more heavily by personal feelings about the prospective justices or the nominating president. A survey item on a Senate amendment to ban the sale of armor-piercing ammunition also is dropped because it was determined to be a Republican substitute for a stronger Democratic amendment and therefore was unlikely to be viewed similarly by survey respondents and Senators. Three survey questions on Senate proposals were not used because they referred to measures that failed to receive sixty votes to invoke cloture (end debate). Therefore, there is no Senate vote that directly corresponds to the policy shown to respondents.

TABLE 3.1. 2004 Survey Questions

Bill Number	Title	Senators Yea-Nay Votes	Respondents Y-N-DK Pct.	Parameters γ_j	α_j
HR 4250	Jumpstart Our Business Strength Act	78–15	44-32-23	.62	-.24
S. Amdt. 1085 to HR 2419	Remove Funding for "Bunker Buster" Nuclear Warhead	43–53	52-41-8	-6.17	.03
S. 1307	Central American Free Trade Agreement	61–34	45-39-15	2.08	-.16
S. 256	Bankruptcy Abuse Prevention and Consumer Protection Act	74–25	54-30-16	3.00	-.52
S. Amdt. 367 to HR 1268	Remove Funding for Guantanamo Bay Detention Center	27–71	46-45-9	-2.32	.10
HR 1308	Working Families Tax Relief Act	92–3	79-10-12	1.69	-1.36
S. Amdt. 2937 to HR 4	Child Care Funding for Welfare Recipients	78–20	50-38-13	-6.01	-.67
S. Amdt. 1026 to HR 2161	Prohibiting Roads in Tongass National Forest	39–59	56-31-13	-5.99	-.27
S. 1626 to S 397	Child Safety Locks Amendment	70–30	75-21-4	-4.91	-.88
S. Amdt. 3584 to S 4567	Stopping Privatization of Federal Jobs	49–47	50-35-16	-5.53	-.11
S. Amdt. 3158 to S 2400	Military Base Closure Delays	47–49	48-36-16	.05	-.18
S. Amdt. 44 to S. 256	Minimum Wage Increase	46–49	67-29-4	-10.76	-.72
S. 397	Protection of Lawful Commerce in Arms Act	65–31	74-19-6	3.82	-.12
S. Amdt. 2799 to S. Con. Res. 95	Cigarette Tax Increase	32–64	59-37-4	-3.21	-.18
S. J. Res. 20	Disapproval of Mercury Emissions Rule	47–51	71-12-17	-5.25	-1.13
S. Amdt. 278 to S. 600	Family Planning Aid Policy (Mexico City Policy)	52–46	50-44-6	-7.35	.17
S. Amdt. 2807 to S. 600	Raise Tax Rate on Income over One Million Dollars	40–57	62-32-6	-7.03	-.37
S. Amdt. 3379 to S. 2400	Raise Tax Rate on Highest Income Bracket	44–53	49-44-6	-4.62	.11
HR 1997	Unborn Victims of Violence Act	90–9	68-24-9	3.28	-.85
S. Amdt. 3183 to S. 2400	Federal Hate Crimes Amendment	65–33	49-42-9	-5.39	.06
S. Amdt. 902 to HR 6	Fuel Economy Standards	28–67	70-22-8	-5.86	-.78
S. Amdt. 826 to HR 6	Greenhouse Gas Reduction and Credit Trading System	38–60	48-36-16	-3.13	-.05
S. Amdt. 1977 to HR 2863	Banning Torture by U.S. Military Interrogators	90–9	57-38-5	-7.90	-.25
S. Amdt. 1615 to S. 397	Broaden Definition of Armor Piercing Ammunition	31–64	70-22-8	-4.39	-.69
S. Amdt. 168 to S. Con. Res. 18	Prohibit Drilling in Arctic National Wildlife Refuge	49–51	48-48-4	-10.52	.42
S. Amdt. 3107 to S. 1637	Overtime Pay Regulations	52–47	44-44-12	.05	-.00
S. 5	Class Action Fairness Act	72–26	53-22-24	1.69	-.63

Table shows Senate vote totals and percentages of 2004 survey respondents supporting, opposing, and saying "don't know" to each surveyed policy. The two rightmost columns show the estimated discrimination and difficulty parameters from the estimation of the model shown in Equation 3.1 with the 2004 survey data and Senate data including all roll call votes cast during 2004 and 2005.

POLL:NGPOINT

S AMDT 44 to S 256: Minimum Wage Increase

- Would raise the minimum wage to $5.85 immediately, then to $6.55 after one year, and to $7.25 in two years.
- The minimum wage before this bill was proposed was $5.15.

How would you vote on this measure?

○ I support this measure and would vote "yes."

○ I oppose this measure and would vote "no."

○ Don't know

Please tell us how you think your Senators will vote on this measure?

	Mel Martinez (Republican)	Bill Nelson (Democrat)
Probably for	○	○
Maybe for	○	○
Maybe against	○	○
Probably against	○	○
Not sure	○	○

FIGURE 3.1. 2004 Survey question example

also were asked how they thought each of their senators would vote on the proposals. Responses to these senator perception questions are not considered here, but are analyzed later in Chapter 7. Figure 3.1 shows an example of the exact question format seen by respondents.

In addition, a second survey was fielded to a nationally representative sample of two thousand likely voters shortly before the 2008 presidential election.[3] Respondents were asked general questions about their political opinions and also were asked to indicate whether they agreed or disagreed with a set of ten specific policy statements that corresponded with issues raised in the presidential campaign. These policies were selected from a wide range of issue areas, including the economy, health care, abortion, and the environment. A full list of the ten policies shown to respondents, along with the overall responses to each question, can be found in Table 3.2. Figure 3.2 shows a portion of the survey screen as seen by respondents.

These two surveys, which I call the 2004 and 2008 surveys, referring to the presidential election they will later be used to study, serve as the main resources on which this book's analyses of ideology and spatial voting

---

[3] The survey was fielded on October 25 to 27 by Polimetrix, Inc. Respondents were selected from the company's PollingPoint panel, an online volunteer respondent pool of more than one million Americans, using a sample matching technique (Rivers 2006) to ensure representativeness at the national level.

TABLE 3.2. *2008 Survey Questions*

Policy Proposal	Candidates Obama	Candidates McCain	Respondents Y-N-DK (%)	Parameters γ_j	Parameters α_j
The United States should begin a phased withdrawal of troops from Iraq.	Yes	No	64-24-12	−6.69	−1.10
The definition of marriage should apply only to relationships between a man and a woman.	Yes	Yes	58-33-10	3.80	−.48
Younger workers should be allowed to invest some of their Social Security contributions in private investment accounts.	No	Yes	51-30-19	3.56	−.40
The Supreme Court's decision in Roe v. Wade, which legalized most forms of abortion, should be overturned.	No	Yes	31-55-14	4.29	.49
A mandatory cap on carbon dioxide emissions by American companies should be imposed, with a credit trading system so that companies who pollute less can sell their credits to other companies.	Yes	Yes	44-28-28	−4.30	−.42
A "windfall profits" tax should be imposed on large profits made by oil companies.	Yes	No	59-25-16	−7.74	−1.16
Tax cuts for those making over $250,000 should be reversed.	Yes	No	50-36-14	−5.26	−.28
The federal government should require that all American children have health insurance.	Yes	No	57-28-14	−6.68	−.83
Same-sex couples should be allowed to form civil unions that give them most of the same legal protections that married couples enjoy.	Yes	Yes	61-29-10	−2.30	−.55
Up to $700 billion dollars should be spent to have the federal government purchase troubled assets from financial institutions in an attempt to remedy current economic troubles.	Yes	Yes	24-50-26	−1.24	.47

Table shows the positions taken by Obama and McCain and percentages of 2008 survey respondents agreeing with, disagreeing with, and saying "don't know" to each surveyed policy proposal. The two rightmost columns show the estimated discrimination and difficulty parameters from the estimation of the model shown in Equation 3.1 with the 2008 survey data along with the positions of Obama and McCain.

POLL:NGPOINT  33%

	Agree	Disagree	Not sure
The definition of marriage should apply only to relationships between a man and a woman.	○	○	○
A "windfall profits" tax should be imposed on large profits made by oil companies.	○	○	○
The Supreme Court's decision in Roe v. Wade, which legalized most forms of abortion, should be overturned.	○	○	○

Please tell us whether you personally agree or disagree with each of the statements below:

FIGURE 3.2. 2008 Survey question examples

are based. Full wordings of all questions used here are given in Appendix A. Before proceeding, however, it seems appropriate to briefly discuss the characteristics of the samples of the two surveys. The 2004 survey was fielded to a large national sample stratified on some basic demographic characteristics, but is not nationally representative. Furthermore, the sample was drawn such that at least one hundred respondents were selected from each state.[4] Accordingly, conclusions reached based on the 2004 survey should be tempered by the fact that its sample is overeducated, contains relatively few minorities, and is otherwise somewhat unrepresentative of the American voter population. The 2008 survey, by contrast, was administered to a sample that has extremely similar demographic characteristics to the American electorate as a whole. Demographic factors, party identification, political information levels, and other measures from the 2008 survey's sample are all similar to those from other national surveys, including U.S. Census studies of voters in the 2008 election. Appendix B contains a more detailed description of the characteristics of these two samples.

Both the 2004 and 2008 surveys were fielded to samples drawn from online participant pools using a sample matching technique (Rivers 2006). Although there has been some debate about the relative benefits and drawbacks of drawing samples from volunteer online panels, this general sampling method has been validated across many recent elections, and data sets drawn using these methods have served as the basis for an increasing number of journal articles and books in recent years. Concerns about this approach typically center on two areas. First, samples of opt-in panelists are sometimes unrepresentative on many demographic or other

---

[4] This sampling procedure was adopted because one of the aims of the survey was to study citizen perceptions of the ideology of their senators (see Jessee and Rivers 2008).

factors. This concern, however, has little to do specifically with Internet samples, as any mode of contact can produce skewed samples. Furthermore, many volunteer online samples have demographic characteristics that very closely mirror the populations under study. The 2008 survey analyzed here has very similar demographic and political characteristics to other studies, such as the Census Bureau's study of the American electorate and the American National Election Studies (see Appendix B). The second level of concern is that the use of such "volunteers" produces a sample that is somehow different, even if its demographic or other characteristics are similar to those of the general population. This second concern raises a valid point, but also is premised on a misguided dichotomization of survey methods. Few surveys, save perhaps the U.S. Census, use anything other than "volunteer" or "opt-in" panelists. The ANES, for example, have typically had response rates in the neighborhood of 60 percent. Although this number is quite high, it clearly does not come close to total participation and emphasizes that all respondents decide for themselves whether they participate in a given survey.

Recent work has attempted to compare the results of these Internet-based surveys to those of more traditional methods, such as in-person or telephone interviews. Although Malhotra and Krosnick (2007) find some differences between Internet surveys and those using other methods, Sanders et al. (2007) find relatively minor differences between Internet-based surveys and the British Election Study. Hill et al. (2007) conclude that the 2006 Cooperative Congressional Election Study sample is similar to those from random digit dialing telephone surveys. Overall, opt-in Internet surveys, especially those using principled and sophisticated sampling methods, have been gaining wide acceptance in political science research in recent years. In particular, their relatively low cost and extreme flexibility have all served as strong selling points. Moreover, the results of these studies have increasingly been validated as similar to, if not better than, those produced by more traditional methods in many cases.

Examining Ideological Constraint across Issues

A prerequisite for spatial voting theory is that the policy views of voters can be accurately summarized by positions in some ideological space. More basic than even this concept, however, is the idea that there exist any sort of meaningful associations between the views of citizens across different types of policies. The discovery of such relationships, which are

TABLE 3.3. *Associations Between Specific Policy Views, 2008 Survey*

	Reverse Tax Cuts for Rich			Overturn Roe v. Wade	
	Support	Oppose		Support	Oppose
Traditional Marriage			Privatize Social Security		
Support	43%	80%	Support	84%	46%
	(439)	(571)		(469)	(424)
Oppose	57%	20%	Oppose	16%	54%
	(483)	(120)		(87)	(492)
TOTAL	100%	100%	TOTAL	100%	100%
	(922)	(691)		(556)	(916)

Note: Cell entries are column percentages with counts underneath in parentheses. "Not sure" and missing responses are omitted.

typically termed constraint, would suggest that the opinions of citizens are more than simply a collection of separate beliefs (or, even worse, a set of random responses with little real thought behind them), but instead are held together by some sort of underlying attitude structure.

The most basic test to detect an attitude structure is to simply examine whether there exist any clear relationships between people's positions on any two different issues. For example, people who support issue A might be more likely to support some other issue B or less likely to support issue C. Table 3.3 shows two examples of such associations, both taken from the 2008 survey. The left side of the table shows the percentage of people who believe that the definition of marriage should apply only to relationships between a man and a woman among those who support reversing tax cuts for people making more than $250,000 per year and among those who oppose it. Supporters of reversing the tax cuts (i.e., people who want taxes on the rich to increase) tend to oppose this traditional view of marriage, with 57 percent believing that the definition of marriage should be broadened. Among those who oppose reversing tax cuts for the wealthy, however, 80 percent support the "one man, one woman" view of marriage. This evidence suggests a powerful association between these two issues, which, on their face, would seem to have little to do with one another in terms of substance. We also see that respondents' opinions on the privatization of Social Security and abortion show strong relationships with each other despite the fact that they deal with dramatically different areas of government policy.

These associations provide evidence that voters' opinions on different issues are related to one another by some underlying structure, but looking at relationships solely between two issues at a time is a fairly basic way of examining these relationships. A common method for exploring richer relationships between sets of variables is to look at their correlation matrices. In particular, scree plots of these correlation matrices are often used to assess the likely dimensionality of the latent structure for data. Loosely speaking, scree plots help researchers determine how much of the variability in a given set of variables can be explained by a latent structure of a certain number of dimensions. Commonly, scree plots are analyzed by looking at the point at which the plot "levels out." It is generally argued that the number of values on a scree plot before it flattens out indicates the number of meaningful dimensions in the unobserved latent structure for the data.

Figure 3.3 shows scree plots for the correlation matrices of issue positions of respondents in the 2004 and 2008 surveys.[5] For both the 2004 and 2008 surveys, scree plots show a relatively high first value, with all further values being much lower. Because both of these scree plots flatten out after one large value, they suggest that one underlying dimension can account for the bulk of the variation in respondents' issue positions for both of these surveys, with any possible further dimensions contributing at most a small amount of explanatory power. In other words, we should be able to explain a large percentage of respondents' stated policy positions using a single liberal–conservative value for each respondent. Furthermore, moving to two or more dimensions does not result in a large increase in our ability to predict these positions.

These results strongly suggest that a single ideological dimension provides a useful and relatively complete description of the political views of respondents across a range of different policy areas. Such findings stand in sharp contrast to earlier works that argued for the general lack of ideological sophistication of ordinary Americans (e.g., Campbell et al. 1960; Converse 1964). Instead of a random collection of views that demonstrate little or no coherent structure, the views expressed by respondents in the two surveys analyzed here show strong evidence of a unidimensional ideological structure. This finding suggests that the policy views of ordinary Americans are in fact structured by some underlying ideology and that

---

[5] Formally, these figures plot the eigenvalues of the double-centered tetrachoric correlation matrices between respondents' support or oppose positions (coded as 0 and 1, respectively) on the policy issues from the surveys.

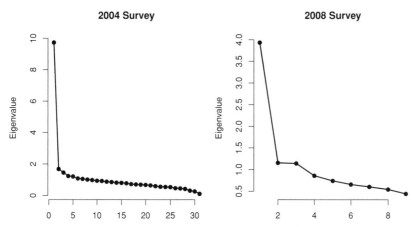

FIGURE 3.3. Respondent policy position scree plots. Graphs plot the eigenvalues of the double-centered tetrachoric correlation matrices between respondents' support or oppose positions (coded as 0 and 1, respectively) on the policy issues from the surveys. These plots, often called "scree plots," help assess the dimensionality of the underlying structure for a given set of data. Because these plots for both the 2004 and 2008 data begin with one relatively large value, with the remaining values being much smaller, these graphs provide strong evidence of a largely single-dimensional structure underlying the policy positions for respondents in both of these surveys.

this ideology can be accurately described by a single liberal–conservative ideological dimension.

It is possible that the samples for the 2004 and 2008 surveys are more politically informed and interested than the samples of previous studies. While this is almost certainly the case for the 2004 survey, the 2008 survey shows relatively similar levels of political information to other studies (see Appendix B). Furthermore, scree plots of the least informed half of each of these survey samples also suggest a strong first dimension, with further dimensions contributing much less explanatory power.

There are several other possible explanations for the divergence between these findings and earlier ones. First, it is possible that the nature of the public's political opinions has changed in recent decades. For example, Bafumi and Shapiro (2009) argue that partisanship has become more ideological and policy based in recent decades. It could be that the ideologically innocent public described in *The American Voter* has been replaced in recent years by one in which policy views are related to each other by strong ideologies. It also is possible that previous authors' findings that respondents were generally incapable of providing any reasonable (at least in the authors' eyes) explanations for their stated policy views are in fact compatible with the findings presented here. Respondents may hold views that are structured by some meaningful ideology even if they are not capable of explaining the basis for this ideological structure. Furthermore, issues with measurement error, which may not have been properly addressed or acknowledged in previous work, may have resulted in earlier findings of a general lack of ideological constraint (see, e.g., Achen 1975; Ansolabehere et al. 2008).

Finally, the approach to assessing dimensionality here is different from that employed in some other studies. I am not centrally interested in whether a second, third, or further ideological dimension exists in the sense that it is statistically significant – that it predicts respondent positions better than randomly generated white noise would be expected to. Instead, I focus on assessing the number of substantively important dimensions – those that explain a large proportion of respondents' issue positions. Stimson (1975) finds evidence of more than one ideological dimension by treating every dimension having an eigenvalue greater than 1 as "real." Stimson himself, however, notes that "factor analysis may also overstate the number of real dimensions" (406). Furthermore, such cutoffs are better suited for assessing the statistical, rather than substantive, significance of these dimensions. The key finding here is that a first dimension can explain an extremely large portion of the variation in respondents' issue positions. While subsequent dimensions explain more, the increase in explanatory power is not large, even if it may be statistically significant.

The findings presented in this section demonstrate clearly that the political opinions of respondents to both of the national surveys analyzed here show strong evidence of ideological constraint. There exist strong and significant associations between people's views on different policies, including those which on their face would seem to have little to do with each other in substantive terms. Furthermore, the specific nature of the relationships between opinions on different policy issues appears to be explained quite well by a single ideological dimension.

Estimating Voter and Candidate Ideology Together

Having established that ordinary citizens do in fact display some amount of constraint between their views on different issues and that this constraint can be explained largely by a single underlying ideological dimension, we can now move on to exploring the specific nature of this dimension. Testing spatial voting theory requires estimates of both voter and candidate ideology on the same scale. As discussed previously, much of the previous work on testing spatial voting has attempted to overcome this issue by relying on strong assumptions and questionable measures. Typical methods for measuring the policy views of citizens produce results that are not comparable with the actual positions taken by candidates or elected officials. For example, when respondents are asked to place themselves on ordinal ideology or policy scales, there is no clear way to determine where candidates would fall on these same measures. For example, would Barack Obama be a one or a two on a five-point ideology scale? Where would John McCain fall on this same measure?

Previous work has attempted to use these or similar measures to locate the ideology of voters and candidates on the same scale, either by looking at respondents' self-placements on ideological scales along with their placements of parties or candidates (e.g., Alvarez and Nagler 1995) or by considering the "true" positions of candidates or parties to be equal to the average perceptions among respondents (Brady and Sniderman 1985). Others have relied on placements of the candidates' positions and electoral medians by experts (Stone and Simas 2010). Taking a somewhat different approach, Schofield et al. (2004) compare party positions in the Netherlands and Germany with voter opinions by leveraging similar questions found in surveys of both party elites and the general public. While these earlier approaches have provided many important insights, they all rest, to some degree or another, on subjective placements, assumptions about aggregate unbiasedness of perceptions, or other strong assumptions. The approach used here attempts to remedy this situation by providing a direct and objective bridge between the estimated positions of candidates and the ideologies of ordinary voters based on specific policy positions. The estimates presented here provide the most direct measures to date of the ideology of voters and candidates on the same scale by obtaining measurements of respondents' policy views in a form that is directly comparable with the roll call votes cast or campaign positions taken by the candidates in recent presidential elections.

Surveying respondents on specific issue positions provides several advantages over simply asking people to quantify their overall ideology. First, these items are more concrete and hence more likely to be perceived in the same way by different respondents, in contrast, for example, to ordinal scale questions, whose response options have no objective definition. Second, surveying respondents on specific policies can allow for the direct comparison of voter ideology with candidate positions, which is generally not possible with ordinal ideology scales or other more traditional measures. Finally, by polling respondents on many proposals across a wide range of issue areas, we are making no a priori assumptions about the nature of the policy dimension that structures their political beliefs. Respondents are allowed, through their stated positions, to reveal how different issues and proposals relate to the primary dimension of policy ideology that underlies their political beliefs.

The technique of ideal point estimation involves estimating the positions of actors on some latent dimension based on some set of positions they have taken. These types of models stem from earlier work in areas such as psychometrics and educational testing (e.g., Rasch 1960, 1966). The most common application of ideal point estimation in political science has been in the estimation of the ideological positions of members of Congress. Because senators and representatives cast a large number of votes in each session of Congress, researchers have a good deal of information with which to estimate their ideological positions, and the estimates produced by various ideal point techniques have served as one of the most useful data sources in modern research on congressional behavior. Several different ideal point models and estimation techniques have been proposed, beginning with the widely used NOMINATE scores of Poole and Rosenthal (1985) and continuing with the factor analytic measures proposed by Heckman and Snyder (1997) and the ideal point model and accompanying Bayesian simulation-based estimation method introduced by Clinton et al. (2004b).

Ideal point estimation generally posits some model for the relationship between actors' ideological positions and their probabilities of supporting a given proposal. Typically, these statistical models are based on some sort of random utility model of decision making. Actors are assumed to have ideological positions (ideal points) in some finite-dimensional, usually one-dimensional, space. On any given vote, an actor is asked to choose between two options – the "yea" and "nay" ("support" and "oppose") positions. It is usually assumed that actors receive greater utility from choosing options that are closer to their ideal points, but that these utilities also involve some random error. Actors thus choose the option that provides them with the most utility, including both the proximity-based utility and this random error term. While ideal point estimation techniques can differ in areas such as the assumed shape of utility functions and error distributions, the resulting differences in the actual ideal point estimates are typically minor (see Clinton et al. 2004a,

360 for an example of various ideal point estimation techniques applied to the same congressional voting data, yielding similar results).

The primary benefit of ideal point estimation is that it grounds the estimation of ideology in a full statistical model. The model's assumptions are clear and direct, and are based around a coherent and well-specified theory of position taking. Furthermore, as in all inference, relying on a full statistical model allows for principled estimation of the quantities of interest and for the quantification of uncertainty about these specific values. In this case, the ideal point framework used results in direct and straightforward tests of specific hypotheses about respondent ideology, and later about the use of spatial voting in presidential elections. It also is comforting to note that more basic analyses using the proportion of time each respondent or candidate took a conservative position on the issues produces largely similar conclusions to the ones reached here, albeit without providing tests as direct as the methods used in the main analyses (see Appendix C for a fuller description of these simplified analyses).

The model of position taking used here follows the work of Clinton et al. (2004a). For this model, policy positions are coded as 1 for support and 0 for oppose. The probability of respondent i supporting some policy proposal j can then be written as

$$P(y_{ij} = 1) = \Phi(\gamma_j x_i - \alpha_j), \tag{3.1}$$

where x_i is respondent i's ideological position, γ_j and α_j are the policy proposal's discrimination and difficulty parameters, and Φ is the cumulative distribution function (cdf) for the standard normal distribution.[6] In other words, an actor's probability of supporting a given policy proposal depends on his or her ideological position as well as the characteristics of the proposal in question. The discrimination parameter γ_j for each bill estimates how strongly and in what direction respondents' ideological positions are related to their probabilities of supporting a given policy.[7] Liberal policies should have negative discrimination parameters, whereas conservative policies will have positive discrimination parameters. Furthermore, policies on which respondent support is strongly related to ideological position will have discrimination parameters that are large in

---

[6] Policy positions y_{ij} are treated as missing for respondents who decline to state whether they support or oppose a given proposal and are randomly imputed by the estimation method based on the values of other unknown parameters.

[7] Clinton et al. (2004a) use the symbol β_j to represent the discrimination parameters. γ_j is instead used here because β will later be used to represent the vector of regression coefficients in a probit model predicting vote choice in presidential elections.

magnitude, whereas policies on which there are not large differences in levels of support between liberals and conservatives will have discrimination parameters close to zero. The difficulty parameters α_j are related to the general level of support for each policy, with higher values of α_j representing more overall opposition holding ideology constant. The underlying ideological scale for ideal points (x_i) will be such that higher values represent more conservative ideological positions, whereas lower ones represent more liberal views.

To obtain ideology estimates for respondents and candidates, the ideal point model shown in Equation 3.1 is estimated for both the 2004 and 2008 survey data. For the 2004 survey, the data used consist of two different partitions. First, we have the roll call records of all Senate votes cast during 2004 and 2005, including President Bush's stated positions for all measures on which he publicly took a stand.[8] Second, we have respondents' views on the twenty-seven surveyed policies used here, each of which corresponds to a specific roll call vote from the Senate data. The surveyed votes, for which we know the positions of respondents, constitute a small percentage of the total number of Senate roll calls. Therefore, respondents are treated as if they were "guest senators," stopping in to vote on a small number of Senate votes but having missing values for all other measures. Because these questions were written to simulate as closely as possible the process of roll call voting on these same bills and amendments, we can assume that meanings of the positions of the "support" and "oppose" response options between which respondents are choosing are the same as the "yea" and "nay" positions on the Senate roll calls that correspond to each survey question. It immediately follows, then, that the bill parameters γ_j and α_j in Equation 3.1 should be the same for a respondent answering a question as for a senator voting on the corresponding proposal. By imposing these restrictions in the model, we can obtain estimates of the ideal points for survey respondents and senators on the same scale, thus bridging the fundamental comparability gap that has, up to this point, prevented direct tests of the spatial voting model. In other words, by assuming that respondents' stated positions on survey questions mean the same thing as do senators' votes on the corresponding Senate roll call votes, we are able to estimate the ideological positions of respondents and senators together on the same scale.

---

[8] The president's position was coded from Congressional Quarterly's online database of Senate votes (http://cq.com). The president is coded as "yea" if he took a public position supporting a given measure and "nay" if he publicly opposed a measure. His position is coded as missing for the majority of votes on which he took no public position.

The 2008 survey again asked ordinary citizens about their views on specific policies. This survey, however, did not ask about policies that had actually been voted on by Congress, but instead included a set of ten policies on which each of the two candidates in the 2008 election had taken public stands. Therefore, while the survey measured respondents' positions on each of these ten policies, the positions of John McCain and Barack Obama on these issues also were known. In order to estimate the ideology of respondents on the same scale as the positions of these two candidates, the ideal point model in Equation 3.1 is estimated for the 2008 survey data along with the positions taken by Obama and McCain, assuming that the positions taken by a respondent supporting or opposing a given policy were the same as those of a candidate taking a public position either for or against that same policy.

For both the 2004 and 2008 data, the model is estimated using the ideal function from the pscl library in R (Jackman 2009). This function estimates the ideal point model shown in Equation 3.1 using a Gibbs sampling procedure.[9] As with all ideal point models, the ideological scale estimated is in a fundamental way undefined. Whereas temperature can be measured in degrees Celsius or Fahrenheit or weight can be measured in pounds or kilograms, there is no objective scale for ideology. A common method of pinning down the ideological scale to be estimated in single-dimensional ideal point models is to fix the ideological positions of two particular actors to specific values. In this case, the scales are identified by restricting the ideological positions of presidential candidates. For the 2004 estimation, it is assumed that John Kerry is located at $-1/4$ and George W. Bush takes a position at $1/4$. Similarly, in 2008, it is assumed that Barack Obama and John McCain take positions at $-1/4$ and $1/4$, respectively. These restrictions do not alter the relative ideological positions estimated for any respondents or candidates, but instead only serve to pin the estimated ideological spectrum down to a specific scale. The reason for the particular choice of these values will become apparent in Chapter 4 when we move on to the predictions of spatial voting theory. Because these restrictions pin down the ideological scale on which the ideal points are estimated, they in effect define the meaning of the scale itself. Accordingly, all other model estimates, including discrimination and difficulty parameters as well as the estimated ideal points of other

---

[9] The models were run in an unidentified state with independent standard normal priors on all actors' ideal points and independent normal priors with mean zero and variance 100 for all difficulty and discrimination parameters. The results of the model were post-processed to impose identification restrictions.

actors, can be interpreted relative to these values. More conservative ideologies are represented by higher ideal point values, and the ideological "center," inasmuch as it may be expected to fall somewhere between the two candidates, will be around zero. It also should be noted that values on the ideological scale estimated for the 2004 survey are not directly comparable with those estimated for 2008. In other words, it is not assumed that Kerry and Obama or Bush and McCain held identical positions. Instead, the two ideological scales estimated for the 2004 and 2008 surveys should be considered separately.

The two rightmost columns of Tables 3.1 and 3.2 show the estimated "discrimination" and "difficulty" parameters γ_j and α_j for each policy question in the 2004 and 2008 surveys, respectively. While the "difficulty" parameter is related to the baseline level of support for a given policy, we can focus on the "discrimination" parameter, which indicates how ideologically divisive a given policy is as well as whether it is a liberal or conservative proposal. This will allow us to get a sense for which issues provide the most structure to the ideological dimension underlying the views of citizens and candidates. We see that for the most part, these results correspond well with conventional notions of liberalism and conservatism in American politics. For example, in the 2004 survey, traditionally conservative proposals such as tax reductions and protections against lawsuits for gun owners and sellers have positive discrimination parameters. Conversely, policies such as reductions in military funding, increases in welfare benefits, and raising the minimum wage all have negative discrimination parameters. In the 2008 survey, supporting a traditional definition of marriage and reversing the Supreme Court's ruling in *Roe v. Wade* are estimated to be conservative positions, whereas imposing taxes on oil company profits and requiring health insurance for all American children are shown to be liberal. These results are reassuring and suggest that the ideological dimensions estimated for both sets of survey data parallel the liberal–conservative spectrum that is commonly discussed in modern American politics.

We can also gain a fuller understanding of these results by examining the specific relationships predicted by the model between ideological position and the probability of supporting various policies. Figure 3.4 shows two examples of these predicted relationships, both taken from the 2008 survey. The left pane of the figure shows the relationship between support for withdrawing troops from Iraq and respondents' ideological positions. We see that there is a strong negative relationship, with more liberals being overwhelmingly supportive of withdrawing troops from

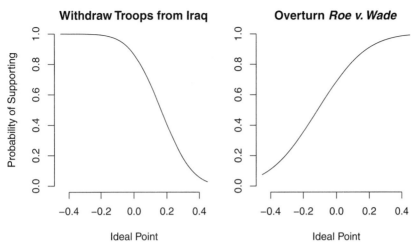

FIGURE 3.4. Ideal point model predicted response probabilities. Plots show examples of the estimated relationship between ideology (ideal point) and an actor's predicted probability of support for two specific policy proposals from the 2008 survey. Support for withdrawing troops from Iraq is highest among liberals and significantly lower among conservatives. Support for overturning the Supreme Court's decision in *Roe v. Wade*, by contrast, is relatively low for liberals and high among conservatives.

Iraq and conservatives being mostly opposed. On the issue of overturning the Supreme Court's decision in *Roe v. Wade*, the right pane of the figure shows that liberals are generally opposed to this proposal, whereas conservatives predominantly support it. In both of these cases, issue positions are strongly related to ideology, and the relationship is generally compatible with common understandings of the liberal–conservative spectrum in American politics.

While examining the difficulty and discrimination parameters for each policy provides a way to understand the nature of the ideological dimension being estimated, the primary quantities of interest from the model are the estimated ideal points of respondents and candidates. Figure 3.5 plots the distributions of estimated respondent ideal points for both the 2004 and 2008 surveys separated by respondent party identification. Here and, unless otherwise stated, for the rest of the book, partisans include both "strong" and "weak" party identifiers as well as those who state that they "lean" toward one party or the other. Independents, therefore, include only those who express no preference for either party (so-called pure independents). As expected, the ideal points of Democrats, denoted by

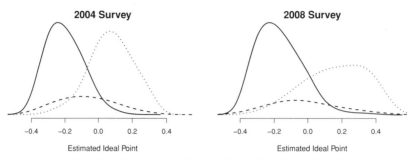

FIGURE 3.5. Density of estimated ideal points. Plots show the density of estimated ideal points for respondents in the 2004 and 2008 surveys separated by party identification, with solid, dotted, and dashed lines indicating Democratic, independent, and Republican respondents, respectively. Note that the estimated ideological scales for the 2004 and 2008 surveys are not directly comparable. Instead, the two scales should be interpreted separately.

solid lines, tend to be the most liberal. Republican respondents (dotted lines) are generally quite conservative. For both surveys, however, there is a decent amount of overlap between the distributions of ideology in the two parties. In the 2004 sample, 11 percent of Democratic respondents are at least as conservative as the average respondent and nearly 14 percent of Republicans are more liberal than the average. In 2008, 15 percent of Republicans are more liberal than the average, while 17 percent of Democrats fall to the right of the mean respondent. Independents fall on average somewhere in between the two parties, but also show a relatively wide range of dispersion. For example, the percentage of independents falling at least one sample standard deviation away from the mean is 17 percent in 2004 and 13 percent in 2008.

The results of these ideal point models also provide another method for assessing the dimensionality of citizen ideology. These one-dimensional models estimated based on the policy items from the 2004 and 2008 surveys fit the data quite well, correctly predicting 78.7 and 82.2 percent of respondent positions, respectively. Estimating these same models but adding a second ideological dimension increases the fit only modestly, correctly predicting 81.4 and 86.5 percent, respectively, of the positions in these two studies. This suggests that while there may be more than one ideological dimension that is statistically significant in the sense of predicting respondent views more strongly than would a set of randomly generated white noise, dimensions beyond this first one are not nearly as substantively important and hence are not extensively analyzed here.

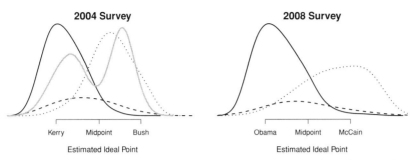

FIGURE 3.6. Density of estimated ideal points with senators and candidates. Plots show the density of estimated ideal points for respondents in the 2004 and 2008 surveys separated by party identification, with solid, dashed, and dotted lines indicating Democratic, independent, and Republican respondents, respectively. The solid gray line in the left pane plots the density of ideal point estimates for senators, with the positions of John Kerry, George W. Bush, and the midpoint between these two candidates shown along the x-axis. The x-axis of the right pane shows the estimated positions of Barack Obama, John McCain, and the estimated midpoint between them.

In addition to estimating the ideological positions of respondents, we also have estimates of the positions taken by candidates in the 2004 and 2008 presidential elections. In 2004, our estimates are in fact not only for Bush and Kerry, but also for all senators who cast roll call votes at any point during 2004 and 2005. The left pane of Figure 3.6 again plots the distribution of estimated respondent ideal points for respondents to the 2004 survey (as in Figure 3.5), this time adding the distribution of estimated senator ideal points, shown with a solid gray line. We see that the estimated ideologies of senators are somewhat similar to those of respondents. Democratic and Republican senators are concentrated roughly in the same areas as Democratic and Republican respondents. Again, it should be pointed out that the 2004 survey's sample is not nationally representative, so conclusions should only be drawn about the particular sample, rather than about the distribution of ideology in the country as a whole. The bottom axis shows the estimated positions of Kerry, Bush, and the midpoint between the two candidates. We see that the two candidates clearly hold divergent positions, with Kerry being located near the center of the distribution of Democratic voter ideology and Bush being even more conservative than most Republicans in the sample. The estimated candidate positions for the 2008 election show somewhat similar characteristics to those in 2004. Obama and McCain are estimated have a clear ideological separation, with both appearing to be positioned near the center of the ideological distribution of their parties' identifiers.

Assessing the Predictions of "Extended" Spatial Voting Models

Spatial voting theory, in its most basic form, is a theory about how voters make decisions. The central axiom of this theory is that citizens will cast their vote (or will be most likely to cast their vote) for the candidate whose position is closest to their own ideal point. This basic setup also has provided the basis for a wide range of what could be called "extended" spatial models, many of which involve assumptions about candidate strategy, the structure of elections, and other factors. In fact, much of the skepticism that has been aimed at spatial voting theory has stemmed from the empirical falsification of implications derived from such extended spatial voting theories. As discussed in Chapter 2, however, many of these predictions rely on an additional set of assumptions above and beyond the basic axioms of spatial voting theory. Furthermore, many of these additional assumptions are objectively false, meaning that the failure of the resulting predictions is largely uninformative about the plausibility of the basic axioms of spatial voting theory.

The most commonly discussed of these extended models is the so-called Downsian model of candidate positioning (Downs 1957).[10] In addition to assuming that voters in elections choose the candidate who takes a position closest to their own ideological location, this setup makes several other assumptions. First, candidates are assumed to choose their positions solely in order to maximize the number of votes they receive. The classic Downsian model also assumes that voter turnout is complete (or at least unrelated to candidate positions) and that candidates win office in a single-stage election process. While some scholars have pointed to divergent candidate positions in real-world elections as a failure of spatial voting theory (see Green and Shapiro 1994 for a notable example), others have argued that by varying the simple assumptions of these extended spatial models, predictions of distinct candidate positions are possible. In a review of this "neo-Downsian" literature, Grofman (2004) identifies fifteen specific assumptions in the Downsian model, describing how modifications to many of these assumptions result in predictions of polarized candidate positions. Multiple constituencies, candidate ambiguity, multistage elections (such as the primary and general elections held for virtually

---

[10] Downs introduces several extended spatial models in his classic book. The variant described here is arguably the simplest but also the most often referenced, particularly with regard to its predictions for candidate positioning.

all federal offices), and several other factors can result in predictions of candidate divergence even under conditions where voters use spatial decision rules. Therefore, findings of candidate divergence in actual American elections, while they do falsify some of what might be termed "extended" spatial models, including the simple Downsian model, do not necessarily provide any direct evidence against the use of spatial decision rules by ordinary voters.

Although the results will not speak directly to the validity of spatial voting theory, we can use the estimated positions of respondents and candidates in the 2008 election survey to examine the positions taken by Obama and McCain relative to the national electorate as a whole.[11] The 2004 survey's estimates are not discussed extensively here because the sample for this survey is not nationally representative. As such, we cannot use it to infer the positions of Bush and Kerry as compared to the national voter population. Because the 2008 survey is broadly representative of the American electorate across many demographic and political variables, the resulting estimates can provide a relatively clear picture of how Obama and McCain positioned themselves relative to voters in the 2008 presidential election.

The most commonly cited prediction of so-called extended spatial theories is that candidates should converge to the position of the median voter's ideal point. According to this prediction, in 2008 the positions for Obama, McCain, and the median voter ideal point should all be the same. In fact, we clearly see that this is far from the truth. First, Obama and McCain are estimated to have distinct positions, with McCain being significantly more conservative than Obama. (Note that this is assumed to be true given the identification restriction of the model, but also is estimated to be true with virtual certainty when the model is estimated in an unidentified state.) As seen in Table 3.4, the median respondent in the 2008 sample is estimated to be located at −.05, fairly close to the midpoint between the two candidates' positions. The prediction of candidate convergence to the median voter's position, then, is clearly falsified by these estimates from the 2008 election. Furthermore, although the 2004 survey data cannot provide reliable estimates of characteristics of the national voter distribution such as the median ideal point, it can still produce estimates of the positions of George W. Bush and John Kerry. As in the 2008 election, we clearly see that the two candidates in 2004 occupied significantly different positions, with Bush being much more conservative than Kerry.

---

[11] See also Jessee (2010b).

TABLE 3.4. *Estimated Respondent Ideal Point Medians,*
2008 Survey

	All Respondents	
	−.05	
	(−.32, .19)	
	Party Identification	
Democrats	Independents	Republicans
−.21	−.04	.21
(−.56, .06)	(−.30, .21)	(−.06, .53)
	Primary Turnout	
Democratic	None	Republican
−.20	−.05	.22
(−.54, .07)	(−.33, .19)	(−.05, .54)

Estimated sample medians are shown for all respondents, along with
those for various subgroups, with 95 percent highest posterior density
regions underneath in parentheses. Note that because of the identification restriction fixing the positions of Obama and McCain at −1/4 and 1/4,
respectively, these 95 percent highest posterior density regions account
for the uncertainty not only of respondents' ideal points, but also of the
candidates' positions. For example, the model actually predicts with virtual certainty that the median Democrat is more liberal than the median
independent and that the median independent is more more liberal than
the median Republican (similarly for primary turnout).

Although some degree of ideological separation between Democratic
and Republican candidates would probably be expected by observers of
modern American elections, we can go further to examine the actual
amount of divergence relative to the distribution of voter ideology in the
2008 election. The positions of Obama and McCain are estimated to
fall approximately one sample standard deviation on either side of the
median. This demonstrates that not only did the two candidates take
ideologically distinct campaign positions, but each candidate took a position relatively far from the ideological center of the nation's voters. In
fact, more than two-thirds of respondents are estimated to have ideal
points between Obama and McCain's positions, further reinforcing the
traditional wisdom that the Democratic and Republican candidates in
presidential elections tend to take positions far from that of the national
median voter.

Several scholars have proposed theories for why candidates may
offer divergent positions in contrast to the predictions of Downsian

convergence. In fact, many of these theories are perfectly compatible with the assumption that citizens cast their votes using spatial decision rules. Most obviously, presidential elections generally consist of a two-stage process, with candidates having to win a primary election in order to secure their party's nomination for the general election. Grofman et al. (2002) demonstrate that such two-stage processes, combined with partisan constituencies with differing ideological characteristics, can produce candidates who come from between each party's median and mode. Therefore, the simplest Downsian models that result in candidate convergence predictions clearly omit a major feature of real-world elections. The failings of their predictions, then, should not be interpreted as a clear falsification of the basic axioms of spatial voting theory.

Some scholars have argued that primary contests should produce nominees who are located between a party's median and the national median (Aranson and Ordeshook 1972; Coleman 1972). Furthermore, voter alienation also could pull the positions taken by candidates away from the national center if voters decide to stay home when no candidate espouses views sufficiently close to the voters' own (Adams and Merrill 2008). On a similar note, candidates or parties may fear that highly mobilized and ideologically extreme constituencies may create or support third-party candidacies when major party nominees move too far to the center. Higher levels of campaign involvement and monetary contributions from more extreme voters also could induce candidates to move to the extremes (Aldrich 1983). In short, while the most basic Downsian models predict complete convergence to the national median voter, several modifications of assumptions regarding candidate incentives or electoral rules can produce predictions of divergence. Directly and formally testing any of these theoretical accounts would likely require estimates of voter ideology and candidate positions across multiple elections and hence is beyond the scope of this study. However, we can still examine how the estimated positions of Obama and McCain in the 2008 election match up with the predictions of these various arguments, which could provide some suggestive evidence regarding the actual degree of ideological divergence that is observed in presidential elections and its possible causes.

Table 3.4 also shows the estimated median positions for respondents by party identification as well as reported primary election participation.[12] The most prominent feature of this table is that the estimated

---

[12] It should be emphasized that these estimates, along with the following discussions, apply to the estimated characteristics of the 2008 survey's sample, rather than the American

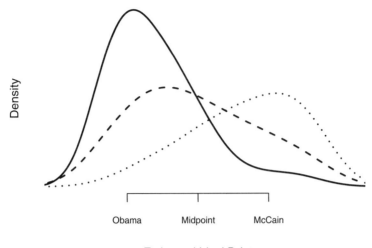

Estimated Ideal Point

FIGURE 3.7. Estimated respondent ideal points by primary participation, 2008 survey. Solid and dotted lines show the weighted density of estimated ideal points for respondents who participated in the Democratic and Republican primaries, respectively, while the dashed line plots the density of estimated ideal points for respondents who reported not voting in either primary election. Respondents who did not recall which primary they voted in and those who skipped or were not asked this question are omitted.

party medians, whether defined by respondents' own identification or by stated primary participation, are estimated to be very similar to the positions taken by Obama and McCain. In fact, the two candidates are estimated to be slightly more extreme than the medians of their partisan and primary constituencies. It may be expected, for example, that competitive primaries, which both Obama and McCain faced in 2008, could drive candidates closer toward the median of their primary constituencies and thus away from the overall median of the electorate. Figure 3.7 plots the density of estimated ideal points by reported primary participation. Solid and dotted lines plot the estimates for respondents who stated that they voted in the Democratic and

voter population as a whole, even though the sample is nationally representative across a relatively broad range of demographic and other characteristics. Attempts to account for the added uncertainty in these median estimates due to sampling error using the bootstrap produced some minor differences, but overall substantive results remained similar.

Republican primaries, respectively, while the dashed line includes respondents who reported not voting in either primary, or who did not provide a response to this question. The positions of Obama and McCain, noted on the x-axis, fall near the middle of their respective parties' primary constituencies.

Overall, these results are compatible with several of the so-called neo-Downsian explanations for candidate divergence. In 2008, both Obama and McCain staked out positions that were clearly more extreme than the median ideology in the national electorate. Even more, the positions of the candidates appeared to be much closer to, if even slightly more extreme than, the positions of their party medians. While commonly cited as an indication of fatal flaws in the spatial voting framework, these observations are actually quite compatible with many models for candidate positioning involving voters who decide purely based on their spatial proximity to candidates. For example, if primary voters cast their ballots based solely on spatial concerns, strategic candidates will be forced to move to the median of their primary electorates in order to win their party's nomination. This prediction is largely compatible with the observed candidate positions in the 2008 election. Obviously, these two observations, taken from only one election, cannot conclusively establish which electoral forces are most prominent in determining candidate positioning, but the results do point to the idea that divergent candidate positions do not constitute prima fascie evidence against the use of spatial decision rules by ordinary voters. Instead, predictions of candidate convergence can generally be shown to result from the questionable validity (or, in some cases, total implausibility) of many of the assumptions used in simple Downsian models.

Discussion

Spatial voting theory is, at its core, a set of assumptions about how voters make decisions. Although the basic ideas and intuitions of spatial voting have been applied extensively across most areas of the political science literature, the theory itself has often been criticized as inadequate or even implausible. These criticisms have often rested on one of two different claims. First, it has been argued that ordinary voters do not possess meaningful ideologies or perhaps even meaningful policy views. If this was true, a theory of voting in which citizens make their decisions based on their ideological proximity to candidates would be on its face implausible – voters cannot base their choices on their ideological positions if they have no ideologies to begin with. Second, critics have pointed to the clear falsification of the candidate convergence predictions of Downsian and other models as evidence that spatial voting represents a fundamentally flawed theory. The evidence and arguments presented in this chapter has demonstrated that both of these criticisms are misguided.

First, the findings presented in this chapter have shown that the specific policy views of American voters are in fact tied together by meaningful relationships – what Converse (1964) termed constraint. Beyond this, the actual form of the relationships between people's views on different issues is described very well by a single liberal–conservative dimension. While this does not, on its own, demonstrate that voters use spatial decision rules in deciding for whom to cast their ballots, it does refute previous findings of an electorate whose political beliefs are largely devoid of any sort of underlying ideology.

Second, this chapter has presented the most direct estimates to date of the ideology of voters on the same scale as the positions taken by candidates in recent presidential elections. These estimates have reinforced the conventional wisdom that candidates tend to take polarized positions rather than converging to the location of the median voter, as would be predicted under simple Downsian models of candidate positioning. This result is commonly cited as a fatal blow to the plausibility of spatial theory generally. In fact, however, this finding casts doubt only on the particular models that produce these predictions. The most commonly discussed of such models is the simple Downsian model in which voters choose spatially, turnout is complete, candidates take positions solely in order to maximize their vote share, and a winner is selected in a single-stage election. The fact that this setup produces a demonstrably false prediction for candidate positions implies only that at least one of its assumptions is incorrect. But this model involves several questionable assumptions, not the least of which is that it ignores the standard two-stage primary and general election process that is used in virtually all contests for federal office, instead assuming that candidates are elected in a single general election. Findings of candidate polarization, such as those presented here for the 2004 and 2008 election, therefore do not constitute direct evidence against the use of spatial decision rules by voters.

This chapter has thus provided strong evidence against two of the most common criticisms against spatial voting theory. What this chapter has not done, however, is provide any direct evidence in support of the spatial model of voter decision making. This is the task that is now turned to in the proceeding chapters. Chapter 4 presents direct tests of the basic spatial voting model in the two most recent presidential elections. Chapters 5 and 6 go further to explore the use of spatial decision rules for voters of different party identifications and of various levels of political information.

4

Linking Theory and Empirics

Testing Spatial Voting Theory

> No matter how elegant or aesthetically pleasing, a model of politics must ultimately be tested against the real world. Otherwise, it remains, at best, an interesting set of abstractions.
>
> (Enelow and Hinich 1984, 169)

One of the main virtues of spatial voting theory is its high degree of both parsimony and precision relative to other theories of voting behavior. Spatial theory posits that a voter's ideological proximity to candidate positions is the sole (or at least the central) determinant of vote choice. Furthermore, most accounts of spatial voting assume a specific, often formally stated relationship between ideology and voting behavior. The clear and rigorous statement of theoretical axioms in the spatial voting framework generally yields strong and specific empirical predictions. Therefore, spatial theory presents more robust opportunities for falsification than do most other approaches to the study of voting as well as most political science theories more generally. To the extent that spatial voting survives these opportunities for falsification, the theory should be viewed as more promising.

Although spatial theory generates clear, testable hypotheses, obtaining the measurements necessary for testing these hypotheses – specifically estimates of the ideology of voters and the positions taken by candidates – generally has not been possible with existing measurement techniques. Previous work attempting to test the empirical implications of spatial voting models has relied on heroic assumptions or rough proxies in order to obtain estimates of the ideology of voters and candidates on the same scale. As the preceding chapter describes, however, two new surveys conducted with the aim of providing direct estimates of the ideology of voters on the same scale as the positions of candidates have provided a bridge across this comparability gap, overcoming the main obstacle to the testing of the empirical predictions of spatial voting theory. In this chapter, the estimates obtained from these two surveys are used to assess the performance of the spatial model in explaining the choices of voters in real-world elections.

The main goal of this chapter is to conduct basic but direct tests of simple spatial voting theory – to expose the theory's predictions about the behavior of actual voters to opportunities for falsification. The chapter begins by describing formal models of spatial voting and deriving testable hypotheses from these models. Next, it is shown how, under appropriate restrictions, the main predictions of spatial voting theory can be tested by estimating a simple binary probit regression predicting vote choice with ideological position. The results of these tests for both the 2004 and 2008 surveys are then presented and the implications for the spatial voting approach are discussed.

Formal Models of Spatial Voting

Spatial models of voting are typically built on formal assumptions about the relationship between the ideological positions of citizens and their vote choices. These models have a wide rage of characteristics, from simple deterministic models of spatial voting to those involving the possibility of random error in voters' choices and those incorporating nonspatial factors into the decision-making rules of voters. This section describes the basic aspects of formalized accounts of spatial voting, building from examples of very simple models up to more complicated ones.

Deterministic Spatial Voting Models
In its simplest form, the spatial voting model is built from a single assump-tion – that voters will choose the candidate who takes a position closest to their own policy views. Thus, voting is deterministic and based solely on a voter's own position in relation to the candidates in a given elec-tion. Beginning with Hotelling (1929) and applied more extensively to voter behavior by Downs (1957), this idealized model of spatial voting provides a useful starting point for the study of voting behavior and its consequences for things such as candidate behavior and policy outputs.

Most accounts of spatial voting begin by specifying utility functions for voters. These utility functions describe how much benefit a voter would receive from casting his or her ballot for a given candidate. Because the central assumption of spatial voting theory is that voters prefer candidates whose ideologies are close to their own, spatial utility functions generally assign the highest values to candidates who take positions near a voter's own ideological ideal point. The most common functional form for these spatial utility functions is the quadratic. Under a simple quadratic utility function, the utility received by some voter i from casting a ballot for some candidate k can be written as

$$U_i(k) = -(x_i - c_k)^2, \tag{4.1}$$

where x_i represents voter i's ideological location and c_k is candidate k's position. This means that a voter will receive the maximum possible utility of zero by choosing a candidate whose position is identical to the voter's own ideological location. As the distance between a voter and a given candidate increases, the utility the voter would receive from casting his or her ballot for the candidate declines (becomes more negative). The quadratic form is chosen for a variety of reasons, most notably mathematical convenience. In practice, deriving properties of spatial models involving quadratic utility functions tends to be relatively straightforward.

Another possible form that could be assumed for voter utility functions is linear. Under this setup, the utility a voter receives from choosing a given candidate can be written as

$$U_i(k) = -|x_i - c_k|, \tag{4.2}$$

where $|\cdot|$ is the absolute value function. While both the quadratic and linear utility functions are single-peaked and symmetric around the voter's ideal point, they do represent somewhat different influences for ideological proximity on voters' utilities. As an illustration, Figure 4.1 shows examples of both quadratic and linear utility functions for a voter with an ideal point of zero. In both cases, the voter's utility is highest when choosing a candidate who takes a position at zero, the voter's own ideal point. As candidates move away from the voter's most preferred position, the voters utility declines under both the quadratic and linear functions. In the quadratic case, however, the utility decline gets steeper as candidates move farther away. For instance, note that for the quadratic utility function, a candidate taking a position at zero offers utility zero, whereas a candidate taking a position at one offers utility negative one. Therefore, this one-unit change in candidate position – from zero to one – results in a one-unit change in utility. A candidate taking a position at two, however,

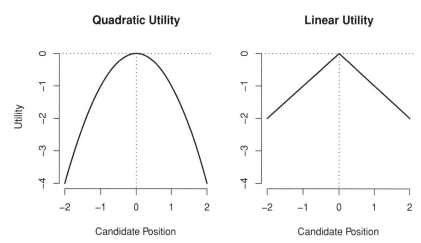

FIGURE 4.1. Examples of possible spatial utility functions. Left pane shows quadratic utility function $U_i(k) = -c_k^2$ and right pane shows linear utility function $U_i(k) = -|c_k|$, both corresponding to $x_i = 0$.

offers utility negative four, meaning that the one-unit change in candidate position from one to two results in a three-unit change in utility. Under the linear utility function, the utility decline is constant, meaning that for each unit of distance a candidate moves away from the voter, the voter's utility declines the same amount – in this case, one unit.

In practice, the simplest spatial models tend to have identical or nearly identical properties regardless of which of these utility functions are chosen. For example, the median voter theorem, discussed in Chapter 1, holds as long as voters have single-peaked utility functions, a set of possibilities that includes quadratic, linear, and many other choices. In this sense, the choice of the specific form for voters' utility functions from among all possible single-peaked functions, while arbitrary, is often largely inconsequential in simple models.

Spatial voting theories generally assume that voters will cast their ballot with the aim of maximizing their utility. In other words, they will vote for the candidate who offers them the highest utility. Assuming that, as in the American case, there are two candidates, a Democrat D and a Republican R, taking positions c_D and c_R, respectively, a voter should cast his or her ballot for the Republican whenever $U_i(R) > U_i(D)$ and should choose the Democratic candidate when $U_i(D) > U_i(R)$. It is typically assumed that voters for whom $U_i(R) = U_i(D)$ (in the case of linear or quadratic utility, someone who holds an ideological position midway between the two

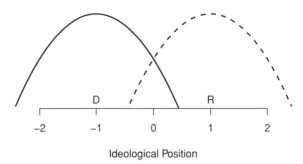

Ideological Position

FIGURE 4.2. Deterministic spatial voting example. Solid (dashed) curve represents the utility that would be received from a voter for casting their ballot for candidate $D(R)$. These curves are a function of the voter's ideal point, following the standard quadratic utility function $U_i(k) = -(x_i - c_k)^2$.

candidate locations) make their decision by simply "flipping a coin," having an equal chance of voting for each candidate. It is easily demonstrated for both the quadratic and linear utility functions that this implies that voters will choose the candidate who takes a position closest to the voter's own ideal point. Therefore, the midpoint between the two candidates' positions, which can be calculated as $\frac{c_D + c_R}{2}$, represents a cut point between voters who will cast their ballots for the Democratic and Republican candidate, respectively. Voters to the left of the midpoint between the two candidates will be closer to, and hence should vote for, the Democratic candidate. Those holding ideologies to the right of this midpoint will be closer to the Republican and will vote for him. In fact, this will be true not just for quadratic and linear utility functions, but for any single-peaked, symmetric utility function.

Because under this quadratic utility function each citizen casts his or her vote for the candidate whose position is closest to the voter's own ideological position, the result is a simple dichotomous function for predicting voter choice. We can simply calculate the midpoint between the two candidates, and all voters to the left should vote for the more liberal candidate, while voters to the right should always choose the conservative candidate. Figure 4.2 illustrates this idea for a hypothetical election in which candidates D and R take positions at -1 and 1, respectively. In this example, if we assume that voters have quadratic utility, we can graph the utility of choosing each candidate as a function of a voter's ideological position. The solid curve shows the utility that voters of various ideological positions would receive from casting their ballot for candidate *D*. We see that this utility is highest for voters who have ideological positions at or near -1, which is candidate *D*'s position. Similarly, the dashed line shows the utility that voters would receive from choosing candidate *R* based on the voter's ideological location. These two curves cross at the ideological position of zero, meaning that voters at this point, whose ideological views are the same distance from either candidate's position, will receive the same utility from voting for either candidate. Furthermore, all voters with ideologies less than zero will obtain more utility from choosing candidate *D*, while all of those with ideological positions to the right of zero will benefit more from casting their ballots for candidate *R*. Most importantly, we see that the utility curves from choosing each of the two candidates cross at the midpoint between the two candidates' positions, which indicates that this is the point that divides citizens into those preferring the Democratic candidate and those preferring the Republican candidate.

The central properties of the simple deterministic spatial voting model in two-candidate elections, then, can be summarized as

(1) If a voter's ideological position is closer to one candidate than to the other, the voter should cast his or her ballot for the candidate he or she is closest to.

(2) Voters whose ideologies fall at the midpoint between the positions of two candidates (and thus who are equally close to both candidates) should be equally likely to vote for either candidate.[1]

Accounting for Randomness: Stochastic Models of Spatial Voting

Although the simple deterministic spatial model discussed in the previous section provides an extremely parsimonious and precise theory about the voting behavior of citizens, its utility in describing the behavior of ordinary voters in actual elections is questionable. In particular, the deterministic model predicts the decisions of any voter with certainty: voters will *always* cast their ballots for the candidate whose position is closest to the voters' own ideological location. This assumption, while useful for exploring basic dynamics and intuitions about spatial politics, is clearly an unrealistic description of behavior in actual elections. In fact, the

---

[1] Again, it should be emphasized that some models of spatial voting violate these properties or at least include cases that could violate these properties. The most notable example would be the possibility of asymmetric spatial utility functions for voters, which would violate the second property here. The models used here, because they use a symmetric, single-peaked utility function – the quadratic – will satisfy these properties.

theory is falsified if only a single voter is found to choose a more ideologically distant candidate instead of a closer one. Therefore, any model of spatial voting that is to be considered as a possible explanation for the behavior of actual voters should allow for the possibility that some voters may not choose the candidate closest to them.

While some scholars have studied spatial voting models involving random error, most of this work has focused on the theoretical consequences of allowing such a stochastic component rather than on testing the empirical plausibility of the assumed models. In particular, much of this work has sought to derive equilibrium conditions for candidate positioning (Enelow and Hinich 1984; Coughlin 1992; Hinich and Munger 1994; Lin et al. 1999; Adams 1999; Schofield 2002). Fewer works have explicitly analyzed voting data within the stochastic spatial voting framework. An important exception is Adams et al. (2005), which employs a conditional logit model to analyze multicandidate elections in the United States and other countries. Additionally, some earlier works have included the ideological characteristics of candidates as a predictor along with other variables such as the state of the economy (see, e.g., Alvarez and Nagler 1995).

Voter behavior could be expected to differ from deterministic spatial voting because of many possible influences apart from ideology. First and foremost, we know that voting, like nearly all human behaviors, is often idiosyncratic, coming as the result not just of large systematic influences such as ideology, but also smaller random forces. Two voters, even if they have exactly the same ideological position, will not always behave in the same way. For example, some people simply may not like the personality of a candidate or may view one candidate as more trustworthy than another.[2] Accordingly, if our goal is to test a model of spatial voting as a possible account of the behavior of actual voters in real elections rather than to simply explore the theoretical consequences of formalized models, we should seek a model of spatial voting that includes some random component.

If deterministic spatial voting is abandoned, however, any stochastic version should preserve the fundamental characteristics of spatial voting. Whereas the spatial voting models without random error generally posit that citizens will always choose the candidate closest to them, stochastic

---

[2] This is different from a valence advantage for one candidate, which will be discussed later, because voters may disagree on the level of trustworthiness or intelligence possessed by each candidate. Valence issues, by contrast, are generally assumed to be both evaluated and valued identically for all voters.

spatial voting should mean that citizens *tend to choose* the candidate closest to them. In other words, given two candidates, a voter should be more likely to cast his or her ballot for the one whose position is closest to the voter's own ideological location. Another characteristic that we might expect from a stochastic variant of spatial voting is that as voters become more conservative, their probability of voting for the Republican candidate should increase (and, correspondingly, their probability of voting for the Democrat should decrease). If we add the seemingly reasonable assumption that the relationship between a voter's ideology and his or her probability of choosing a given candidate is continuous, then the two aforementioned criteria imply that voters holding ideologies at the midpoint between the two candidates' positions should have a 50 percent chance of voting for either candidate. Therefore, the ideological location at which a voter is predicted to have an equal chance of choosing each candidate, which can be called the *implied indifference point* (following Jessee 2009), provides the stochastic spatial voting analog for the perfect cut point we would observe between voters who choose the liberal or conservative candidates, respectively, under perfect (errorless) spatial voting.

These three properties provide a set of directly testable hypotheses that we can consider minimally sufficient for the existence of spatial voting with random error:

(1) As voters become more conservative, their probability of voting for the conservative candidate should increase.
(2) A voter should be most likely to choose the candidate to whom he or she is ideologically closest.
(3) Voters holding ideologies at the midpoint between the two candidates' positions should have an equal probability of voting for either candidate.

These three criteria will provide the basis for the evaluation of spatial voting in real-world elections in this and subsequent chapters. If stochastic spatial voting theory provides a realistic depiction of voter behavior in American presidential elections, we should observe that these properties hold in actual elections.

As in most discussions of deterministic spatial voting, the formulation of stochastic voting theory used here will be built from utility functions for voters. The stochastic spatial model used here will closely follow the utility functions used in the deterministic models discussed previously. Specifically, voters' utility functions are assumed to be quadratic in their distance from candidates as before, but now include a random error term. Formally, the utility that voter i, who holds an ideal point of x_i, receives from casting his or her ballot for candidate k, who takes a position c_k, is written as

$$U_i(k) = -a(x_i - c_k)^2 + e_{ik}, \tag{4.3}$$

where e_{ik} is drawn independently across both voters and candidates from a normal distribution with mean zero and variance $1/2$. The reason for this particular choice of distribution will become apparent in the next section when a statistical model of voting is derived from this setup. The parameter a, which would be expected to be positive, represents a policy weight determining how strongly a citizen's utility from voting for a given candidate is related to the citizen's ideological proximity to the candidate's position.[3] In the deterministic spatial utility models shown in Equation 4.1, this policy weight parameter is omitted because any positive value of a will result in identical vote predictions.[4] In the probabilistic framework employed for this stochastic spatial voting model, however, predictions will differ for different values of a.

The deterministic part of this expression (omitting the random error e_{ik}) is identical to, and thus has the same properties as, the deterministic utility function from Equation 4.1. It attains its highest value of zero when the candidate and voter hold the same ideological position. As the distance between the voter's ideal point and the candidate's position increases, the nonrandom part of the expression becomes more negative, indicating that the voter receives less utility on average from casting a ballot for the candidate. This means that, on average, a citizen would get the most utility from choosing a candidate holding the same views as the citizen himself does. A voter is assumed to vote for the candidate who offers him or her the most overall utility, including the random error term e_{ik}. Without this random error term, the voter would always choose the candidate closest to him or her. In this stochastic setup, however, the voter will usually choose the candidate whose position is closest to him or her, but the inclusion of an error term allows for the possibility that he or she will vote for the farther-away candidate if the utility shock for

---

[3] The use of the term "policy weight" here is not to be confused with its use in the literature on issue importance in vote choice. While important, this topic is not considered here. The term "policy weight" is instead meant to describe the weight that voters place on policy concerns or ideology as a whole in making their vote choices.

[4] To see this, simply note that $-(x_i - c_1)^2 > -(x_i - c_2)^2 \iff -a(x_i - c_1)^2 > -a(x_i - c_2)^2$ for any x_i, c_1, c_2 whenever a is positive.

doing so is sufficiently large or if the utility shock for choosing the closer candidate is sufficiently small.

Because we will be analyzing elections between a Democratic and Republican candidate (ignoring third-party and independent candidates), we will have two positions c_D and c_R for the candidates. Assuming this utility function, the probability of voter i choosing the Republican candidate is simply the probability that the utility voter i receives from voting for the Republican candidate is greater than the utility voter i receives from voting for the Democrat. Therefore, this can be written as

$$P(v_i = R) = P(U_i(R) > U_i(D))$$
$$= P(-a(x_i - c_R)^2 + e_{iR} > -a(x_i - c_D)^2 + e_{iD}). \quad (4.4)$$

It is straightforward to verify that the spatial voting model defined by this utility specification satisfies the three requirements stated above for spatial voting in the stochastic case whenever $a > 0$. Voters will become more likely to vote for the Republican candidate as their ideal points become more conservative. Voters also will be most likely to vote for the candidate closest to their own ideal point. Finally, voters positioned at the midpoint between the positions of the Democratic and Republican candidates will have an equal probability of voting for either candidate.

Spatial Voting with Bias

While the spatial voting models discussed in the previous sections assume that the only systematic determinant of vote choice is a voter's ideological proximity to candidates, it also is possible that one candidate may enjoy certain advantages that go above and beyond his or her ideological proximity to voters. The stochastic utility function shown in Equation 4.3, for example, assumes that voters will be more likely to choose candidates who take positions closer to their own ideal points and also that, aside from their ideological proximity to each of the candidates, voters are not on average biased toward one candidate or the other. In other words, while the random error in the utility functions of any individual voter may push him or her toward voting a certain way above and beyond his or her ideological proximity to the candidates, neither candidate should enjoy an advantage *on average* in the population as a whole. That such a condition should hold in real-world elections is not necessarily obvious. In fact, several scholars have argued that in any given election, a so-called valence dimension may exist on which a specific candidate may enjoy an advantage. This advantage may be based on qualities fully independent of ideological position, such as charisma or intelligence, that could be valued more or less equally by all voters (Stokes 1963; Ansolabehere and Snyder 2000; Groseclose 2001).

To allow for the possibility that the choices of voters may be systematically skewed to the advantage of one candidate or the other, we can specify a model of voting behavior that, in addition to accounting for spatial proximity and random error, also includes a non-policy advantage for one particular candidate. This can be accomplished through the introduction of a bias term b_k for each candidate, which will allow for the possibility that voters are predisposed toward choosing them above and beyond their ideological proximity to the candidate's position. The utility that voter i obtains for choosing candidate k can now be written as

$$U_i(k) = -a(x_i - c_k)^2 + b_k + e_{ik}, \tag{4.5}$$

where, again, x_i is the voter's ideal point, c_k is the candidate's ideological position, a is a policy weight indicating how strongly voters' utilities are related to their ideological proximity to a candidate, and e_{ik} is a normal random error term that is assumed to be independently distributed across both voters and candidates with mean zero and variance $1/2$.

When these bias terms are equal to zero, this model reduces to the model in Equation 4.3.[5] If one candidate enjoys an advantage in terms of a larger bias term b_k, however, this model predicts that voters will tend to be biased toward that candidate above and beyond their spatial proximity to each candidate. In these cases, the model will not satisfy the properties described previously for stochastic spatial voting models. As in the previous model without a bias term, a positive value for the policy weight a will satisfy the first condition of a positive relationship between a voter's conservatism and the probability of casting their ballot for the more conservative candidate. The second and third conditions, however, will not be satisfied if voters are biased systematically toward one particular candidate. In this case, voters with certain positions may be ideologically closer to one candidate yet be predicted to vote for the other candidate with probability greater than one-half. Such biases would imply that the ideological position at which voters are equally likely to choose either candidate does not fall at the actual midpoint between the two candidates' positions.

---

[5] In fact, in terms of the probabilities of selecting each candidate, the model including this bias term (Equation 4.5) will generate identical predictions to the simple stochastic model without bias (Equation 4.3) whenever the bias terms b_k are the same for both candidates.

Under this new model, as with previous models, it is assumed that each voter will cast his or her ballot with the aim of maximizing his or her utility. This means that voters will choose the candidate who offers them the most utility, including policy proximity, bias, and random error terms. Accordingly, for elections involving a Democratic candidate D and Republican candidate R, the vote probability of respondent i can be written as

$$P(v_i = R) = P(U_i(R) > U_i(D))$$

$$= P(-a(x_i - c_R)^2 + b_R + e_{iR} > -a(x_i - c_D)^2 + b_D + e_{iD}).$$

$$(4.6)$$

This is this stochastic model of spatial voting with bias that is the focus of the investigation of spatial voting in the 2004 and 2008 elections. Estimating the parameters of this model will establish whether the three properties of spatial voting described previously can be said to hold in recent presidential elections. In particular, as will be see in the following section, the values of the policy weight parameter a and the bias terms b_k indicate whether these properties hold.

Directional Voting Theory

A related approach to the study of voting behavior is the directional theory proposed by Rabinowitz and Macdonald (1989). This theory argues that on any given issue, voters who take a given side most prefer candidates who are strongly to that same side. In other words, a voter who is just left of center on an issue would prefer a candidate who is far to the left on that issue to one who is slightly to the right, even if the latter candidate is actually closer to the voter's position. Directional theories have been elaborated on to include so-called regions of acceptability in which voters may penalize candidates who stray too far toward the extremes, even if the candidate is on the same side of the issue as the voter. The specific predictions generated by directional theory, however, are somewhat ambiguous. How to define the "center" on a given issue or how to determine where the "region of acceptability" lies is not necessarily clear. Furthermore, recent studies such as Tomz and Van Houweling (2008) estimate, based on simplified survey experiments, that only a small fraction of voters are likely to use directional decision-making rules. Finally, when candidates are spaced roughly equally around the center of the ideological spectrum, as is likely the case in both elections studied here, the predictions of directional theory, to the extent that they can be clearly identified, are largely consistent with those of proximity or spatial theories. For these reasons, and because spatial theory has been significantly more influential in the modern political science literature, directional theories are not focused on in this book's analyses.

Connecting Theoretical and Statistical Models of Spatial Voting

In order to conduct direct tests of the spatial voting model, we must derive a statistical model from the random utility model assumed in Equation 4.5. The model for voter utility functions employed here has two central parameters: a policy weight, a, and a bias term, b. The values of these parameters describe how voters' decisions are related to their ideological proximity to candidates and, more importantly, dictate whether the behavior of voters satisfies the three properties of stochastic spatial voting described in the previous section. In this section, a connection is made between the utility function assumed for voters in Equation 4.5 and a statistical model predicting vote choice, which will allow for the estimation of the spatial utility parameters and ultimately for the direct testing of the empirical implications of spatial voting.

Deriving a Statistical Model of Spatial Voting

The spatial utility function assumed in Equation 4.5 combined with the assumption that voters will cast their ballot for the candidate who offers them the most utility, as shown in Equation 4.6, implies a probabilistic model of vote choice based on a voter's ideal point in relation to the positions taken by the two candidates in a given election. To obtain a useful expression for this probabilistic model, we can expand the expression in Equation 4.6 for the probability of voter i choosing the Republican candidate by plugging in the assumed utility function and attempting to simplify the resulting expression. Doing this, we obtain the following result:

$$
\begin{aligned}
P(v_i = R) &= P(U_i(R) > U_i(D)) \\
&= P(-a(x_i - c_R)^2 + b_R + e_{iR} > -a(x_i - c_D)^2 + b_D + e_{iD}) \\
&= P(-a(x_i - c_R)^2 + b_R + a(x_i - c_D)^2 - b_D > e_{iD} - e_{iR}) \\
&= P(-a(x_i^2 - 2x_i c_R + c_R^2 - x_i^2 + 2x_i c_D - c_D^2) \\
&\quad + b_R - b_D > e_{iD} - e_{iR}) \\
&= P(2ax_i(c_R - c_D) + a(c_D^2 - c_R^2) + b_R - b_D > e_{iD} - e_{iR}) \\
&= \Phi(\lambda x_i + \pi + \delta), \quad\quad\quad\quad\quad\quad\quad\quad\quad\quad (4.7)
\end{aligned}
$$

where $\lambda = 2a(c_R - c_D)$, $\pi = a(c_D^2 - c_R^2)$, $\delta = b_R - b_D$, and Φ represents the standard normal cdf. The last line of this expression holds because the random error terms e_{iD} and e_{iR} are drawn independently from normal distributions with mean zero and variance $1/2$. Therefore, their difference $e_{iD} - e_{iR}$ has mean $0 - 0 = 0$ and variance $1/2 + 1/2 = 1$, and thus follows a standard normal distribution.

It may not be immediately apparent why the expression in the last line of Equation 4.7 is useful. What has been shown, however, is that the probability of a voter choosing the Republican candidate under this spatial model can be written as a standard probit regression on the voter's ideal point.[6] If we were to estimate a probit regression predicting vote choice in a presidential election with each respondent's ideal point, where 1 indicates a vote for the Republican candidate and 0 indicates a vote for the Democrat, it would take the form

$$P(v_i = 1) = \Phi(\beta_0 + \beta_1 x_i), \tag{4.8}$$

where, as before, x_i is respondent i's ideal point and Φ is the cdf for the normal distribution. Under our spatial utility model, the coefficients from this probit regression should have the following correspondence with the parameters of the spatial utility model from Equation 4.5:

$$\beta_1 = \lambda = 2a(c_R - c_D)$$
$$\beta_0 = \pi + \delta = a(c_D^2 - c_R^2) + (b_R - b_D). \tag{4.9}$$

If we did not know the positions of the two candidates on the same scale as the ideology of voters, we would have four unknowns – a, c_D, c_R, and δ – and only two equations. Therefore, we could only solve for our parameters of interest a and δ in terms of the unknown candidate positions. In particular, we could not directly estimate the actual values of a and δ and hence would not be able to directly test the conditions of spatial voting theory. This has been the central problem in testing accounts of spatial voting. Because previous work has generally not been able to obtain estimates of candidate positions on the same scale as the ideology of voters, there has been no way to directly connect estimates of vote choice regressions with the underlying parameters of spatial utility models. Even making the sensible assumption that the position of the Republican candidate is more conservative (greater) than that of the Democratic candidate, we can only know that the sign of a will be the

---

[6] Perhaps the earliest recognition of this general type of correspondence appears in Hinich (1977), which derives the general expression for vote probability for arbitrary error distributions and spatial utility functions (including linear, quadratic, and others).

same as the sign of the coefficient β_1. Furthermore, there is no way to learn about the relative size of the biases for the two candidates, c_D and c_R.

With the positions of both candidates known, however, the problem reduces to one with two equations and only two unknowns – a and δ. From this setup, we can easily solve these equations to obtain the value of these two central parameters of interest as well as the parameter π. This would yield

$$a = \frac{\beta_1}{2(c_R - c_D)}$$

$$\delta = \beta_0 - a(c_D^2 - c_R^2)$$

$$= \beta_0 - \frac{\beta_1(c_D^2 - c_R^2)}{2(c_R - c_D)}$$

$$\pi = a(c_D^2 - c_R^2)$$

$$= \frac{\beta_1(c_D^2 - c_R^2)}{2(c_R - c_D)}. \tag{4.10}$$

With estimates for both candidate positions and probit regression coefficients predicting vote choice with voter ideal points, we could then solve for the values of the parameters of the spatial utility model from Equation 4.5 using the formula in Equation 4.10.

As discussed in Chapter 3, the scale on which respondent ideal points are measured is inherently undefined. Just as temperatures can be measured in degrees Celsius or Fahrenheit and weight can be measured in pounds or kilograms, we can rescale these ideology measures without fundamentally changing their meaning. This means that we can define this scale in a way that causes the expressions from Equation 4.10 to take the most useful form possible. If, as in Chapter 3, a scale for measuring ideology is adopted such that the Democratic and Republican candidates in a given election hold positions at $-1/4$ and $1/4$, respectively, this will imply that $c_R - c_D = 1/2$ and $c_D^2 - c_R^2 = 0$, which would reduce the expressions in Equation 4.10 to

$$a = \beta_1$$

$$\delta = \beta_0$$

$$\pi = 0. \tag{4.11}$$

This provides a simple correspondence between the estimated coefficients of the probit regression in Equation 4.8 and the parameters of the spatial utility voting model.

Thus, we have established a direct link between the parameters of the theoretical random utility model of spatial voting specified in Equation 4.6 and the coefficients from a probit regression using the ideal point estimates presented in Chapter 3 to predict respondents' vote choice. Bridging this gap is made possible by the availability of measures of voter and candidate ideology on the same scale. It has therefore been established that estimates of the parameters of voter utility functions can be recovered by simply estimating a probit regression of vote choice predicted by voter ideal point given suitable identification restrictions on the ideological scale on which citizen and candidate ideology are estimated.

Understanding the Parameters of the Spatial Utility Model

The parameters of the spatial utility function shown in Equation 4.6 determine how citizens' vote choices depend on their ideological positions. The focus of the empirical analyses in this chapter is on estimating the values of these parameters in actual elections. This will provide the most direct tests to date of the spatial theory of voting behavior in real-world elections. Accordingly, the first question of interest is whether voters appear to satisfy the criteria for unbiased spatial voting. Beyond this, however, we also should be interested in the general dynamics of vote choice indicated by the values of these parameters. The three unknown parameters of the stochastic spatial voting model are the policy weight, a, and the bias terms, b_D and b_R, for the Democratic and Republican candidates, respectively.

The first criterion of spatial voting states that as voters become more conservative, their probability of voting for the more conservative (here, Republican) candidate should increase. Because the normal cdf Φ is always increasing, this will be true whenever $\lambda = a(c_D^2 - c_R^2)$ is greater than zero. Assuming that $c_R > c_D$ (i.e., the Republican candidate is more conservative than the Democratic candidate), this will occur if the policy weight a is positive. Therefore, the test of whether a (and hence λ) is positive will provide a direct test of the first condition of spatial voting.

In substantive terms, the policy weight parameter represents how strongly a respondent's ideological proximity to each candidate affects the utility that he or she receives from choosing that candidate. Therefore, the magnitude of a also indicates how steep the relationship is between voters' ideal points and their probabilities of voting for either candidate.

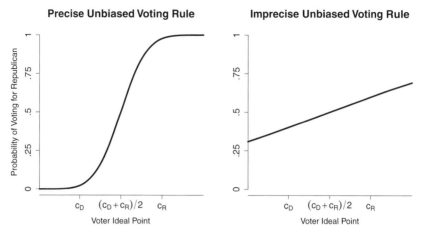

FIGURE 4.3. Precise and imprecise spatial voting examples. Examples of possible decision rules relating voters' ideal points (measured in relation to the positions of candidates D and R, who hold positions at c_D and c_R, respectively to probabilities of voting for the more conservative candidate R. The curve on the left shows a relatively precise voting voting rule while the one on the right is fairly imprecise.

We can think of this as the *precision* of the voting rule in discriminating ideologically between the two candidates. At one extreme, the policy weight could be equal to zero. This would mean that voting decisions are not affected at all by citizens' policy positions. Votes would depend only on the overall bias voters have toward each candidate and the random errors each voter is affected by, and voters would effectively ignore the ideological positions of candidates. Alternatively, a could be positive and very large. This would indicate that voters' utilities are strongly affected by ideological proximity to the candidates. As the value of a approaches infinity, voting would approach the perfect, or errorless, spatial voting discussed previously in which all voters to the left of the midpoint between the two candidates would vote for the Democratic candidate and all those to the right would vote for the Republican.

As an illustration, Figure 4.3 shows two examples of stochastic spatial voting rules, one that is relatively precise and another that is imprecise. The left pane shows a precise voting rule, corresponding to a large positive value for the policy weight a. Under this voting rule, voters with ideologies near the Democratic candidate's position are very likely to vote for him, while those with more conservative ideologies are very likely to choose the Republican. The probability of choosing the Republican candidate increases steeply as voters' ideal points become more conservative, with only voters having ideal points near the midpoint between the two candidates being predicted to have a significant chance of voting for either candidate. The right pane of the figure shows an imprecise voting rule. Under this rule, voters are more likely to choose the Republican candidate as they become more conservative, but this relationship is fairly flat. Liberal voters still have a significant chance of voting for the Republican, and conservatives will still vote for the Democrat fairly often. This example corresponds to a value for the policy weight a that is positive, but not large in magnitude. As a gets closer to zero, the voting rule would approach a horizontal line where voters' probabilities of casting their ballot for the Republican candidate was unaffected by their ideological position. While both of the voting rules shown in Figure 4.3 satisfy the first property of spatial voting, they differ in the overall picture they paint about the influence of voters' ideological positions on their ultimate decisions.

While the sign of a will determine whether the first criterion of spatial voting is satisfied, the value of the parameter provides information more generally about how responsive voters' decisions are to their spatial proximity to the two candidates in a given election. Larger values of this policy weight indicate that voters are able to more precisely determine which of the two candidates is closest to their own ideal point. A value of a close to zero would imply that, even if the other conditions of stochastic spatial voting were satisfied, voters would be only mildly responsive to their proximity to each candidate and would vote with a great deal of randomness. This would suggest a less optimistic conclusion about the capabilities, or at least the level of attention and effort, of ordinary voters.

The second and third properties of spatial voting relate to bias in voters' choices above and beyond their spatial proximity to each candidate. In a two-candidate election between a Democrat and a Republican, we have two such bias terms b_D and b_R. Each represents the amount of utility that voters receive for choosing a given candidate independent of the voters' ideological proximity to the candidate's position. What is important, however, is not the specific values of each of these terms, but rather the difference between them. This is because the important concern for a voter is not the actual values of the utility given by each candidate, but simply which candidate would provide them with the *most* utility. Adding a given value to both of these terms will not change the predictions of the model.[7]

---

[7] For a given constant κ, we can see that $\delta = (b_R + \kappa) - (b_D + \kappa) = b_R + \kappa - b_D - \kappa = b_R - b_D$. Therefore, adding any constant to both of the candidate bias terms will not change the value of δ and hence will not change the model's predictions for the choices of any voters.

In other words, if a voter has two units of bias toward the Democratic candidate and also has two units of bias toward the Republican, then these biases will cancel out, resulting in the same predictions for the voter's behavior as if he or she had no bias toward either candidate. Therefore, we cannot estimate the biases b_D and b_R independently and will instead focus on the difference $\delta = b_R - b_D$. This can be thought of as the "net spatial bias" that voters display toward the Republican candidate. If voters on average are biased toward the Democratic candidate, this parameter will be negative.

When δ equals zero, the vote probability in Equation 4.6 reduces to the expression from Equation 4.4. Voters with no net bias toward either candidate or, equivalently, with equal bias toward either candidate, will necessarily satisfy the final two criteria for unbiased spatial voting whenever $a > 0$. They will be most likely to choose the candidate closest to their own ideal point, and they will be equally likely to vote for either candidate if their ideal point falls midway between the two candidates' positions. As an illustration, the left pane of Figure 4.4 shows an example of an unbiased spatial voting rule. Because voters using this decision rule have no net bias toward either candidate ($\delta = 0$), voters holding an ideal point at $c_D + c_R/2$, the midpoint between the two candidates' positions, have a 50 percent chance of choosing either candidate. The right pane of Figure 4.4, by contrast, shows an example of a biased spatial voting rule. This decision rule corresponds to $\delta > 0$, meaning that voters are biased toward the Republican candidate. While this voting rule does depend on voters' ideological location, with more conservative voters being more likely to choose the Republican candidate (i.e., $a > 0$), we clearly see that the rule is biased. Voters with ideologies at the midpoint between the two candidates, for example, are shown to have a probability well above one-half of casting their ballots for the Republican. Furthermore, voters holding ideological positions in the shaded area of the graph are predicted to be most likely to vote for the Republican even though they are ideologically closer to the Democratic candidate.

Therefore, under the spatial utility model presented in Equation 4.5, we have established two central hypotheses that will allow for the testing of the properties of spatial voting used here. First, if voters with more conservative ideologies are more likely to cast their ballots for the Republican candidate, we should observe that the policy weight a is positive. Second, respondents will be most likely to choose the candidate closest to them, and the ideological position at which voters will be equally likely to vote for either candidate will fall at the midpoint between the two

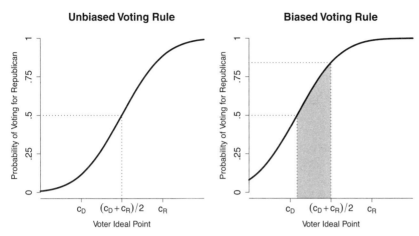

FIGURE 4.4. Biased and unbiased spatial voting examples. Examples of possible decision rules relating voters' ideal points (measured in relation to the positions of candidates D and R, who hold positions at c_D and c_R, respectively) to probabilities of voting for the more conservative candidate R. The curve on the left presents an unbiased voting rule, while the one on the right shows significant bias. Specifically, all voters whose ideal points lie in the shaded region of the righthand side plot are ideologically closer to the Democratic candidate, but are predicted to be more likely to cast their vote for the Republican.

candidates' positions when δ is equal to zero. These two hypotheses will allow for direct empirical tests of the properties of spatial voting.

Estimating the Parameters of the Spatial Voting Model

Using the survey data collected regarding citizens' policy views and vote choice in the two most recent presidential elections, we can now go about directly estimating the central parameters of interest in our spatial voting model. The values of these parameters – the policy weight, or precision, term (a) and the net spatial bias term (δ) – will indicate whether the theory of spatial voting provides a realistic description of citizen decision making in real-world elections. Furthermore, we can assess how precisely citizens discriminate between the candidates along ideological lines and whether their decisions are more favorable on average toward a particular candidate apart from the citizens' ideological positions.

To estimate these parameters, we simply estimate a probit regression model of the form in Equation 4.8, predicting vote choice with respondents' ideological positions where, as described previously, choice coded 1

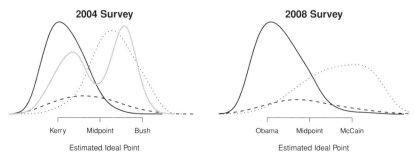

FIGURE 4.5. Distributions of estimated voter ideology. Plots show the density of estimated ideal points for respondents in the 2004 and 2008 surveys separated by party identification, with solid, dotted, and dashed lines indicating Democratic, independent, and Republican respondents, respectively. The solid gray line in the left pane plots the density of ideal point estimates for senators, with the positions of John Kerry, George W. Bush, and the midpoint between these two candidates shown along the x-axis. The x-axis of the right pane shows the estimated positions of Barack Obama, John McCain, and the estimated midpoint between them.

for the Republican candidate and 0 for the Democratic candidate. In order to take advantage of the direct correspondence derived in Equation 4.11 between the estimated probit coefficients and the policy weight and bias terms of the spatial utility model, the ideology estimates are scaled, as in Chapter 3, so that the Democratic and Republican candidates in each election have positions $-1/4$ and $1/4$, respectively.[8] Therefore, all coefficients and other estimated quantities should be interpreted with reference to the ideological scales defined by these restrictions in each election.

As a reference, Figure 4.5 plots the estimated distributions of voter ideology in each election as presented in the previous chapter (again, recall that the 2004 election estimates should be thought of as, at best, a rough approximation of the distribution of ideology in the voter population as a whole because of the lack of representativeness in this sample, while the 2008 results are based on a highly representative national sample and thus can be interpreted as a good description of the ideology of American voters generally). We again see that the candidate positions are generally closer to their party medians than the median of the full electorate. While

---

[8] It should again be noted that, strictly speaking, we have no way of comparing the ideological scales that are separately estimated for each of the two elections. The assumption that Kerry and Obama both hold ideologies at $-1/4$ and that Bush and McCain both take positions at $1/4$ should not be construed to mean that these candidates have the same ideologies. Instead, the ideological scales estimated for the 2004 and 2008 elections should be thought of as separate scales, not as directly comparable.

TABLE 4.1. *Estimated Spatial Utility Model Parameters*

Coefficient	Utility Model Parameter	2004 Estimates (Standard Errors)	2008 Estimates (Standard Errors)
Intercept	δ	.72 (.03)	.13 (.05)
Ideal Point (x_i)	a	10.09 (.23)	7.87 (.33)
	Log-likelihood	-1663.1	-572.9
	N	5,568	1,739

Table shows results of probit regression model predicting presidential vote choice in 2004 and 2008 elections (coded as 1 for Republican and 0 for Democratic votes) using respondent ideal point. Coefficient estimates correspond to spatial utility parameters as shown in Equation 4.11.

Democratic voters tend to be more liberal than Republicans, there is a fair degree of ideological overlap between the two parties. Independents, as expected, are on average more moderate, but also show a fairly wide distribution, overlapping those for both parties.

Table 4.1 presents the coefficients from the probit regression model of vote choice, estimated for the 2004 and 2008 elections. Each of these models predicts the vote choices of respondents using their estimated ideal points.[9] Recall that because of the identification restrictions used for the ideal point scale, these coefficient estimates will correspond directly to the underlying parameters of the spatial utility model as shown in the second column of the table. We can first examine the estimated value of the policy weight (or precision) parameter (a). In both elections, this parameter is estimated to be positive, large, and highly significant. A movement of one unit on the ideological scale would be expected to produce a change of 10.09 on the probit scale for the 2004 election and 8.09 for the 2008 election. This means that, for example, moving from zero, the midpoint between the two candidates' positions, to the same position as one of the candidates, either $-1/4$ or $1/4$, would produce a change on the probit scale of 2.52 units in the 2004 election and 2.02 in the 2008

[9] In all results presented here, the estimated ideal points presented in Chapter 3 are included in regression models as if they were known. Clearly, these ideal points are estimated with some error. For the sake of simplicity, however, I do not use any statistical adjustments to account for this estimation error. Similar regression models presented in Jessee (2009) and Jessee (2010a) employ more elaborate methods to take these uncertainties into account, but generally reach very similar overall conclusions, as do the results presented here. This issue also is discussed in Chapter 5.

election. Both of these values represent very large changes on the probit scale, indicating that, on average, the choices of voters in both elections were highly sensitive to their ideological positions relative to those of the candidates. These findings provide strong validation of the first condition for spatial voting – that as voters become more conservative they become more likely to cast their ballot for the conservative, in this case Republican, candidate. This relationship is both highly statistically significant and also substantively large in magnitude for both election years.

We also can examine the estimates of the net spatial bias term δ, which describes the difference between the biases voters show toward the Republican and Democratic candidates. Recall that positive values indicate a net bias toward the Republican and negative values imply an overall advantage for the Democrat. In the 2004 election, voters are estimated to be somewhat biased toward Bush on average. Our estimate of δ is .72, with a standard error of .03. This means that we can conclude with some certainty that voters on the whole were predisposed toward voting for Bush above and beyond what their ideological proximity toward each candidate would suggest under unbiased spatial voting. In the 2008 election, by contrast, voters show relatively little bias on average. The estimated value of δ is .13, which, while statistically significant, is not very large in a substantive sense. In other words, voters on average appeared to be slightly more favorable toward McCain, but their behavior departed only slightly from what would be predicted under unbiased spatial voting.

The net bias term δ also can be thought of as a net valence advantage for the Republican candidate. Valence issues (see, e.g., Ansolabehere and Snyder 2000; Groseclose 2001) are conceptualized as characteristics that are valued (and usually perceived) identically by all voters. Examples include honesty, intelligence, or physical attractiveness. Valence issue differ from spatial ideology in the sense that while all voters may prefer a more honest candidate, voters will differ, for example, on whether they prefer a more liberal candidate. A benefit of the spatial model assumed here is that it allows for the separation of the vote equation into a spatial term, whose importance is described by the policy weight a, and a valence term δ. The estimated biases of voters toward Republican presidential candidates in 2004 and 2008 are both positive and statistically significant, but differ in magnitude. These results suggest that while Bush may have enjoyed a meaningful valence advantage over Kerry, McCain's net valence advantage over Obama was relatively small.

Another, perhaps more intuitive, way to understand the results of these models is to examine the predicted probabilities of voting for the

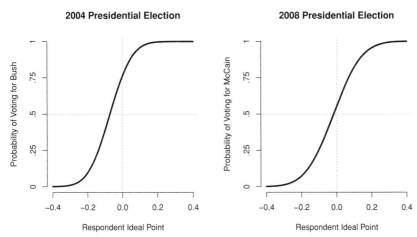

FIGURE 4.6. Predicted vote probabilities from simple spatial voting model. Plots show the predicted probabilities of voting for the Republican candidate as a function of respondent ideal point based on the estimates shown in Table 4.1.

Republican candidate for voters as a function of their ideological position. Figure 4.6 plots these predicted probabilities estimated for voters in both the 2004 and 2008 elections. The most obvious feature of these graphs is the relatively steep increases in the probability of choosing the Republican candidate that result from voters becoming more ideologically conservative. In both the 2004 and 2008 elections, these predicted vote probabilities are highly sensitive to voters' ideologies, as would be expected given the large values estimated for a, which demonstrates that voters seemed in general to vote quite precisely based on ideological concerns.

Beyond this, we can consider the predicted behavior of voters whose ideologies fall precisely at the midpoint between the two candidates' positions. Because the ideological scale has been defined such that the Democratic and Republican candidates in each election take positions at $-1/4$ and $1/4$, respectively, this midpoint will fall at zero. In both panes of Figure 4.6, a vertical dotted line has been plotted at zero, allowing for the easy identification of this midpoint. Furthermore, a horizontal dotted line is drawn at .5. As discussed previously, under unbiased spatial voting, voters at this midpoint, because they are equally close to each of the two candidates, should have an equal chance of choosing either the Republican or the Democrat. Graphically, this would imply that under unbiased spatial voting, the predicted probability curves in Figure 4.6 should pass through the intersection of these lines at the point (0, .5) on these graphs.

TABLE 4.2. *Estimated Implied Indifference Points*

	2004 Presidential Election	2008 Presidential Election
Estimate	−.07	−.02
95% Confidence Interval	(−.08, −.07)	(−.03, −.01)

Cells show the ideological location at which a voter would be predicted to have an equal chance of casting their ballot for either candidate according to the estimates presented in Table 4.1. Ninety-five percent confidence intervals underneath in parentheses are calculated using the bootstrap procedure.

The curve estimated for voters in the 2004 election passes above this point, indicating that, on average, voters at the midpoint between the two candidates are predicted to have a .76 probability of casting their ballots for Bush. This is a relatively significant departure from the predictions of unbiased spatial voting. Voters in the 2008 election, by contrast, are predicted to have a .56 probability of voting for McCain when they are equally close to the two candidates. While this predicted probability is not exactly the .5 predicted by unbiased spatial voting theory, it represents a much smaller departure than the 2004 election and demonstrates that although we can reject the hypothesis that the spatial bias term δ is equal to zero, in substantive terms, the magnitude of the departure from unbiased spatial voting seems rather small.

As a final way of understanding these results, we can look at the estimated *implied indifference point* between the two candidates in each election. This value is the ideological position at which voters, according to the estimates of our probit model, are predicted to have an equal chance of voting for either candidate. Under our third condition for unbiased spatial voting, this point should fall at the actual midpoint between the two candidates' positions. To calculate the implied indifference point, we can simply solve Equation 4.8 to find the point at which the probability of voting for the Republican candidate is equal to one-half. Because the normal cdf Φ gives a value of one-half when evaluated at zero, we simply need to solve for the value of x_i at which $\beta_0 + \beta_1 x_i = 0$. Doing this, we find that the implied indifference point can be calculated as $-\beta_0/\beta_1$.

Table 4.2 shows the estimated values of these implied indifference points for the 2004 and 2008 election analyses along with 95 percent confidence intervals calculated using the bootstrap procedure (see Efron 1979). In 2004, we see that the estimated value is −.07, meaning that voters having ideologies at this position are predicted to be indifferent between the two candidates even though they would be much closer to Kerry than to Bush (.18 versus .32). Furthermore, a wide range of voters (all of those with ideological positions between −.07 and 0) will be ideologically closer to Kerry and yet be more likely to vote for Bush. This implies that voters can be nearly twice as close to Kerry than to Bush and yet still be equally likely to cast their ballot for either candidate. These estimates clearly represent a violation of the second requirement of unbiased spatial voting.

In the 2008 election analyses, the implied indifference is estimated to be −.02. Again, this point deviates from the precise value of zero that we would get under strictly unbiased spatial voting, and we can reject the hypothesis that the true value is equal to zero. But this implied indifference point is much closer to its expected value under unbiased spatial voting than is the estimate for 2004. In the 2008 analyses, voters predicted to be indifferent between the two candidates will be only slightly closer to Obama than to McCain (.23 versus .27 units away). Therefore, those voters between −.02 and 0 are closer to Obama while being more likely to cast their ballots for McCain, and their deviations from the strict predictions of unbiased spatial voting are significantly less severe than those found in 2004. In fact, only 2 percent of this sample is predicted to be closer to Obama, but more likely to vote for McCain, while the other 98 percent of respondents are predicted to be most likely to vote for the candidate to whom they are actually closer.

Overall, the results presented in this section have shown support, albeit somewhat mixed, for the empirical implications of spatial voting theory in recent presidential elections. Voters on the whole are clearly influenced by their ideological proximity to each candidate, with more conservative voters being much more likely to cast their ballots for the Republican candidate. Voters also appear to make their decisions with a relatively high degree of precision. The two elections analyzed paint somewhat different pictures, however, about the level of bias relative to the spatial voting standard. In 2004, voters appeared to be biased toward choosing Bush, with some voters who were significantly closer to Kerry being more likely to choose the Republican. In 2008, by contrast, the estimated bias was relatively small. Only a tiny fraction of respondents were predicted to cast their ballot for the candidate farthest from their own position. These results suggest that the basic logic of spatial voting theory appears to apply relatively well to the decisions of actual voters in real-world elections.

The Predictive Structure of Issues

One of the ways that scholars have sought to evaluate whether American politics can be said to be ideological has been to look at the impact of ideology on important political behaviors. The results presented in this chapter have reinforced the conclusions of earlier works that ideology has a strong and meaningful impact on vote choice, which is arguably the most important political behavior in a democratic political system. When these results are combined with the findings presented in Chapter 3 of a high degree of constraint tying together people's beliefs on different issues, the only possible conclusion is that American politics, at least at the national level in recent years, is quite ideological. There exists a strong set of relationships between citizens' views on different issues, which can be accounted for by a single-dimensional ideology. Furthermore, these ideologies powerfully predict vote choice in a manner largely consistent with the predictions of spatial voting theory.

In addition to these findings, however, we can examine the relationship between respondents' views on individual issues and their vote choices. The estimates of ideology derived in the previous chapter are based only on the relationships between respondents' views on different issues and are not at all influenced by respondents' vote decisions. These ideology estimates are produced, loosely speaking, by finding the single dimension that can best explain respondents' positions on the given set of issues. A logical question to ask, then, is whether the dimension structuring people's views on these issues is the same as the dimension that relates the individual issues to a respondent's vote choice. It is possible, for example, that citizens' views across different issues are related to each other in one way, while their vote choices are related to the individual issues in a different way.

To explore these possibilities, respondents' vote choices are first predicted using their positions on these individual issues. Table 4.3 shows the estimated coefficients of a probit regression of vote choice in the 2008 presidential election (again coded 1 for McCain and 0 for Obama) on respondents' positions on each of the ten policy proposals included in the survey (coded 1 for support and 0 for oppose). Only the 2008 survey is analyzed here because the 2004 questionnaire contains many more issues, with each respondent being surveyed only on a subset of these issues (no respondents were asked to take positions on all of the policy proposals in the survey).[10] These issue positions generally have strong relationships with vote choice, with many of the estimated coefficients being

---

[10] Even in the 2008 survey, a very large number of people failed to take a position on at least one of the ten surveyed issues. Because these people were somewhat less politically informed on average, the results presented here may be somewhat less informative about low-information respondents.

TABLE 4.3. *2008 Individual-Issue Voting Model*

Coefficient	Estimate (Standard Error)
Intercept	1.74
	(.38)
Iraq Withdrawal	−1.86
	(.26)
Traditional Marriage	.66
	(.20)
Privatize Social Security	1.18
	(.19)
Overturn *Roe v. Wade*	.50
	(.20)
Carbon Emissions Cap	−.63
	(.20)
Windfall Profits Tax	−.69
	(.25)
Reverse Tax Cuts for Rich	−.06
	(.20)
Universal Child Health Care	−.82
	(.22)
Homosexual Civil Unions	−.15
	(.20)
Economic Bailout Bill	−.44
	(.19)
Log-likelihood	−457.5
N	622

Note: All issue positions are coded as 1 or 0 for support or oppose, respectively. Dependent variable is presidential vote, coded as 1 for McCain and 0 for Obama. Results are based only on respondents with non-missing values for presidential vote and all ten issue questions.

large and eight of the ten being statistically significant. These significant findings should be all the more impressive given the strong correlations observed between respondents' positions on different issues (see Table 3.3). Furthermore, the estimated signs of the coefficients are generally in accord with the ideological nature of the proposals. Liberal policies such as withdrawing troops from Iraq or capping carbon emissions tend to have negative coefficient estimates, whereas conservative proposals such as overturning *Roe v. Wade* have positive estimates.

Interestingly, significant coefficients appear on two of the three surveyed issues on which Obama and McCain took identical positions. At first glance, it would seem that this does not make sense. Respondents who, for example, supported a cap on carbon dioxide emissions are agreeing with both Obama and McCain on this issue. This position, then, may not be expected to push them toward either candidate. But respondents who support this one form of environmental protection are also, in all likelihood, more supportive on average of other environmental protections. They would then tend to agree with Obama more often than with McCain, at least on these types of issues. There also are several other possibilities for these effects, such as that respondents may tend to misperceive Obama or McCain as taking the "traditional" liberal or conservative positions associated with their party.

These results also combine respondents' stated positions across these ten different issues into one underlying scale that represents their likelihood of voting for McCain as opposed to Obama. The latent scale fitted values, often called the linear predictor, which can be calculated by multiplying the coefficient estimates by a respondent's positions on each issue (1 or 0 for support or oppose) and adding them all to the intercept, represent the structure of the way in which these issue positions are related to vote choice. To assess whether this relationship between issues and vote choice is similar to the relationship between the issues themselves, we can compare the value of this linear predictor to the ideal point estimated in Chapter 3 for each respondent.

Figure 4.7 plots this linear predictor against the estimated ideal point for all respondents who have non-missing values for vote choice and all ten surveyed policy proposals. The results show an extremely strong association between these two quantities, with a correlation of .98, suggesting the latent scale that ties together people's views on different political issues is nearly identical to the scale that relates their issue positions to vote choice. In other words, the scale that best explains variation across the individual policy views of respondents is nearly identical to the scale that relates these policy views to their vote choices. This finding suggests that ideology is fundamental to political thought and actions more generally. One scale can describe both the primary connection between different issues as well as the primary connection between issues and the vote.

Voting "Spatially Correctly"

The simplest spatial voting models, such as the deterministic models discussed earlier, are based on the idea that voters should cast their ballots for the candidate whose position is ideologically closest to their own ideal

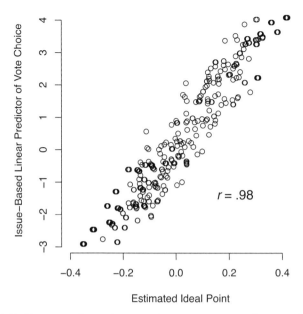

FIGURE 4.7. Correspondence between issue structure and vote relationships. Relationship between issue-based linear predictor of vote choice and estimated ideal point. Fitted values on the latent (probit) scale are from the coefficient estimates of the probit regression of vote choice on issue positions shown in Table 4.3 are plotted against estimated ideal points for respondents in 2008 survey described in Chapter 3.

point. Generalizations of this simple spatial model, such as the stochastic models analyzed throughout most of this chapter, relax this prescription to state that people should simply be more likely to vote for a candidate who takes a position closest to them than they are to vote for a more ideologically distant candidate. In either case, spatial voting models define a clear criterion for voting "correctly": choosing the candidate whose ideological position is closest to one's own ideal point. How do the decision rules used by voters correspond to the spatial standard of "correctness"? What types of voters seem most likely to cast their ballot according to the prescriptions of spatial theory? This section explores these questions using the ideology estimates presented in Chapter 3.

Previous research has attempted to evaluate whether people vote correctly, albeit usually with a different focus. The most notable example of this is Lau and Redlawsk (1997), which investigates whether voters would have decided differently under complete information. It is estimated that, by this standard, approximately three-quarters of American voters choose correctly. Alternatively, Boatright (2008) examines the self-reported seven-point ideological scale positions of ANES respondents from 1972 to 2004 and concludes that between 9 and 15 percent of voters are "spatial voting violators." He further concludes that these voters are less educated, less politically active, and less interested in politics more generally.

The estimates and analyses presented here allow for a different, perhaps more principled and more precise examination of "correct voting" according to the spatial standard. First, we can look at the predicted probability from the models estimated that voters of various ideological positions will cast "spatially correct" votes (i.e., that they will vote for the candidate whose position is ideologically closest to themselves). Because we have estimated voter ideology on a scale on which the Democratic candidate is located at $-1/4$ and the Republican candidate has a position of $1/4$, voters with ideal points of greater than zero are ideologically closer to the Republican candidate and thus would "correctly" vote for him, while those with ideal points less than zero should vote for the Democratic candidate.

The probit model shown in Equation 4.8 predicts vote choice, with 1 representing a vote for the Republican and 0 indicating a vote for the Democrat. Therefore, we can look at the estimated coefficients presented in Table 4.1 for this vote choice model for the 2004 and 2008 survey data to determine the predicted probability of voters at different ideological locations voting correctly. For voters to the left of zero, the probability of voting correctly will be the probability of voting for the Democratic candidate. Therefore, this probability is calculated as $1 - \Phi(\beta_0 + \beta_1 x_i)$, in other words, one minus the predicted probability of voting for the Republican candidate. Respondents with ideal points greater than zero will be predicted to vote correctly whenever they choose the Republican candidate, which can be calculated as $\Phi(\beta_0 + \beta_1 x_i)$.

Figure 4.8 plots the probability of voting correctly according to this spatial standard as a function of voters' ideological positions for the 2004 and 2008 elections. In 2004, most voters are predicted to have relatively high likelihoods of voting correctly, with the clear exception of voters with ideal points falling slightly to the left of zero. As expected, voters with relatively extreme ideal points are the most likely to vote correctly. Extremely liberal voters are almost certain to vote for Kerry, and very conservative voters will almost always vote for Bush. This makes sense given that the choice should be fairly obvious to these voters – they tend

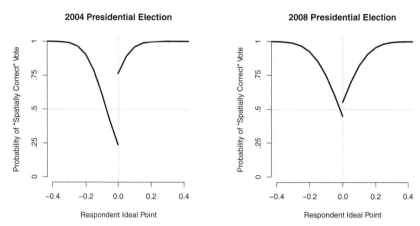

FIGURE 4.8. Predicted probability of casting "Spatially Correct" vote from simple spatial model. Plots show predicted probabilities of voting for the candidate whose position is ideologically closest to a voter's own ideological position as a function of voter's ideal point, based on the results presented in Table 4.1.

to be relatively close to one candidate and very far from the other. More moderate voters, however, are less certain to cast their ballots correctly. In fact, as suggested by the implied indifference point estimate in Table 4.2, voters between −.07 and zero are actually more likely to vote incorrectly than correctly. Furthermore, some voters even further to the left are almost equally likely to vote correctly as incorrectly. These findings are reflective of the general bias estimated toward Bush that is observed in the 2004 data.

In 2008, the probability of voting correctly is estimated to be greater than one-half for virtually all respondents. Again, ideologically extreme voters are estimated to vote correctly with probability near one. As respondents' ideologies move closer to zero – the midpoint between the two candidates' positions – their probability of voting correctly decreases, eventually approaching approximately one-half around the midpoint between the two candidates' positions. This should not seem unexpected given that voters holding ideologies near zero are almost equally close to either candidate. They may therefore be more likely to be swayed by random idiosyncratic forces given that their policy distance from the two candidates is virtually identical. Under the properties of spatial voting described earlier in this chapter, voters would always be predicted to have at least a 50 percent chance of voting for the candidate closest to their ideal point. In fact, this is very nearly the case in the 2008 election.

TABLE 4.4. *Proportions of Respondents Casting "Spatially Correct" Votes*

	2004 Survey			2008 Survey		
All Respondents		.84			.87	
Party ID	Dem	Ind	Rep	Dem	Ind	Rep
	.95	.83	.75	.89	.80	.86
Info Level	Low	Med	High	Low	Med	High
	.74	.87	.91	.75	.91	.92

Note: Table entries show the proportion of respondents voting for the candidate whose position is closest to the voter's own estimated ideal point for all respondents and by party identification and level of political information for the 2004 and 2008 surveys.

The estimated probability of casting a "spatially correct" vote dips only slightly below .5 for a very narrow range of respondents – those with ideal points between −.02 and 0.

In both the 2004 and 2008 elections, voters with more ideologically extreme positions are the most likely to cast their ballot for the candidate who is closest to them. More moderate voters, by contrast, are much more likely to vote incorrectly, which is to be expected under the spatial utility model given that moderates will be presented with smaller utility differences between the two candidates. In addition to these baseline findings, the relationships between correct voting and other factors also can be examined. In particular, we may suspect that two key variables – party identification and political knowledge – may strongly affect how ideology relates to the vote choices of ordinary citizens.

Table 4.4 shows the proportions of respondents casting "spatially correct," votes. The vast majority of respondents in both the 2004 and 2008 surveys voted for the candidate whose ideology was closest to their own position. In both surveys, these estimates are significantly higher than the three-quarters reported by Lau and Redlawsk (1997). On the whole, it seems reassuring that somewhere near 90 percent of voters appeared to cast their ballots for the candidate closest to their position. In addition to the normative appeal of this finding, these results also demonstrate the predictive power of spatial voting theory. Using only the single variable of ideological position, this theory correctly predicts the vote choices of all but a relatively small subset of voters. If, as suggested by the quote at the beginning of this chapter, theories of voting should be evaluated according to the quality of their predictive statements, spatial voting theory seems to fare quite well.

As a comparison, the vote choices of approximately 85 percent of respondents in both the 2004 and 2008 surveys could be predicted by assuming that they cast their ballots for the candidate of the party with which they identify.[11] This is because, although well over 90 percent of partisans vote for their party's candidates, 13 and 11 percent of voters did not express any identification with either party in the 2004 and 2008 surveys, respectively, identifying as independents. Purely party identification – based theories of vote choice make no predictions about these pure independents. This difference in predictive power of spatial theory over party identification is even more impressive given that the ideology in spatial voting theory is estimated without any direct information about feelings toward candidates or the parties they represent.

A related question to the *relative* predictive power of ideology and partisanship according to these two theories is how well the votes of respondents of different party identifications conform to the predictions of spatial theory. Accordingly, Table 4.4 also presents the percentage of respondents voting "spatially correctly" by respondents' party identifications. In both 2004 and 2008, Democratic respondents have the highest percentage of correct voting. In 2004, Republicans vote correctly at the lowest rates, while in 2008, independents fare the worst according to this standard. Considering partisanship by itself, however, is clearly misleading because this measure is heavily correlated with ideology, as seen in Figure 4.5. Therefore, to truly examine the independent effects of partisanship and ideology on vote choice, we should seek a model of spatial voting that also includes a possible role for party identification.

In addition to party identification, there is good reason to suspect that a voter's level of political information may moderate the effects of spatial proximity to candidates on vote choice. For example, voters with higher levels of information are likely to be better able to judge the distances between their own ideological positions and those of candidates, making it easier for them to determine which candidate is closest to them. As Table 4.4 shows, for both surveys, there is a clear positive relationship between information level and the probability of casting a "spatially

---

[11] Predicting vote choice using probit regressions on either ideology or party identification (Democrat, independent, and Republican) results in similar likelihoods, with party identification faring better in some cases. It is important to note, though, that the predictive accuracy of these regressions is not the same as the predictive accuracy of the theories themselves.

correct" vote. While approximately three-quarters of low-information respondents voted correctly, more than 90 percent of high-information respondents chose the candidate closest to their own ideal point in both the 2004 and 2008 surveys.

These findings would initially suggest that more informed voters are better spatial voters than those having less information. But it also is a well-known fact that less informed voters tend to be more ideologically moderate than those with higher levels of political knowledge, which is the case for respondents in the two surveys used here. The average ideological distance from zero (the midpoint between the two candidates' positions) in the 2004 survey was .13, .17, and .18 for low-, medium-, and high-information respondents, respectively. For the 2008 survey, the corresponding numbers are .13, .21, and .22. It is unclear, therefore, how much the differences in the bottom row of Table 4.4 reflect the moderating effects of political information on the conduct of spatial voting and how much they result from the higher percentage of ideological extremists among more informed voters.

Overall, though, these results clearly demonstrate the strong predictive power of even the simplest spatial voting models. Assuming that each voter will choose the candidate closest to them results in predictions that are correct 84 and 87 percent of the time in the 2004 and 2008 surveys, respectively. These predictions are more accurate even than predicting that respondents will vote for the candidate whose political party they associate themselves with. In addition to providing strong support for the basic logic of spatial voting, these findings are also quite appealing from a normative perspective. While there are clearly factors other than ideology that may be important in choosing a president, it should be comforting to note that the vast majority of voters seem to cast their ballots for the candidate who holds views closest to their own.

Discussion

This chapter has demonstrated how the measurements of the ideology of voters and candidates presented in Chapter 3 can be used to directly test spatial voting models. From a generalized stochastic model of spatial voting, three empirically testable propositions have been derived that should hold if voters are employing unbiased spatial voting. First, as voters become more ideologically conservative, they should become more likely to vote for the conservative candidate, which in our study of American presidential elections will be the Republican. Second, while we have abandoned the absolute predictions of the deterministic spatial voting model, we expect that voters should be more likely to choose the candidate to whom they are ideologically closer. Finally, voters whose ideologies fall precisely at the midpoint between the two candidates, and who therefore are equally close to either candidate, should be equally likely to cast their ballots for the Democrat or the Republican.

This chapter has derived the conditions under which the precision and bias parameters of the stochastic spatial utility model can be estimated through a probit regression model predicting vote choice with respondent ideology. Using the ideology estimates discussed in Chapter 3 for both voters and candidates, these parameters are estimated for both the 2004 and 2008 presidential elections. The results show that in both elections, the first condition of spatial voting is strongly confirmed. Voters become significantly more likely to vote for the Republican candidate in each election as their ideologies become more conservative. While this represents a strong validation of ideological, or policy, voting, further conditions are required to verify whether voters meet the more specific requirements for spatial voting. Although the second condition of spatial voting – that voters are more likely to choose the candidate closest to them – is validated for the vast majority of voters, in each election a segment of the electorate is identified in which voters are more likely to choose the candidate who is ideologically *farthest* from them. In the 2004 election, this class of voters represents a small but nontrivial portion of the survey sample. In 2008, however, only a tiny fraction of the voter population is ideologically closer to one presidential candidate yet is predicted to be more likely to vote for the other. Finally, the third condition of unbiased spatial voting, that voters at the midpoint between the two candidates' positions should be equally likely to vote for either candidate, was found to be violated in the 2004 election, with such voters having a 75 percent chance of casting their ballots for Bush. In the 2008 presidential election, these voters were estimated to have a 56 percent chance of choosing McCain, suggesting a relatively close approximation of this condition.

These conclusions also hold under a wide range of statistical specifications and do not result from the specific setup or assumptions used here. Appendix C presents the results of simplified analyses of spatial voting relying on simple additive measures and nonparametric models. The findings based on these simplified analyses are nearly identical to those presented in this chapter, strengthening the results and demonstrating that they do not derive solely from the particular setup or assumptions employed here.

Overall, the results presented in this chapter show that voters on average came fairly close to satisfying the conditions for unbiased spatial voting. These results, however, also point to some important exceptions to these findings. Perhaps more importantly, these results represent only a first step in understanding the dynamics of spatial voting in actual elections. The proceeding chapters attempt to generalize the results presented here. Chapter 5 presents an expanded model of spatial voting that includes the possibility of differing biases that result from partisanship, while Chapter 6 examines the effects of political information levels on the use of spatial voting.

5

Partisanship versus Proximity

The Effect of Party Identification on Spatial Voting

> Most Americans have this sense of attachment with one party or the other. And for the individual who does, the strength and direction of party identification are facts of central importance in accounting for attitude and behavior.
>
> (Campbell, Converse, Miller, and Stokes 1960, 121)

Perhaps the most influential work on voting behavior in the United States is *The American Voter* by Campbell, Converse, Miller, and Stokes (1960). While the book touches on a number of areas of political behavior, it is most widely cited for its emphasis of party identification – longstanding and largely unchanging loyalties to a political party, usually developed by voters at a young age – as the primary determinant of vote choice and other political actions. *The American Voter* stands as the central work of the so-called Michigan school of political behavior, which argues that voters are overwhelmingly unsophisticated, making political decisions without much planning or reason, and guided mostly by a sense of personal loyalty to one of the two major political parties.

Most works categorized under the Michigan school umbrella downplay policy ideology not only as a meaningful predictor of vote choice, but also as existing in the first place for the majority of voters:

> We have seen that the stable qualities of the public's response to political affairs have to do primarily with long-term loyalties to the parties rather than ideological commitments against which current acts or policies of the parties could be evaluated. The forces not based on party loyalty that influence the decisions of the American electorate appear almost wholly free of ideological coloration. (550)

103

The spatial theory of voting paints an almost diametrically opposed picture of voter reasoning. According to the basic spatial model, vote choices are determined solely by voters' ideological proximity to the positions of candidates, rather than based on longstanding attachments to political parties. The previous two chapters suggest powerful counterarguments to the "Michigan school" line of thought. First, a single latent dimension can account for the vast majority of the variation in the specific policy views of respondents to both the 2004 and 2008 surveys. Furthermore, the decisions of voters in both the 2004 and 2008 presidential elections are shown to depend strongly on their ideological positions, with the specific relationship closely matching the predictions of simple theories of spatial voting.

The models tested in Chapter 4, however, posit no direct role for party identification in affecting decisions of voters. Furthermore, because policy views and ideology are known to be strongly correlated with party identification (see Figure 3.5 and Table 3.4), the exclusion of partisanship from statistical models predicting vote choice may systematically bias estimates of the effects of ideology. In particular, it could be the case that once the effects of partisanship are accounted for, ideology no longer plays a significant role in determining vote choice or that it plays a much smaller role than previous findings would suggest. Furthermore, the relatively low amount of spatial bias estimated for voters in Chapter 4 could be the result of strong partisan biases, pushing Democrats and Republicans in opposite directions, which cancel out in the aggregate when party identification is not taken into consideration.

This chapter generalizes the simple spatial model analyzed in the previous chapter in order to explore variation in the use of spatial voting across party identifications. The findings demonstrate that while strong effects of ideology on vote choice remain even after controlling for party identification, the magnitude and direction of spatial bias among voters is strongly affected by their partisan affiliations. These results suggest that while simple theories of spatial voting describe the average relationship between ideology and vote choice quite well, they also mask important partisan variation in the relationships between ideological proximity and vote choice.

Modeling Spatial and Partisan Voting Effects

In order to directly test the competing predictions of spatial and partisan voting theories, this section proposes a model that allows for the simultaneous influence of both of these factors on vote choice. The model is built on the same spatial utility framework employed in Chapter 4, but also allows for voters to receive benefits from casting their ballots for the candidate from the party with which they identify.

Previous studies have examined the consequences of allowing voters to differ in their use of these nonpolicy factors (Chapman 1967, 1968; Adams 2001; Adams et al. 2005). As pointed out by Erikson and Romero (1990), the inclusion of such measured nonpolicy factors would generally be expected to affect the properties of the stochastic spatial voting model if they are correlated with voters' policy views. The most prominent example of such a factor is party identification, which is known to exhibit very high correlations with ideology and is generally thought to have a fundamental relationship with vote choice (e.g., Campbell et al. 1960). For example, in the 2004 and 2008 surveys, the correlations between respondents' estimated ideological positions and their seven-point party identifications are .68 and .67, respectively. Accordingly, it is appropriate to expand the spatial voting framework to include the influence of partisanship, which could be hypothesized to influence vote choice above and beyond citizens' ideological proximity to each candidate.

Moreover, including party as well as ideology in models of vote choice may be thought to create a stronger test for the influence of ideological position on voter behavior. Party is often assumed to be causally prior to ideology (Campbell et al. 1960, 24–32). If this is the case, then demonstrating that ideology has a strong effect on vote choice even after controlling for partisanship should be all the more impressive. Conversely, if ideology affects partisanship, the effects reported could underestimate the overall impact of ideology on vote choice because they do not include the indirect effects of ideology on the vote that operate through partisanship. Overall, a fuller model of vote choice including both ideology and partisanship will provide a richer picture of the specific effects of each factor.

A Random Utility Model of Spatial Voting with Partisanship

The primary way in which the impact of partisanship on the vote is conceptualized is through some form of loyalty – a desire (perhaps a compulsion) to cast one's ballot for the candidate from the political party with which one identifies. If we seek to measure the effects of this party loyalty along with the impact of ideological proximity, we must specify a model in which both of these factors can play a role in determining voters' preferences between the two candidates. Here, a strategy previously employed by other scholars (see, e.g., Adams 2001; Adams et al. 2005) is followed and the effects of partisanship are included as additive terms in respondent utility equations. Under this setup, voters obtain utility from each candidate's proximity to their ideal points and from the random error term just as in the model presented in Chapter 4. Under this new setup, however, a partisan utility term b_{ik} also is included, which represents the amount of utility that person i gets from voting for candidate k above and beyond the candidate's ideological proximity to the voter. This term can be thought of as capturing the aspect of partisan loyalty that the Michigan school argues is central to voting behavior. It will be assumed that respondents within party identification grouping (here Democrats, independents, and Republicans) have the same values of b_{ik} for a given candidate k (i.e., $b_{ik} = b_{jk}$ for all candidates k whenever respondents i and j have the same party identification). Therefore, our equation for the utility voter i receives from voting for candidate k becomes

$$U_i(k) = -a(x_i - c_k)^2 + b_{ik} + e_{ik}. \tag{5.1}$$

This model again assumes that each voter i will choose the candidate who offers him or her the most utility. In the elections analyzed here, voters choose between the Democratic and Republican candidates whose ideological positions again denote c_D and c_R, respectively. Therefore, a respondent's probability of voting for the Republican candidate can be written as

$$P(v_i = R) = P(U_i(R) > U_i(D))$$
$$= P(-a(x_i - c_R)^2 + b_{iR} + e_{iR} > -a(x_i - c_D)^2 + b_{iD} + e_{iD})$$
$$= \Phi(\lambda x_i + \pi + \delta_{pty(i)}), \tag{5.2}$$

where $\lambda = 2a(c_R - c_D)$, $\pi = a(c_D^2 - c_R^2)$, and $\delta_{pty(i)} = b_{iR} - b_{iD}$. The direct correspondence to a probit model is again obtained by assuming that $e_{iD} - e_{iR}$ follows a standard normal distribution. The main parameters of interest in this utility-based model of voting are the policy weight a and partisan biases b_{ik} toward the candidates.

As before, the policy weight parameter a represents how strongly a respondent's ideological proximity to each candidate affects the utility that he or she receives from choosing that candidate. The partisan bias term $\delta_{pty(i)}$ can be thought of as the net bias of a respondent i toward the Republican candidate. Negative values of this parameter, conversely, will indicate biases toward the Democrat. These bias terms are assumed to relate to respondents' own party identifications, with the net bias being the same for voters within each party identification category: Democrat, independent, or Republican.

The Michigan school and the spatial voting approach to the study voting behavior offer starkly different predictions for the values of these parameters of the utility model in Equation 5.1. According to the Michigan school, vote choice should be centrally determined by partisanship. In other words, the net biases of Democratic and Republican identifiers, described by the parameter δ_D and δ_R, should be large in magnitude and should be negative for Democrats (indicating a net bias against the Republican candidate and hence toward the Democratic candidate) and positive for Republicans (indicating a net bias toward the Republican and against the Democratic candidate). Furthermore, most of the work in the Michigan school tradition argues that the effects of policy views on the vote, particularly after party identification is accounted for, should be minimal. This would imply a value for the policy weight (or precision) parameter a that is relatively close to zero.

By contrast, the simplest spatial voting theories assume that the sole determinant of vote choice is a voter's relative ideological proximity to the candidates in a given election. Therefore, the impact of partisanship should be small, corresponding to values for δ_D and δ_R that are close to zero. δ_I, which denotes the net bias among independent voters, also should be nearly zero. Spatial voting also would presumably imply a large positive value for a, indicating that the decisions of voters are strongly affected by their ideological proximity to candidates, with voters being much more likely to select the candidate closest to themselves.

The left and center panes of Figure 5.1 plot the predictions of the "Michigan school" party identification theory of voting and the spatial theory in terms of the predicted vote probabilities for Democratic, independent, and Republican voters, shown with solid, dashed, and dotted lines, respectively. Under the simplest versions of the party identification voting model, citizens would have their vote choices affected by only party identification, with ideology having little or no effect. This is represented by horizontal lines for voters of each party identification, with Democrats being very likely to vote for the Democratic candidate, Republicans being very likely to vote for the Republican candidate, and independent voters falling somewhere in between. The center pane of the figure shows the predictions of simple unbiased spatial voting. Under this theory, voters' choices are based on their relative ideological proximity to each candidate. Voters closer to the position of the Democratic candidate (c_D) are likely to vote for him, those closest to the Republican candidate's

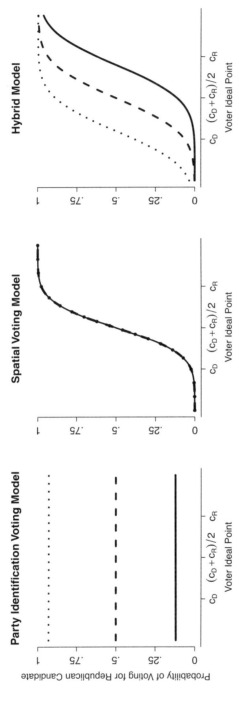

FIGURE 5.1. Simple baseline vote choice models. Simplified predictions of "Michigan school" party identification model of voting, simple unbiased spatial voting model, and hybrid model of voting for Democratic (solid lines), independent (dashed lines), and Republican (dotted lines) voters. Note that in the center pane ("Spatial Voting Model"), the predictions for voters of all party identifications are identical, shown by overlapping curves.

ideological location (c_R) generally vote for him, and voters with ideal points at the midpoint between the two candidates are equally likely to vote for either one. Furthermore, according to this basic spatial setup, vote choices are not affected by partisanship after controlling for ideology, as shown by the overlapping dotted, dashed, and solid lines. In other words, this simple version of spatial voting assumes that a Democratic, independent, and Republican voter will all have the same vote probabilities if they hold precisely the same ideology.

These two competing theories, while often framed in absolute terms, are in some ways two ends of a spectrum on which the truth almost certainly falls somewhere near the middle. One theory argues that voting is purely partisan, while the other assumes that vote choice is solely the result of voters' ideological proximity to candidates. While the goal of the models analyzed here will be to arbitrate between these two accounts of voter behavior by looking at the actual decisions of voters in recent presidential elections, the results can be thought of as indicating the relative importance of party and ideological proximity on vote choice. For example, the right pane of Figure 5.1 shows an example of a possible compromise between the partisan and spatial theories of vote choice. Under this hybrid model, both ideology and partisanship exert independent effects on vote choice. As voters of all party identifications become more conservative, they become more likely to cast their ballots for the Republican candidate. But voters having the same ideological positions will differ in their probabilities of voting for the Republican candidate if they identify with different political parties. An important question is what kind of balance the actual decisions of voters reveal between the influences of spatial proximity and partisanship.

Estimating Spatial and Partisan Effects on Vote Choice

As before in Chapter 4, we can derive the correspondence between the latent utility model assumed in Equation 5.1 and the coefficients of a probit model, this time predicting presidential vote with respondents' ideal points and party identification. Under this new model, we can estimate a probit regression, which, as before, includes an intercept and a coefficient on voter ideology. In this case, however, the intercept term is allowed to vary, being estimated separately for Democratic, independent, and republican voters. The probability of a voter i casting his or her ballot for the Republican candidate can now be written as

$$P\left(v_i = R\right) = \Phi\left(\beta_{pty(i)} + \beta_x x_i\right), \tag{5.3}$$

TABLE 5.1. *Estimated Spatial Utility Model Parameters, Varying Intercept Model*

Coefficient	Utility Model Parameter	2004 Estimates (Standard Errors)	2008 Estimates (Standard Errors)
Democrat Intercept	δ_{Dem}	−.97	−.78
		(.07)	(.08)
Independent Intercept	δ_{Ind}	.31	.09
		(.06)	(.13)
Republican Intercept	δ_{Rep}	2.00	1.17
		(.07)	(.09)
Ideal Point (x_i)	a	7.09	5.59
		(.32)	(.39)
	Log-likelihood	−736.1	−360.4
	N	5,411	1,715

Cells show estimated probit coefficients, with corresponding spatial utility model parameters from Equation 5.2, with standard deviations underneath in parentheses.

where $pty(i)$ is voter i's party identification, resulting in separate intercepts being estimated for Democratic, independent, and Republican voters (β_D, β_I, and β_R, respectively). The identification of the ideology scale to place the positions of the Democratic and Republican candidates in both elections at $-1/4$ and $1/4$, respectively, yields the following correspondence between the parameters of Equations 5.2 and 5.3:

$$\delta_D = \beta_D \qquad \delta_I = \beta_I \qquad \delta_R = \beta_R$$

$$a = \beta_x \qquad \pi = 0 \qquad\qquad\qquad\qquad (5.4)$$

This indicates that we can simultaneously estimate the effects of partisanship, through the bias terms δ_D, δ_I, and δ_R, and of ideological proximity, through the policy weight term a, on vote choice.

Table 5.1 presents the results of these estimates for both the 2004 and 2008 surveys. These estimates reveal substantively large and statistically significant differences between the behavior of Democrats, independents, and Republicans in both the 2004 and 2008 presidential elections, even after controlling for their ideological positions. This means that two voters with exactly the same policy views will have dramatically different vote probabilities if they do not identify with the same political party.

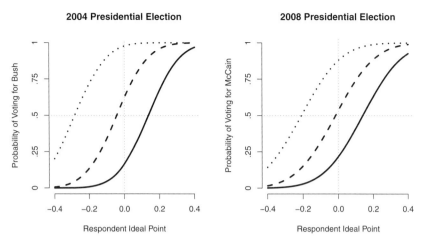

FIGURE 5.2. Predicted vote probabilities, varying intercept model. Curves show the predicted probabilities of voting for the Republican candidate in the 2004 and 2008 elections as a function of a voter's ideological position for Democrats (solid lines), independents (dashed lines), and Republicans (dotted lines). Probabilities are calculated based on the estimates presented in Table 5.1 for the parameters in Equation 5.3.

These findings strongly support the well-accepted notion that partisanship exerts a strong independent effect on vote choice. We also see, however, that in both 2004 and 2008, voters were strongly influenced by their ideology above and beyond their party affiliations. The estimates for the policy weight a is quite large and highly significant in both elections, taking values of 7.09 in 2004 and 5.59 in 2008, demonstrating that while the choices of voters are clearly affected by their partisan loyalties, they also are strongly influenced by their ideological proximity to candidate positions as predicted by spatial theories of voting. Although the estimated effects of ideology are slightly weaker once partisanship has been controlled for, we still see an important role for ideological proximity in vote choice. As before, independent voters are estimated to have relatively low amount of bias by the standards of spatial voting. The estimates of δ_I are .31 and .09 in 2004 and 2008, respectively. In fact, we cannot reject the hypothesis in 2008 that independents vote without any spatial bias at all. Partisan voters, by contrast, show an extremely high amount of bias, with Republican and Democratic identifiers being pushed strongly toward their party's candidate above and beyond the influence of ideology.

Figure 5.2 plots the predicted probability based on the estimates presented in Table 5.1 of Democratic, independent, and Republican identifiers voting for the Republican presidential candidate in 2004 and 2008 as a function of respondents' ideological positions. The most obvious feature of these plots is the relatively large amount of divergence between the predicted behavior of partisans and independents, even those having similar ideological positions. In both the 2004 and 2008 analyses, Democratic voters (shown with solid lines) are much less likely to vote for the Republican candidate than are independents (dashed lines) or Republicans (dotted lines), even when they have the same ideological positions. For example, the predicted probabilities of voting for George W. Bush in 2004 for Democratic, independent, and Republican voters who all have ideal points at zero – precisely midway between the positions of the two candidates – are estimated to be .17, .62, and .98, respectively. In other words, partisan voters who, based on their ideological positions, should be equally likely to vote for either candidate according to spatial voting are overwhelmingly likely to vote for their party's candidate. The estimates in 2008 show similar results, predicting that Democrats, independents, and Republicans with ideal points of zero will have .22, .54, and .88 probabilities of voting for McCain. Despite this large partisan divergence in vote probabilities, we still clearly see that ideological position and, as a consequence, relative ideological proximity to the candidates has a large impact on vote choice. These results suggest important modifications to spatial voting theory in order to take into account the effects of partisanship in addition to spatial concerns.

An important implication of the partisan divergence uncovered here is that the implied indifference points of voters discussed in Chapter 4 will vary with respondents' party identification. Recall that a voter's implied indifference point is the ideological position at which he or she would be estimated to be indifferent between the two candidates in a given election, having a 50 percent chance of voting for both the Republican and the Democrat. Under the new model specification in Equation 5.3, the decisions of voters depend on both ideology and partisanship. Accordingly, both must be taken into account when solving for a voter's implied indifference point. We can calculate this value, using the estimates presented in Table 5.1, as

$$\text{Implied Indifference Point}_i = \frac{-\beta_{pty(i)}}{\beta_x}. \tag{5.5}$$

Table 5.2 presents estimates of these values along with 95 percent confidence intervals. These estimates provide a powerful illustration of the strength of partisanship even after controlling for the ideological

TABLE 5.2. *Estimated Implied Indifference Points*

	2004 Presidential Election		
	Democrats	Independents	Republicans
Estimate	.14	−.04	−.29
95% Confidence Interval	(.11, .16)	(−.06, −.03)	(−.31, −.25)
	2008 Presidential Election		
	Democrats	Independents	Republicans
Estimate	.14	−.01	−.21
95% Confidence Interval	(.11, .18)	(−.06, .03)	(−.26, −.17)

Cells show the ideological location at which voters of different party identifications would be predicted to have an equal chance of casting their ballot for either candidate according to the estimates presented in Table 5.1. Ninety-five percent confidence intervals underneath in parentheses are calculated using the bootstrap procedure.

proximity of voters to each candidate. In both 2004 and 2008, Democratic voters who are more than three and a half times closer to the Republican candidate, having an ideal point of .14, would be indifferent between the two candidates. Republican voters in 2004 would be more likely to choose Bush even when they had an ideological position identical to that of Kerry. The implied indifference point of these voters actually falls to the left of Kerry's position. In 2008, the implied indifference point for Republican voters is still very far to the left, implying that Republican identifiers who are almost as liberal as Obama will still be indifferent between the two candidates.

Independent voters, by contrast, are estimated to have implied indifference points in both elections that fall very close to the true midpoint between the two candidates. In 2004, while we can reject the hypothesis that the implied indifference point of independents is equal to zero, the amount of divergence from this midpoint appears quite small. In 2008, the implied indifference point of independents is estimated to be −.01, and we cannot reject the hypothesis that it is actually zero. These results show mixed support for the unbiasedness criterion of spatial voting discussed in Chapter 4. The ideological position at which partisans are predicted to be indifferent between the two candidates falls quite far from the actual midpoint between the two candidates in both 2004 and 2008. Independents, however, very closely approximate this spatial unbiasedness condition in both elections studied.

The estimates presented here clearly show that both partisanship and ideology play an important role in determining the vote choices of citizens in recent presidential elections. The strong associations uncovered in the previous chapter between ideology and vote choice remain, albeit in somewhat weakened form, even after controlling for partisanship. This suggests that what is often viewed as a competition between two distinct frameworks – the "Michigan school," in which partisanship is key and ideology has little if any significant role, and the spatial voting tradition, in which ideology is the central determinant of vote choice – is in fact more of a compromise between or a combination of these viewpoints.

Disentangling the Influence of Valence Issues

Apart from spatial proximity and partisanship, scholars have proposed that there may be some considerations that are evaluated identically by all voters. It is often argued that these so-called valence issues may confer an overall advantage on a particular candidate based on qualities such as charisma or intelligence (e.g., Stokes 1963). These valence issues may include superficial qualities such as attractiveness or more substantive ones such as judgment, leadership, or competence. The key distinguishing feature of valence issues is that they are valued equally by all voters. This property stands in sharp contrast to ideology, which, under the spatial setup, is judged differently by different voters. For example, a candidate who moves to the right (becomes more conservative) will please conservative voters but displease liberals. A candidate who becomes more competent, by contrast, may be thought to improve his or her standing with all voters. The effects of valence also differ importantly from those of partisanship for similar reasons. While affiliation with the Democratic party may cause a candidate to be viewed more favorably among Democratic voters, it is likely to represent a strike against the candidate in the minds of Republicans. Such valence issues have been demonstrated to have important theoretical consequences for the properties of spatial models, mainly with regard to candidate strategy (Feld and Grofman 1991; Macdonald and Rabinowitz 1998; Ansolabehere and Snyder 2000; Groseclose 2001; Roemer 2001; Miller and Schofield 2003; Schofield 2003, 2004).

While the estimates presented in the previous chapter suggested a slight valence advantage for Bush in 2004 and little or no influence for valence issues in 2008, these findings were based on models that did not include any possible effects for partisanship. Therefore, we may worry that the net advantages they estimate are just an average of the effect of partisanship across the samples being analyzed. The analyses presented in this chapter estimate separate intercepts, which also can be considered as spatial bias terms, for respondents of each partisanship. These terms, however, should account for the overall net bias toward the Republican candidate after controlling for voters' ideological positions. These predispositions toward a particular candidate may be thought to include not only partisanship, but also any possible valence effects that differentiate the two candidates. An important question is what part of these terms is due to partisanship and what can be attributable to a net valence advantage for one candidate or another. Accordingly, we can seek to separate the effects of partisanship, which will affect Democrats and Republicans differently, and of valence issues, which should affect all voters in the same way. To do this, we modify the model presented in Equation 5.1 to include a valence term. Under this new specification, we can write the utility that voter i receives from casting his or her ballot for candidate k as

$$U_i(k) = -a(x_i - c_k)^2 + b_{ik} + v_k + e_{ik}, \qquad (5.6)$$

where, as before, x_i is voter i's ideal point (or ideological location), c_k is the position taken by candidate k, a is a policy weight, and b_{ik} is a partisan bias term. The newly introduced term v_k represents a valence advantage or disadvantage for candidate k. The fact that this advantage is valued the same by all voters is implied by the fact that it has no i subscript.

The valence and partisan bias terms v_k and b_{ik} cannot be separately estimated without some restriction. This is because adding any constant to v_k and subtracting that constant from b_{ik} will result in identical utilities. We can only estimate the total net spatial bias for each type of voter – what we have previously called δ_D, δ_I, and δ_R. An obvious assumption, however, is that any bias shown by independent voters cannot be due to partisanship, but should instead be attributed solely to a valence advantage for one candidate. This implies the formal restriction that $b_{ik} = 0$ for independent voters, which means that the estimated intercept term δ_{Ind} for independents in Table 5.1 represents the net valence advantage for the Republican candidate in a given election. Furthermore, accounting for this valence advantage changes the estimates for partisan bias, which should now be equal to $\delta_D - (v_R - v_D) = \delta_D - \delta_I$ for Democrats and $\delta_R - (v_R - v_D) = \delta_R - \delta_I$ for Republicans.

TABLE 5.3. *Estimated Valence and Partisanship Effects*

	2004 Estimates	2008 Estimates
Valence	.31	.09
	(.06)	(.13)
Democratic Partisanship	−1.28	−.87
	(.09)	(.15)
Republican Partisanship	1.69	1.08
	(.09)	(.16)

Cells show estimated values of the net valence advantage for the Republican candidate and the partisan biases (apart from valence effects) of Democratic and Republican voters toward the Republican candidate in the 2004 and 2008 presidential elections. These estimates are derived from those presented in Table 5.1.

Table 5.3 shows the estimated values of the valence and partisanship effects for the 2004 and 2008 elections. The valence term represents the advantage held by the Republican candidate across all voters apart from both ideology and partisanship. Furthermore, it is assumed that independents are not affected by any form of partisan bias, implying that the bias shown by these voters is attributable entirely to valence factors. This is why the estimated valence term for both elections is equal to the net bias term δ_I from Table 5.1. The partisanship terms are the biases that remain after adjusting the net bias terms for Democrats and Republicans (δ_D and δ_R, respectively) by subtracting the valence effect in each election. This can be thought of as partitioning these overall spatial bias terms into valence and partisanship.

The most apparent feature of these estimates is the huge difference in magnitude between the valence and partisanship effects. In 2004, the effect of valence is estimated to be less than one-fourth the size of that for Democratic partisanship and well under one-fifth the size of the effect of partisanship for Republican voters. In 2008, the differences are even more stark, with the effects of partisanship for both parties being estimated to be in the neighborhood of ten times the size of the net valence effect. These results suggest that while valence issues may play some role in presidential elections, their overall impact on individual vote choice is dwarfed by that of partisanship.

This, however, does not necessarily mean that individual valence issues do not have large effects on vote choices, only that the overall influence of valence issues is small. It could still be the case, however, that several different valence issues each had a large impact on the choices of voters, but the impact of these issues worked in opposite directions. For example, we could imagine that in 2008, voters may have perceived McCain to be more experienced and a stronger leader, while Obama was more charismatic and intelligent. In this case, each of these issues could have a large impact on voters, but if they worked in opposite directions and were of similar magnitudes, the overall impact of valence issues could be small.[1]

Thinking of parties as strategic, we may suspect that a huge valence advantage for one party or another may be unlikely, particularly in a presidential election. Assuming that both parties have a relatively large pool of potential presidential candidates, it stands to reason that they would be most likely to choose nominees who score highly on valence issues. Absent any strong reason for one party to have better candidates, this may be thought to produce Democratic and Republican nominees with similar valence characteristics. Furthermore, the increasing intra-party homogeneity that has been observed in recent decades could lead to even more optimization of the valence characteristics of party nominees because of the fact that there is likely to be little ideological variation between potential candidates and hence selection can focus more on other candidate traits. While these arguments are somewhat speculative, they do raise important points about the prominence that valence issues may play in American presidential elections, particularly in light of the findings from Table 5.3.

Another finding from Table 5.3 is that the effects of partisanship appear much more similar in magnitude after separating out valence effects than they were looking solely at the overall spatial biases. For example, Table 5.1 suggests that in Republicans exhibited biases that were roughly twice and 1.5 times the size of those for Democrats in 2004 and 2008. When these total biases are separated into valence and partisan effects, however, the resulting partisan biases appear much more similar, suggesting that Democrats and Republicans display roughly equal amounts of bias according to the standards of spatial voting.

Comparing the Effects of Ideology, Valence, and Partisanship

The estimated effects of valence issues and partisanship shown in Table 5.3 are on the scale of voters' utilities. While this is interesting in its own right, another way of understanding the substantive size of these effects is

---

[1] This example is not meant to objectively characterize voters' views on this subject, but is merely meant as an illustration of the logic of overall valence effects.

TABLE 5.4. *Equating the Effects of Valence, Partisanship, and Ideology*

	2004 Estimates	2008 Estimates
Valence	.04	.01
	(.03, .06)	(.00, .06)
Democratic Partisanship	.18	.16
	(.15, .21)	(.10, .21)
Republican Partisanship	.24	.19
	(.21, .27)	(.13, .26)

Cell entries show the estimated amount of ideological movement required to affect respondent utilities (and hence vote choices) an equal amount to the effects of valence and partisanship. Bootstrapped 95 percent confidence intervals are shown underneath in parentheses.

to attempt to equate them with the effects of moving a voter's ideology. To do this, we can divide the valence and partisan effect terms by the coefficient on ideology. This will, in a sense, provide some conversion that will relate the effects of valence, partisanship, and ideology on a comparable scale. These quantities will describe how much ideological movement would be required to have an effect equal to that of either the valence term or of the Democratic or Republican bias terms.

Table 5.4 shows the estimated ideological movement that would be required to offset the effects of valence and partisanship, along with corresponding 95 percent confidence intervals for these quantities. In both elections studied here, we see that valence issues exerted a very minor impact in comparison to that of ideology. In 2004, an ideological movement of just .04 units would have a comparable effect to the overall influence of valence issues. In 2008, moving just .01 units on the ideology scale would offset the net valence advantage (recall that we cannot even reject the null hypothesis that the net valence advantage for McCain in 2008 is zero). These two estimates emphasize that while valence issues may play some role in voter choices, they appear to have had at most a small effect in the two most recent presidential elections.

By contrast, the effects of partisanship remain significant, even in comparison to those of ideology. In 2004, movements of .18 and .24 units on the ideological scale would be required to offset the impacts of Democratic and Republican party identification, respectively, on vote choice. Recall that the ideology scales analyzed here have been normalized so that the Democratic and Republican candidates have positions at $-1/4$ and $1/4$, respectively. This means that, for example, a voter in the 2004 election changing from being an independent to identifying with the Republican party would have his or her vote probability affected in a manner roughly comparable to moving his or her ideology from zero (the midpoint between the two candidates) to $1/4$ (the same ideological position taken by McCain). This represents a huge ideological shift – effectively, the voter is transformed from being a moderate to a fairly strong conservative. The corresponding results for the 2008 survey suggest a slightly smaller effect of partisanship relative to that of ideology, but on the whole paint a very similar picture. The effects of party identification are as large as or larger than those of significant shifts on the ideological scale.

Does Ideology Affect Partisans and Independents the Same Way?

A final question that can be asked about the impact of partisanship on the use of spatial voting rules is whether partisans have their vote choices affected by their ideological proximity to the candidates in the same way that independents do. For example, is it the case that independents pay a good deal of attention to the policy positions of candidates, while partisans largely ignore these things, focusing instead only on their party labels? If this were the case, our estimates for the policy weight term *a* could be misleading. In particular, the finding of significant effects for ideology on vote choice could apply only to independents and not partisans or could apply differently to these types of voters.

To assess this possibility, we can reestimate the statistical model of vote choice from Equation 5.7, this time allowing not only the intercept term, but now also the coefficient on ideology, to be estimated separately for Democrats, independents, and Republicans. We then obtain the expression

$$P(v_i = R) = \Phi(\beta_{0,pty(i)} + \beta_{1,pty(i)}x_i), \tag{5.7}$$

where for each voter i, v_i denotes vote choice, either Democrat (D) or Republican (R), $pty(i)$ represents party identification, and x_i is ideological position. This new model specification will allow for the estimation not only of different spatial bias terms (what we have previously called $\delta_{pty(i)}$), but also of different policy weights (now written with a party subscript as $a_{pty(i)}$) for voters of each party identification.

Table 5.5 shows the estimated coefficients for this new vote choice model. The estimated partisan bias terms $\delta_{pty(i)}$ are generally similar to

TABLE 5.5. *Estimated Spatial Utility Model Parameters. Varying Intercept and Slope Model*

Coefficient	Utility Model Parameter	2004 Survey			2008 Survey		
		Dem	Ind	Rep	Dem	Ind	Rep
Intercept	$\delta_{pty(i)}$	−1.06	.44	1.94	−.82	.12	1.17
		(.08)	(.08)	(.07)	(.08)	(.14)	(.09)
Ideal Point (x_i)	$a_{pty(i)}$	6.02	8.88	6.23	5.15	6.27	5.89
		(.59)	(.61)	(.54)	(.55)	(.98)	(.70)
	Log-likelihood	−242.5	−237.0	−248.9	−187.6	−55.9	−116.3
	N	2,325	645	2,441	878	130	707

Cells show estimated probit coefficients, with corresponding spatial utility model parameters from Equation 5.7, with standard deviations underneath in parentheses.

those presented in Table 5.1. Partisans exhibit strong biases toward their party's candidate. Independents in 2004 show some moderate amount of bias toward Bush, while in 2008 they show little if any detectable bias. The estimated policy weight terms $a_{pty(i)}$ are all large in magnitude, positive, and highly significant, suggesting that voters of all party identifications respond strongly to the spatial proximity of candidates.

There is some evidence that independents show stronger relationships between ideology and vote choice. In both 2004 and 2008, the estimated policy weight for independents is estimated to be larger than those for Democrats and Republicans. For the 2004 survey, these differences are statistically significant, but in 2008, they are not. Although not conclusive, this suggests that independent voters may be slightly more responsive to the ideological positions of candidates. Overall, though, these differences are not substantively large. For comparison, Figure 5.3 plots the predicted probabilities of voting for the Republican candidate for Democratic (dotted lines), independent (dashed lines), and Republican (solid lines) voters in both the 2004 and 2008 surveys. Looking back to Figure 5.2, it is apparent that the overall substantive results are not meaningfully changed by allowing the policy weights of voters to vary by party identification.[2] The main difference between the decision rules used by partisans and independents, then, is clearly their spatial biases rather than the influence of ideology.

[2] Furthermore, estimates of implied indifference points (not shown here) are nearly identical under these two setups.

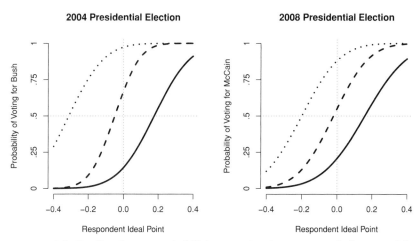

FIGURE 5.3. Predicted vote probabilities, varying intercept, and slope model. Curves show the predicted probabilities of voting for the Republican candidate in the 2004 and 2008 elections as a function of a voter's ideological position for Democrats (solid lines), independents (dashed lines), and Republicans (dotted lines), allowing for different policy weight terms for each party identification. Probabilities are calculated based on the estimates presented in Table 5.5 for the parameters in Equation 5.7.

The Effects of Measurement Error

The topic of measurement error, although quite important, has largely been ignored in the preceding discussions. In particular, although the estimates of ideology first described in Chapter 3 are just that – estimates – they have been treated in subsequent analyses as if they were known with certainty. The main reason for this decision has been convenience: we cannot measure citizens' ideologies without some error, so we simply use the uncertain measures as the best guess we have. But measurement error can have dramatic effects on coefficient estimates in regression models. While we cannot know exactly how our conclusions would differ from those using perfect measures of ideology, we can get a basic sense for the likely direction of the biases that impact the preceding analyses.[3]

The consequences of measurement error depend crucially on the nature of the errors in question. Generally, measurement error in a dependent variable can be absorbed into the random error term of a regression

---

[3] For an excellent discussion of the consequences of measurement error in regression models, see Achen (1983).

model, avoiding serious consequences aside from a decrease in the overall precision of estimates. Measurement error in independent variables, however, can be more pernicious. In bivariate regression models (i.e., those predicting some dependent variable using only one independent variable), the main consequence of measurement error in X is an attenuation, or biasing toward zero, of the slope coefficient. If we are predicting vote choice using estimated ideology (i.e., measures of ideology that contain some random error), we would expect the coefficient on ideology to be biased toward zero. Therefore, the estimates shown in Table 4.1 may be thought of as being something like a lower bound for the actual effect of ideology. The true impact of ideology on the vote choice is likely to be larger than our estimates given the downward bias that comes with measurement error.

In multivariate regression models in which one independent variable is measured with error, the consequences are more complicated. The coefficient on the variable measured with error should be attenuated as in the bivariate case. But measurement error in one independent variable also will bias the estimated coefficients on the other independent variables in the regression. While the direction and magnitude of the biases for these other coefficients are not as straightforward to understand, it is possible to make educated guesses about whether these coefficients should be biased upward or downward.

One way to think of the situation in which one explanatory variable is measured with error is as a milder form of omitted variable bias. Because one X is only known with some error, it is as if that variable has been "partially omitted," with the degree of omission depending on the relative amount of signal to noise in our imprecise measure of the true variable. Including noisy measures of some independent variable instead of the true variable itself will tend to have the same consequences on other estimated coefficients in the model, albeit to a milder degree, as if the noisy variable were omitted altogether. The specific direction and magnitude of these biases will depend on the sign of the true coefficient on the variable that is measured with error, the magnitude of the measurement error, and the correlation between the different predictors in the regression.

In the analyses presented in this chapter, ideology and partisanship have been used to predict vote choice in presidential elections. Ideology is clearly measured with error. Specifically, it is assumed that respondents' individual policy views are generated probabilistically based on their ideological positions and the characteristics of each policy proposal.

Therefore, while we can estimate each respondent's ideology from his or her issue positions, these estimates will contain some random measurement error. The larger the number of policy positions we know for each respondent, the more precisely we can measure his or her ideological position. Basing these ideology estimates on a larger number of policy questions could decrease the magnitude of this error and, in the limit eliminate it altogether. But for any finite number of policy questions, including the fifteen and ten positions known for each respondent in the 2004 and 2008 surveys, respectively, our measure will contain a nontrivial amount of random error.

Partisanship, on the other hand, may be assumed to be measured with little if any error. In particular, partisanship is generally defined as a person's feeling of attachment to or membership in a political party. Consequently, asking respondents whether they think of themselves as a Democrat, Republican, or independent is likely to be a fairly precise measure of partisanship. While all survey responses necessarily contain some stochastic element, it seems safe to assume that partisanship is less error prone because of the more direct correspondence between the quantity being measured and the measurement instrument.

We can then think of the model from Equation 5.3 as one in which partisanship (included through the separate intercepts for Democrats, independents, and Republicans) is measured with little or no error, while respondent ideology contains significant measurement error. In multivariate regression with measurement error, the coefficient on the variable containing error should be attenuated (biased toward zero). The biases for other coefficients in the model, here the differing partisan intercepts, are less straightforward. These biases depend both on the sign of the true coefficient on the variable that is measured with error and on the correlations between the variable measured with error and each of the other variables in the regression.

Although we cannot know the precise amount of bias in each estimated coefficient, we can, at a minimum, come up with educated guesses as to the direction of each of these biases if we know the sign of the true coefficient on ideology and the correlation between partisanship and ideology. Because ideology is measured with error, any other variables in the regression that are correlated with ideology should "absorb" some of the effects of ideology on vote choice into their own estimated coefficients. The three partisan intercepts can be thought of as coefficients on dummy (binary zero-one) variables for membership in each partisan grouping. We also know the direction of correlation between

Democratic or Republican identification and respondents' true ideology. Membership in the Democratic party is negatively correlated with ideology and membership in the Republican party is positively correlated with it.

Because we would clearly hypothesize that the true coefficient on ideology predicting likelihood of voting for the Republican candidate is positive, measurement error in ideology should result in some of the effects of ideology "spilling over" into the estimated coefficients on the other variables. Because ideology is positively correlated with identification with the Republican party (i.e., the average ideology for Republican identifiers should be greater, meaning more conservative, than the average for non-Republicans), we would expect the estimated coefficient on Republican identification (i.e., the estimated intercept for Republican identifiers) to be biased upward. Republican identification, through its positive correlation, can serve as a sort of proxy for "partially omitted" portions of ideology that result from the random error. Democratic identification, by contrast, is negatively correlated with ideology, meaning that its coefficient (i.e., the estimated intercept for Democratic identifiers) is biased downward. Independent identification would not be expected to have much correlation with respondents' true ideology (in fact, the correlation between *estimated* ideology and independent party identification in these data sets is virtually zero), so we would not expect a high degree of bias in the estimated intercept for independents.

The coefficient estimates presented in Table 5.1, then, should be reinterpreted in light of these new concerns related to measurement error. In particular, the estimated effect of ideology (i.e., the coefficient on respondents' ideal points x_i or what we have called the policy weight a in our random utility model of spatial voting) may represent something of a lower bound on the likely effect of ideological position on vote choice. Because the estimated coefficient is, in all likelihood, biased downward, we may expect that the true effect of ideology is actually greater than our coefficient estimate. In other words, ideology may be an even more important determinant of vote choice than most of the preceding analyses would suggest. By contrast, the fact that the Democratic intercept is biased downward and the Republican intercept is biased upward implies that partisanship may actually have a smaller effect on vote choice than previously thought. If we were somehow able to measure respondent ideology without error, it is quite likely that partisanship would be revealed to be less important, perhaps much less so.

Because we cannot estimate ideology without error, it is not possible to know the exact magnitude of the biases that exist in each of these coefficient estimates. If we could add more policy questions with which to estimate respondents' ideologies, we could decrease the measurement error in this variable and reduce the biases of all coefficients in the model. For the 2004 and 2008 surveys, however, all suitable questions, meaning those for which positions of respondents and candidates were both known, were included in the analyses. What we can do, however, is get an idea of how increased measurement error affects the estimated coefficients in the vote choice model from Equation 5.3 by computing ideology estimates omitting some questions. This would increase the measurement error of these ideology estimates.

To accomplish this, I estimate respondent ideology based on all possible combinations of the ten policy questions in the 2008 survey.[4] For each possible combination of these policy questions, the ideology estimates are used in a probit regression predicting the probability of voting for McCain with respondent ideology and separate intercepts for Democratic, independent, and Republican identifiers just as in Equation 5.3, but using the new ideology estimates. Figure 5.4 shows a boxplot of the estimated coefficients on respondent ideal point from each of these regressions as a function of the number of policy questions used to estimate the ideal points.[5] The horizontal lines in each of the boxes denote the median estimated coefficient for all models with a given number of items used in the ideology estimation. For example, there is only one possible way to estimate respondent ideal points using ten of the total of ten policy questions. Therefore, the horizontal line segment for this value simply represents the estimated coefficient on ideology from the full model in Table 5.1. There are, however, ten different ways to estimate respondent ideology using a subset of nine of the total ten policy issues.

The most obvious characteristic of this boxplot is that the coefficient estimates for respondent ideal point tend to be larger on average as the number of questions used to estimate ideal points increases. This is because using more questions reduces the amount of measurement error in the ideal point estimates, thus reducing the bias of the estimated

---

[4] The 2004 survey was not used because each respondent was asked only a random subset of the policy questions, making it less straightforward to analyze in this way.

[5] Ansolabehere et al. (2008) conduct a similar exercise, plotting the estimated over-time correlations of various measures of policy views, including larger or smaller numbers of policy questions in these measures.

Ideal Point Coefficient

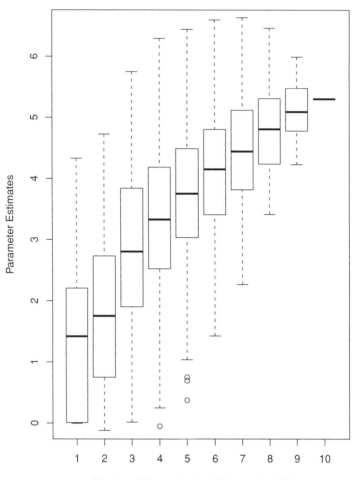

FIGURE 5.4. Estimated effects of ideology on vote choice. Boxplots of estimated coefficients from probit regressions predicting 2008 presidential vote with respondent ideal point, estimating respondent ideal point with all combinations of the ten policy issues included in the 2008 survey.

coefficient on ideology. Because this coefficient would be biased toward zero in the presence of measurement error, reducing this error results in a larger estimated coefficient.

Presumably, if we had eleven or twenty or one hundred questions with which to estimate respondent ideology, we could measure ideology even more precisely (with even less measurement error). This would be expected to increase the estimated coefficient on ideology even more. Eventually, these increases for β_x would taper off, but we have no way of knowing exactly when this would happen. For example, if ideology were measured without any error, would the effects of party identification go to zero or would strong partisan differences still remain? The most conclusive thing we can say based on these analyses is that the effect of ideology on the vote is quite likely to be underestimated.

We can also use this same exercise to explore the consequences of measurement error in ideology on the estimated effects of partisanship. Figure 5.5 plots the estimated intercepts for Democrats, independents, and Republicans based on these same probit regressions using all possible combinations of the ten policy proposals to estimate respondent ideal points. Boxplots of the estimated intercepts are presented based on the number of policy items used to estimate the ideal points used in the regressions. Looking first at the Democratic intercept, we see that as the number of items used increases, thus decreasing the amount of measurement error in the ideal point estimates, the effects of Democratic partisanship move toward zero. Similarly, the effects of Republican partisanship also tend to move toward zero as the number of items used increases. The estimated intercepts for independents show little systematic movement as the number of items used varies. These results illustrate the dynamics of measurement error discussed earlier. Partisanship will appear more important in the presence of measurement error in ideology. The intercept for Democratic identifiers should be biased downward and the Republican intercept should be biased upward – biases that increase the magnitude of both of these coefficients. If we were able to know respondents' ideological positions without error, we would expect the estimated impacts of partisanship to be weaker than those presented in Table 5.1.

The results of this chapter have shown that ideology is likely to be more important than previously acknowledged by much of the political behavior literature. A corollary of this statement may be that partisanship does not play as important a role as the literature would suggest. In fact, the importance of partisanship relative to that of ideology, as it has been estimated and discussed earlier in this chapter, may be thought to paint too rosy of a picture for the "partisanship matters" school of thought in light of this section's discussion. These results also may more broadly call into question the claimed effects of partisanship whenever ideology is measured with error.

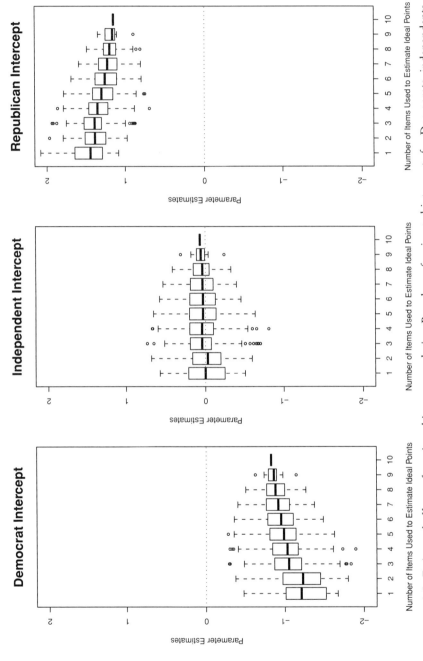

FIGURE 5.5. Estimated effects of partisanship on vote choice. Boxplots of estimated intercepts for Democrats, independents, and Republicans from probit regressions predicting 2008 presidential vote with respondent ideal point, estimating respondent ideal point with all combinations of the ten policy issues included in the 2008 survey.

Discussion

Partisanship is perhaps the most widely studied individual characteristic in American political behavior. As a predictor, it has been argued that partisanship plays a role in a wide range of areas, most notably vote choice. This chapter has sought to formally assess the impact of partisanship, putting it on equal footing with ideological proximity to candidates as a predictor of vote choice. The results have clearly demonstrated that while partisanship plays an important role in affecting the vote, it does not do so to the exclusion of ideological position.

The results presented here demonstrate that a realistic depiction of voter choice must combine the insights of the partisanship-centered Michigan school with those of the spatial voting approach. In particular, both partisanship and ideology have clear independent impacts on vote choice. It is not the case, as the simplest versions of partisan voting theory would say, that ordinary voters fail to demonstrate any responsiveness to the ideological locations of candidates, basing their decisions almost purely on partisan affiliations. It also is not the case, as the simplest versions of spatial theory may argue, that the vote choices of citizens are the product of a purely ideological evaluation of candidates.

Beyond simply showing that both partisanship and spatial ideological proximity exert strong effects on vote choice, the results presented here also have provided a direct assessment of the relative strength of these two forces and of the impact of so-called valence issues. In both 2004 and 2008, the impact of partisanship is equivalent to the effects of significant moves on the ideological spectrum. For instance, in 2004, the effect of identification with the Republican party is roughly similar to the effect of moving from an ideological position at the midpoint between Bush and Kerry to having the same ideological position as Bush. While other partisanship effects are estimated to be slight smaller in magnitude, they remain a very large determinant of vote choice. Valence effects, by contrast, appear to have at most a small impact on individual vote choices.

A natural question stemming from these results is whether the effects of ideology and partisanship vary systematically across voters. For example, do some voters tend to rely more on spatial proximity to candidates while others base their vote choices more on party identification? In particular, it may be thought that the story of the stereotypical voter of the Michigan school, who has little political thought other than a simple affective orientation toward the major political parties, may do a better job describing less informed voters. Conversely, spatial voting theory, with its requirements that voters form accurate perceptions of the positions taken by candidates and compare the relative distances between each of these distances and their own ideal points, may do a better job describing the decision making of high-information voters. These are the questions addressed in the following chapter.

6

Political Information and Spatial Voting

> Does it make sense, [that] two very different sorts of people – one extremely
> well informed and sophisticated about politics, the other not – make up
> their minds about how to vote in the same way?
>
> (Sniderman, Brody, and Tetlock, "Reasoning and Choice," 1991, 20)

A key criticism of spatial voting theory, and also of the somewhat weaker
theories of ideological or policy voting, is that it assumes a set of skills
far beyond the capacities of most voters. According to this line of argument, the vast majority of citizens do not possess the information or
conceptual capacities necessary to make decisions in this way. The preceding chapters have rebutted many key aspects of these criticisms: that
most voters do not possess any sort of real ideological constraint, that
voters cannot intelligently relate their own ideological positions to the
actual locations of candidates in elections, and that partisanship exerts a
predominant influence on vote choice, largely to the exclusion of other
factors. What previous chapters have not done, however, is to assess the
extent to which political information serves as a moderator of the effects
of ideology and partisanship on vote choice. To put it differently, do the
overall results presented in Chapters 4 and 5 mask significant differences
between uninformed and highly informed citizens in terms of their use of
spatial or partisan voting? Is a high level of political information a prerequisite for employing spatial voting rules? Is it, for example, the case that
uninformed voters rely predominantly on partisanship, whereas highly
informed voters more closely approximate the spatial voting ideal? This
chapter addresses these questions by elaborating on the voting models

previously considered with the aim of analyzing variation in the decision rules used by low-, medium-, and high-information voters.

Political information (along with its close relatives political sophistication and political expertise) has long served as a central variable in political behavior.[1] Its specific impact on the relationship between ideology and vote choice, however, has been the subject of some scholarly debate. According to some works, the vote choices of more informed citizens are more strongly affected by their ideological positions (e.g., Stimson 1975; Knight 1985; Goren 1997). Others, however, find no significant interaction between ideology and political information or sophistication in predicting vote choice (e.g., Campbell et al. 1960; Rahn et al. 1990). In particular, Ansolabehere et al. (2008) suggest that previous findings of an interaction between information and ideology are the result of measurement error under which the ideologies of more informed voters are estimated more precisely, particularly in studies relying on a single-item ideology measure.

There are several mechanisms by which political information may be thought to moderate the effects of ideology and partisanship on vote choice. First, citizens must presumably have some understanding of the ideological positions of candidates in order to engage in any form of spatial voting. Clearly, there may exist important differences between more informed voters, who may understand with a high degree of certainty where candidates stand, and uninformed voters who may have little or no specific knowledge about candidate positions. Second, less informed voters may attempt to substitute for their lack of knowledge by using simpler, more accessible rules of thumb, often called heuristics (Popkin 1991; Lupia 1994; McDermott 1997; Lupia and McCubbins 1998; Lau and Redlawsk 2001). Whereas some of these heuristics may lead to reasonably accurate inferences (at least on average), others may systematically mislead voters. In particular, party identification is likely to serve as an especially powerful heuristic for many voters, leading to the question of whether the impact of partisanship is conditional on voters' information levels.

This chapter begins by describing a procedure for estimating the knowledge levels of citizens using their responses to factual questions related to politics. The vote choices of respondents to the 2004 and 2008

---

[1] I do not make sharp distinctions between these three related concepts, but rather think of them in general terms, largely because a similar proxy – knowledge of political facts – has often been used to measure all three. See Luskin (1987) for a deeper discussion of measurement in this area.

surveys are then analyzed in order to estimate the effects of both ideology and partisanship for voters at various levels of political information. The results reveal that the relative influence of ideological proximity and party identification vary considerably across knowledge levels. While highly informed respondents are strongly influenced by ideology, those with less political knowledge show significantly smaller effects for ideology. In fact, some of the least informed voters show no detectable relationship between ideology and vote choice after controlling for partisanship. Information levels also seem to affect the severity of the spatial bias exhibited by partisan voters. These results underscore important differences in the use of spatial voting between high- and low-information voters.

Measuring Political Information

The measurement of political knowledge generally entails posing factual questions to respondents and computing knowledge scores, either by adding up the number of correct answers from each respondent or through some more elaborate statistical technique. The benefits of moving to a full statistical model of political knowledge are similar to those of estimating ideology using an ideal point model. The results of these models represent more principled estimates than do arbitrarily calculated summary statistics; valid measures of uncertainty and precision can be obtained; and the testing of hypotheses is typically more straightforward and direct. The most common statistical approach to estimating knowledge dates back to the work of Rasch (1960). Originally applied to the field of educational testing, the Rasch model posits that responses to questions are a function of both the knowledge level of individual respondents and the characteristics of a given question. A key result under the simple Rasch model is that the number of questions correctly answered is a sufficient statistic for a respondent's knowledge level, meaning that this value provides all the information that can be gleaned from a given set of data about the quantity being estimated. This property, although not often cited in political science applications, provides strong justification for using the "total correct" measure of political knowledge.

Despite the intuitive and statistical appeal of using the number of questions correctly answered as a measure of political knowledge, this approach can be improved upon in several ways by estimating full statistical models of political knowledge. First, on a more technical note, the standard Rasch model assumes that while knowledge questions can vary in their baseline level of difficulty, all questions tap knowledge in the same way. This is often referred to as discriminating equally well between high- and low-knowledge respondents. To the extent that this assumption is violated, there will exist more efficient ways of using the data to estimate knowledge. The estimation of full statistical models of these responses also provides an approach for assessing the usefulness and appropriateness of various items. Finally, estimating full statistical models of political knowledge produces measures such as standard errors that allow for the quantification of the level of uncertainty in each value.

The approach taken here relies on a statistical model that is a generalization of the Rasch method. Under this model, the probability of a respondent i correctly answering a knowledge question j is written as

$$P\left(q_{ij} = 1\right) = \Phi\left(\lambda_j \theta_i - \eta_j\right), \tag{6.1}$$

where q_{ij} is respondent i's answer to question j (coded 1 if correct and 0 otherwise), θ_i is respondent i's level of political information, and λ_j and η_j are the discrimination and difficulty parameters for question j.[2] This model actually has an identical specification to the one used to measure respondents' ideology, but here the latent dimension is assumed to be political knowledge, with higher values indicating more informed voters.

Each of the two surveys analyzed here includes a battery of political knowledge items. The 2004 survey contains nine questions, shown in Table 6.1, designed to tap political information including items on party control of the House of Representatives and the Senate and whether tax rates went up or down since the year 2000. The 2008 survey contains a battery of five political knowledge items, shown in Table 6.2, following the recommendations of Delli Carpini and Keeter (1993), including the requirements for overriding a presidential veto, and recognition of Dick Cheney's occupation (vice president at the time of the survey).

Although respondents in the 2004 survey are clearly more informed than the electorate as a whole, levels of knowledge in the 2008 survey are quite similar to those suggested by other national surveys such as the ANES.[3] For example, in the 2008 ANES, 67 percent of respondents stated

---

[2] "Don't know" responses are treated as incorrect. Although there has been some debate about this topic (Malhotra and Krosnick 2007; Mondak 1999, 2001; Sturgis et al. 2008), Jessee (2011) estimates a multinomial latent traits model of political knowledge, which demonstrates that "don't know" responses are actually strongly suggestive of less political information than not only correct, but also incorrect answers.

[3] Unfortunately, the open-ended political information items from the 2008 ANES, such as recognition of Dick Cheney as the vice president, had not been coded at the time of writing and so cannot be compared with the results of the 2008 survey.

that the Republican party was more conservative than the Democratic party. The ANES, however, is a study of the American public as a whole. The surveys analyzed here, by contrast, focus on voters in presidential elections. When looking only at 2008 ANES respondents who reported voting for president, the proportion correctly recognizing the Republican party as more conservative jumps to 74 percent, which is quite similar to the percent of respondents in the 2008 survey analyzed here who correctly answer this question.[4]

One notable difference is in the proportion of respondents demonstrating knowledge of House party control. In the 2008 survey, 76 percent of respondents correctly identified Democrats as currently (at the time of the survey, which was late October 2008) controlling the House. The corresponding ANES numbers are quite different: 46 percent for voters and 40 percent for all respondents. A couple of key differences bear noting, though. First, the ANES asks about House party control in the post-election wave of the survey, whereas the 2008 survey analyzed here takes place entirely before the election. Second, and perhaps more importantly, the ANES question wording asks, "Do you happen to know which party had the most members in the House of Representatives in Washington BEFORE the election (this/last) month?" Although House party control did not change hands after the 2008 election, it stands to reason that the ANES wording would make confusion, and hence incorrect or "don't know" responses, more likely. Furthermore, as shown in Appendix B, the proportion of respondents to other surveys, such as the Pew Research Center for the People and the Press report titled "What Americans Know: 1989–2007," who correctly identify the Democratic party as controlling the House is nearly identical to the 76 percent from the 2008 survey.[5]

For each survey, the model in Equation 6.1 is estimated on the set of all political knowledge questions. In order to aid interpretation, the resulting knowledge estimates are transformed so that they have mean zero and variance one, with higher scores representing more political knowledge. The resulting estimates for question parameters suggest that

---

[4] ANES response percentages reported here are calculated as the weighted percentage of correct responses of all non-missing (i.e., correct, incorrect, or "don't know") responses for purposes of comparison with the results in Tables 6.1 and 6.2. Note that the 2008 survey does not include the "Neither" option, which should presumably, by removing an incorrect response option, increase the proportion of people answering the question correctly relative to that of the 2008 ANES.

[5] http://people-press.org/reports/pdf/319.pdf.

TABLE 6.1. *2004 Survey Political Knowledge Items*

Question	% Correct	% Incorrect	% DK	λ_j	η_j
Have federal income tax rates increased or decreased since 2000?	52	33	15	.49	−.04
Has the federal budget surplus increased or decreased since 2000?	69	25	6	.18	−.50
Who provides most of the money to run public schools in the United States? [Federal government, State and local governments, About equal]	71	22	7	.14	−.56
When people are charged with a crime such as burglary, driving while intoxicated, or murder, what type of law are they usually charged with violating? [Federal law, State law]	88	09	3	.24	−1.22
Who favors developing a national missile defense shield? [Democrats, Republicans]	82	10	8	.52	−1.07
Who favors raising the minimum wage? [Democrats, Republicans, Both, Neither]	82	22	6	.63	−1.14
Who favors putting restrictions on businesses? [Liberals, Conservatives, Both, Neither]	83	21	6	.50	−1.08
Who currently controls the U.S. House of Representatives? [Democrats, Republicans]	95	2	3	.53	−1.90
Who currently controls the U.S. Senate? [Democrats, Republicans]	95	3	2	.53	−1.95

Text and response options for political information items from 2004 survey are shown with response percentages and discrimination (λ_j) and difficulty (η_j) parameters estimated using the political knowledge model shown in Equation 6.1.

the latent scale corresponds well to common understandings of political knowledge. First, all estimated discrimination parameters (λ) for both 2004 and 2008 are positive, indicating that more informed respondents are more likely to answer the questions correctly. The questions differ somewhat in both estimated difficulty level and in their ability to

TABLE 6.2. *2008 Survey Political Knowledge Items*

Question	% Correct	% Incorrect	% DK	λ_j	η_j
Do you happen to know what job or political office is currently held by Dick Cheney? [Speaker of the House, Senate Majority Leader, Vice President, Supreme Court Justice]	89	10	1	.87	−1.80
Whose responsibility is it to determine if a law is constitutional or not? [President, Congress, Supreme Court]	81	18	1	.88	−1.26
How much of a majority is required for the U.S. Senate and House to override a presidential veto? [one-half, two-thirds, three-fourths, nine-tenths]	77	31	2	.74	−.96
Do you happen to know which party currently has the most members in the House of Representatives? [Democratic, Republican]	76	22	2	.80	−.99
Would you say that one of the political parties is more conservative than the other at the national level? Which party is more conservative? [Democratic, Republican]	78	20	2	.85	−1.10

Text and response options for political information items from 2008 survey are shown with response percentages and discrimination (λ_j) and difficulty (η_j) parameters estimated using the political knowledge model shown in Equation 6.1.

discriminate between high- and low-knowledge respondents. In the 2004 survey, most questions relate to political knowledge in a similar manner, having roughly equal discrimination parameters. Questions on fiscal policy, however, seem to show a somewhat lower ability to discriminate between high- and low-information respondents. In 2008, the discrimination parameters for all questions are roughly similar. For both surveys, difficulty parameters (η_j) differ across questions. This simply reflects the fact that some questions are harder or easier than others.

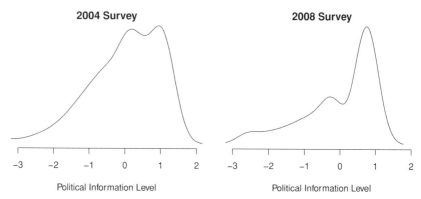

FIGURE 6.1. Distribution of estimated political information levels. Density plots of political information levels estimated according to the model from Equation 6.1 using political information items from 2004 and 2008 surveys. Estimates are normalized to have mean zero and variance one, with higher values indicating more knowledge.

Figure 6.1 plots the distribution of political information estimates for respondents in the 2004 and 2008 surveys. As mentioned previously, these estimates have been transformed so that they have mean zero and standard deviation one within each survey. In both surveys, the distributions have a negative skew, with a longer tail to the left than to the right. This should not be surprising, however, given that all of the political knowledge questions used were multiple choice. Accordingly, it is much more likely that respondents will get all (or almost all) of the questions correct than that they would get all (or almost all) of them wrong. This is because even blind guessing should result in a one in four chance of a correct answer. As seen in Tables 6.1 and 6.2, the percentage of correct answers is greater than 50 percent for each question and is greater than 70 percent for all but one. The estimates are also somewhat lumpy, particularly for the 2008 survey, which contains only five political knowledge questions as opposed to nine for the 2004 survey.

These estimates will provide a key measure for analyzing the relationship between political information and vote choice. They will also allow for the investigation of whether the effects of both ideology and partisanship differ between high- and low-information voters. For example, we will be able to assess whether the precision with which more informed voters discriminate between candidates is higher than for lower-information voters. The following section expands the spatial voting model with partisanship that was analyzed in the previous chapter in order to incorporate the possibility of both direct and moderating effects for political information on vote choice.

Estimating the Moderating Effects of Political Information on Spatial Voting

Using the estimates shown in Figure 6.1 of respondents' political knowledge levels together with measures of respondent ideology, party identification, and vote choice, we can now proceed to generalize the spatial voting models considered in Chapters 4 and 5 in order to assess the impact of political information on the use of spatial and partisan voting rules. The spatial voting models presented in previous chapters provide strong support for the hypotheses that voters use some form of spatial (proximity-based) voting rules and that the decisions of independent voters in particular correspond strongly with the predictions of unbiased spatial voting. These models, however, have been somewhat restrictive. Specifically, these models have not allowed for the possibility that political knowledge affects the decision rules by which citizens choose how to cast their ballots. Considering the quote at the beginning of this chapter, it may not make sense to assume that one voter who is very highly informed about politics will use the same process to arrive at a vote choice as another person who knows little at all about the political world.

There are several reasons why we may suspect that decision-making processes and, in particular, the use of spatial voting may differ for more and less informed voters. Less informed voters, for example, may lack the basic political knowledge to make decisions based on candidates' actual policy positions and may instead rely on partisanship or other informational shortcuts, often called heuristics or "low information rationality" in the political science literature (e.g., Popkin 1991). More informed voters may be more able to form perceptions of the policies supported and opposed by each candidate (a topic that is revisited in more depth in Chapter 7) and to compare these positions with their own issue preferences, allowing for stronger spatial voting.

Incorporating Political Information into the Spatial Model
The model of vote choice used here is similar to those employed in previous chapters in that vote choice is modeled as a function of a voter's ideological position and party identification. Here, however, both ideology and partisanship are interacted with information level to allow for

different relationships for voters with different amounts of knowledge. Formally, vote choice is modeled using the probit regression specification for the probability of voting for the Republican candidate:

$$P(v_i = R) = \Phi(\beta_{0,pty(i)} + \beta_{1,pty(i)}x_i + \beta_{2,pty(i)}info_i + \beta_{3,pty(i)}x_i info_i),$$

$$(6.2)$$

where v_i is voter i's vote choice, $pty(i)$ is voter i's party identification (Democrat, independent, or Republican), x_i is voter i's ideal point (ideological position), and $info_i$ is voter i's political information level. Recall that the ideal point scale is identified so that the Democratic and Republican presidential candidates in any given election have positions $-1/4$ and $1/4$, respectively, and estimated political information levels have mean zero and standard deviation one within each survey. Again, only votes for the Democratic and Republican candidates are included, with votes for other candidates or reports of not voting dropped from the analysis.

Under this expanded version of the model, we again obtain correspondences between the parameters of the utility-based spatial model and the probit regression coefficients for the model in Equation 6.2. Recall that the random utility model including partisanship from Chapter 5 takes the form

$$U_i(k) = -a_i(x_i - c_k)^2 + b_{ik} + e_{ik}.$$

$$(6.3)$$

Previous versions of this model allowed the policy weight term a_i and partisan bias term b_{ik} to vary across party identifications. Under this new specification, both of these terms also are allowed to vary by respondents' levels of political information. In fact, by estimating the probit regression model of vote choice shown in Equation 6.2, we can estimate these precision and partisan bias terms as a function of respondents' political knowledge, obtaining the correspondence for each term as

$$\delta_i = \beta_{0,pty(i)} + \beta_{2,pty(i)}info_i \qquad (6.4)$$

$$a_i = \beta_{1,pty(i)} + \beta_{3,pty(i)}info_i,$$

where $\delta_i = b_{iR} - b_{iD}$ is the net bias of voter i toward the Republican candidate. In other words, we are now allowing both the net partisan bias terms δ_D, δ_I, and δ_R, and the policy weight term a_i to vary by respondent political information level. Both terms also will be estimated separately for each party identification grouping.

TABLE 6.3. *Estimated Spatial Utility Model Parameters, Party and Information Model*

	2004 Survey			2008 Survey		
	Dem	Ind	Rep	Dem	Ind	Rep
Intercept $(\beta_{0,pty(i)})$	−1.07	.40	1.91	−.72	.11	1.16
	(.09)	(.08)	(.07)	(.10)	(.16)	(.09)
x_i $(\beta_{1,pty(i)})$	6.21	9.96	6.77	5.61	6.40	5.64
	(.66)	(.74)	(.57)	(.66)	(1.05)	(.74)
$info_i$ $(\beta_{2,pty(i)})$	.01	−.03	−.14	.34	.05	.05
	(.08)	(.07)	(.08)	(.09)	(.12)	(.11)
$x_i info_i$ $(\beta_{3,pty(i)})$	1.42	2.30	.98	3.08	1.24	.94
	(.63)	(.59)	(.58)	(.67)	(.98)	(1.01)
N	2,325	645	2,441	878	130	707
Log Likelihood	−237.6	−222.9	−239.9	−175.1	−55.1	−115.9

Cells show estimated probit coefficients, with corresponding spatial utility model parameters from Equation 6.2, with standard deviations underneath in parentheses.

Estimating the Effects of Ideology, Partisanship, and Political Information

Table 6.3 shows the estimated coefficients from the expanded probit model of voting from Equation 6.2. Because information levels within each survey are normalized to have mean zero, the terms $\beta_{0,pty(i)}$ and $\beta_{1,pty(i)}$ can be interpreted as the estimated partisan bias terms (δ_i) and precision or policy weight terms (a_i), respectively, for respondents of average information levels.[6] This can be seen by substituting the average information score of zero for $info_i$ in Equation 6.4. We see that the estimated spatial biases for voters of average information levels are similar to the results found in Chapter 5 (omitting political information level from the analyses). At average political knowledge levels, Democrats in both 2004 and 2008 show large biases toward the Democratic candidate, while Republicans show even larger biases toward their party's nominee in both elections. Independents with average levels of political information show much smaller biases than do similarly informed partisans, being slightly biased toward Bush in 2004 and showing little if any bias in 2008.

Turning to the coefficients on ideology $(\beta_{1,pty(i)})$, we clearly see that these values are all estimated to be positive and quite large in magnitude.

---

[6] Note that these are average information levels within the sample, not necessarily the population of all voters in the 2004 and 2008 presidential elections. While the sample of the 2004 survey is overeducated and overinformed relative to the voter population as a whole, the 2008 sample corresponds closely with characteristics from other representative surveys on political knowledge measures.

This indicates that voters with average levels of political information show strong relationships between ideological position and vote choice. This finding holds across all partisan groups for both the 2004 and 2008 elections. These estimates are very similar to those presented in Chapter 5, not including political knowledge. The estimated coefficients on voter ideology do exhibit some significant variation across party identification, with independent voters being estimated to have the largest policy weight terms in both surveys. We can reject the hypothesis that the coefficients on ideology $(\beta_{1,pty(i)})$ are identical for independents and either Democrats or Republicans in the 2004 survey. In the 2008 survey, although the estimated coefficient on ideology is largest for independents, the differences between partisan groups is not statistically significant. These findings suggest that independent voters are likely to be more strongly influenced by ideology than are partisans, at least at average levels of political information.

The central question of the analyses presented in this chapter, however, is whether the decision rules used by voters show important differences across political information levels. On this note, the results are suggestive, but not completely conclusive. The main effect of political information, indicated by the coefficient $\beta_{2,pty(i)}$, is estimated to be relatively small and insignificant in most cases. The main exception to this is that for Democratic voters in 2008, the effect is estimated to be .34 and is statistically significant. In 2004, the coefficient for Republicans comes somewhat close to achieving significance at the conventional .05 level, but is not as large in magnitude. In both of these cases, however, it seems likely that higher information levels may attenuate the impact of partisanship, reducing the level of spatial bias exhibited by Republican voters in 2004 and Democratic voters in 2008. In all other cases, the main effect of information appears to be negligible. In other words, political information does not seem to meaningfully affect the net spatial biases (δ_i) shown by Democratic or independent voters in 2004 or by independent or Republican voters in 2008.

Overall, then, the main effect of political information is somewhat ambiguous. It seems that political knowledge may have some direct effect on vote choice for some types of voters, but it is unclear when this will occur. In 2008, Obama was a heavy favorite, having solid leads in most polls during the time leading up to the election. The large effect for information estimated for Democrats could represent the larger effects of this Democratic tide on less informed Democrats. Alternatively, in 2004, there was no strong favorite. Bush and Kerry seemed closely matched throughout the campaign. Any inferences about the cause of these differences in coefficients, however, are largely speculative because we have data from only two elections.

A second important question regarding the role of political information in vote choice is whether the effects of ideology vary for voters with different levels of political information. For example, are more informed voters more sensitive to their relative ideological proximity to the two candidates? To examine this, we can look at the estimated coefficient on the interaction between ideology and political information ($\beta_{3,pty(i)}$). As seen in Equation 6.4, this coefficient describes how a voter's policy weight a_i varies by his or her level of political information. If more informed voters are more strongly influenced by their ideological proximity to candidates, we would expect this coefficient to be positive. If the use of spatial voting rules were unrelated to political information, this coefficient should be zero. If (unexpectedly) less informed citizens had their vote choices more strongly influenced by ideology, this estimate would be negative.

Table 6.3 shows that these estimated coefficients on this ideology–information interaction term are all positive and relatively large in magnitude for all partisan groups across both elections. These estimates are statistically significant at the .05 level in four of the six cases. For Republican voters in the 2004 survey, the coefficient comes somewhat close to reaching conventional significance levels ($p = .09$), but we cannot conclusively reject the hypothesis that the coefficient is equal to zero in this case. In 2008, this interaction term for Republicans is much less precisely estimated. While the estimate is positive and of very similar magnitude to the corresponding 2004 estimate, it does not come close to achieving statistical significance ($p = .35$). These results suggest that political information serves an important moderating role in spatial voting. Although the finding is somewhat tentative for Republican voters, it appears that more informed voters base their vote choices more strongly on their ideological proximity to the candidates in a given election than do less informed voters. It should not be that surprising that it is difficult to obtain precise estimates of these interaction terms because both ideology and information level are estimated rather than known exactly. In particular, political information is estimated using a relatively small number of questions – nine in the 2004 survey and five in the 2008 survey. Accordingly, it is estimated fairly imprecisely for each individual respondent.[7]

---

[7] See Jessee 2009, 2010a for examples of analyses employing more elaborate statistical approaches to account for the fact that these predictors are measured with error. Overall substantive results from these works are similar to those presented here and elsewhere in the book.

Because probit regression models are interactive on the probability scale, the effects of one variable on the probability of voting for the Republican candidate will be contingent on the values of all other variables in the model. This can make the interpretation of these models somewhat complicated when the values of interest are the relative probabilities of choosing a given candidate. In order to better understand the substantive implications of the estimates presented in Table 6.3, we can examine predicted vote probabilities for voters across different partisanship groups, ideological positions, and political information levels.

Figure 6.2 plots the predicted probability of voting for Bush for low-, medium-, and high-information respondents in the 2004 survey, defined as the .05 percentile, mean, and .95 percentile of sample political information, respectively, separated by party identification. Looking across these three plots, the most obvious feature is the convergence of the voting behavior of partisans toward that of independents as information levels increase. For low-information respondents, there is an enormous gap between the predicted probabilities of voting for Bush for Democrats and Republicans, with independents falling somewhere in between. The voting behavior of Democrats and Republicans still shows large amounts of divergence at medium-information levels. For the most informed voters, these gaps remain, but are much smaller.

As Figure 6.3 shows, these dynamics are similar in the 2008 survey. Low-information respondents show significant divergence, with Democratic voters actually being estimated to have a negative relationship between ideal point and probability of voting for Bush. This would imply that among the least informed Democrats, being more liberal actually *decreased* the probability of voting for Obama. This estimated effect for low-information voters, however, does not come close to statistical significance. Therefore, this result merely suggests that among the least informed Democrats, we cannot be sure whether ideology has any effect on vote choice.[8] Medium-information respondents show large gaps, albeit much smaller than those for low-information voters, while the most informed voters show the lowest amount of divergence across partisan groupings.

---

[8] Another consideration is that the distribution of political information estimates in 2008 (as well as in 2004) is heavily skewed, with the .05 quantile falling much farther from the mean than does the .95 quantile. As a result, predicted probabilities for the least informed respondents are likely to depend much more heavily on the functional form of both the interaction and the probit model. Accordingly, the implications for low-information respondents may be less clear.

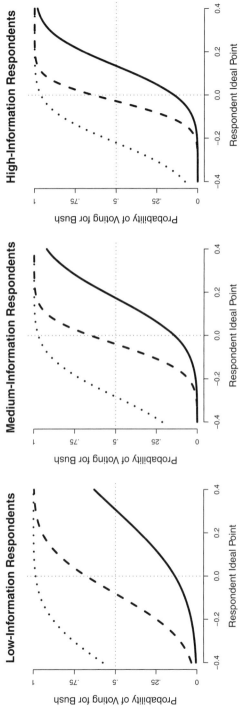

FIGURE 6.2. 2004 predicted vote probabilities from partisan spatial model. Curves show the predicted probabilities of voting for the Republican candidate in the 2004 election as a function of a voter's ideological position for Democrats (solid lines), independents (dashed lines), and Republicans (dotted lines) at low-, medium-, and high-information levels defined as the .05 quantile, mean, and .95 quantiles, respectively, of political information for the sample. Probabilities are calculated based on the estimates presented in Table 6.3.

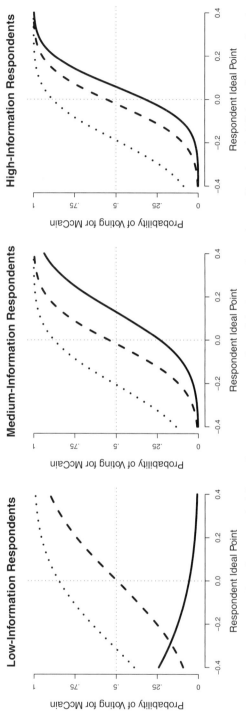

FIGURE 6.3. 2008 Predicted vote probabilities from partisan spatial model. Curves show the predicted probabilities of voting for the Republican candidate in the 2008 election as a function of a voter's ideological position for Democrats (solid lines), independents (dashed lines) and Republicans (dotted lines) at low, medium and high information levels defined as the .05 quantile, mean and .95 quantiles, respectively, of political information for the sample. Probabilities are calculated based on the estimates presented in Table 6.3.

Based on these new results, we can revisit the simple typology of voting models previously discussed in Chapter 5. The main competing models of vote choice – the Michigan school party identification voting model and the spatial (or proximity) voting model – offer strong but competing accounts of how vote choice should relate to both partisanship and ideology. The Michigan school model, at least in its simplest form, argues that party identification is the chief determinant of vote choice (and, in fact, of most other political attitudes and behaviors as well). Furthermore, most of the classic works in this school argue that very few voters possess true ideological views or have the capacity to judge the ideological distance between themselves and the candidates in a given election. Accordingly, there should exist little if any relationship between citizen ideology and vote choice, largely because the vast majority of voters have no real ideology. The left pane of Figure 6.4 illustrates these predictions, plotting an example of the probability of voting for the Republican candidate for Democratic, independent, and Republican voters (indicated by dotted, dashed, and solid lines, respectively) as a function of their ideological positions. According to this party identification voting model, partisans should have a very high likelihood of voting for their party's nominee, while independents should fall somewhere in between. Ideology should not have a meaningful impact on vote choice, as indicated by the horizontal lines relating ideology to vote probability.

The simple spatial voting model paints an almost diametrically opposed picture of voter behavior. Under this theory, illustrated by the center pane of Figure 6.4, vote choice is determined solely by voters' ideological proximity to candidates. The most basic spatial voting theories posit no role for partisanship in vote choice. Accordingly, the behavior of Democrats, independents, and Republicans is identical given their ideological positions. It is important to note that even this simplified theory of spatial voting does not predict that Democrats, independents, and Republicans will all vote the same way on average, only that Democrat, independent, and Republican voters, all having the same ideological positions, will all have the same vote probabilities. The fact that Democratic voters tend to be more liberal and Republicans tend to be more conservative will still imply that more Republican voters will vote for the Republican candidate.

The right pane of Figure 6.4 plots an example of a possible combination of party identification and spatial theories of voting that could be called the hybrid model. Under this model, the choices of voters are influenced by both their party identifications (as in the Michigan model) and their

148

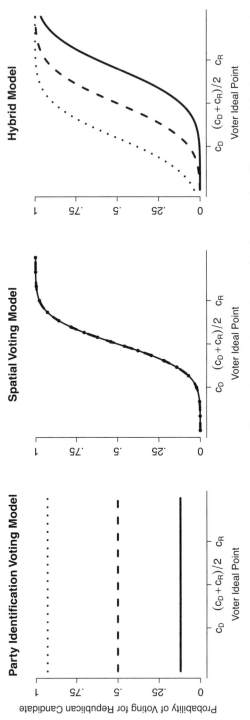

FIGURE 6.4. Simple baseline vote choice models. Simplified predictions of "Michigan school" party identification model of voting, simple unbiased spatial voting model, and hybrid model of voting for Democratic (solid lines), independent (dashed lines), and Republican (dotted lines) voters. Note that in the center pane ("Spatial Voting Model"), the predictions for voters of all party identifications are identical, shown by overlapping curves.

ideological proximity to each candidate (as in the spatial model). The results presented in Chapter 5 suggested that a hybrid model, including the effects of both partisanship and ideology, described the behavior of voters in the 2004 and 2008 presidential elections quite well. But the new findings shown in Figures 6.2 and 6.3 demonstrate that while the vote choices for virtually all voters are the result of a combination of partisanship and ideology, the relative balance of these two influences is strongly related to political information.

Among the least informed voters in 2004 and 2008, partisanship dominates the decisions of Democratic and Republican identifiers. The predicted vote probabilities of these low-information partisans are wildly divergent, with virtually all Democrats being overwhelmingly likely to vote for the Democratic candidate and almost all Republicans voting for the Republican candidate with near certainty. Although there exists some evidence of ideological influence among low-information partisans, these results lend relatively strong support to the Michigan school line of thought. Independent voters, however, even at the lowest levels of political knowledge, seem to have their vote choices affected by ideology. These results are not completely conclusive – the estimated effects of ideology in both the 2004 and 2008 surveys for independents at the fifth percentile of political information are positive and large in magnitude – but while this result is highly significant in 2004, it does not achieve conventional significance levels in 2008. The 2008 sample, however, contains approximately one-third as many independents as the 2004 sample, so the relative lack of precision in these estimates should not be unexpected.

Although voters with moderate levels of political information are more strongly influenced by ideology than the least informed respondents, partially offsetting the strong influence of partisanship, the effects of partisanship among these voters are still quite strong. As information approaches its highest levels in the 2004 and 2008 samples, the effects of ideology begin to overtake those of party identification. Even among the most highly informed respondents, however, there exists meaningful divergence between the behavior of Democrats, independents, and Republicans, even those having precisely the same ideological positions. For example, among high-information respondents in the 2008 survey with ideal points of zero, meaning they are equally close to the positions of Obama and McCain, the probability of voting for McCain is .32, .56, and .89 for Democratic, independent, and Republican voters, respectively.

Overall, the results from these two sets of analyses demonstrate that not only is the behavior of voters best described by a combination of partisan and spatial models, but the relative balance between these two models is strongly related to voters' levels of political information. Voters having less information about politics tend to base their decisions mostly on partisan cues. Even at these low levels of knowledge, however, we do see some relationship between ideology and vote choice, with this relationship being particularly strong for low-information independents. More highly informed voters exhibit much stronger relationships between ideology and vote choice. While the effects of partisanship appear similar across information levels for most voters, these effects on the probability scale are strongly attenuated by the increased importance of ideology as political information levels increase.

The Effects of Political Information on Implied Indifference Points

Yet another way to examine the effects of partisanship and ideology on voters is through the concept of implied indifference points first introduced in Chapter 4. A voter's implied indifference point is defined as the ideological position at which he or she would be predicted to be indifferent between the Democratic and Republican candidates, having a 50 percent chance of voting for either. Under simple unbiased spatial voting, this point would be predicted to fall at the actual midpoint between the two candidates, which has been defined here as zero. Furthermore, these implied indifference points provide a way of comparing the relative impacts of ideology and partisanship. For example, for a partisan voter with a given level of political knowledge, his or her implied indifference point will represent the amount of ideological movement away from the midpoint of zero between the two candidates that would offset the spatial bias his or her partisanship has produced.

Because the effects of both partisanship and ideology are allowed to vary by voters' level of political information under the vote choice model from Equation 6.2, the estimated implied indifference point for voters also will be a function of political information levels. Formally, for a respondent i with political information level $info_i$ and party identification $pty(i)$, his or her implied indifference point can be calculated as

$$\text{Implied Indifference Point}_i = \frac{-\beta_{0,pty(i)} - \beta_{2,pty(i)}info_i}{\beta_{1,pty(i)} + \beta_{3,pty(i)}info_i}. \tag{6.5}$$

This can be seen by setting the expression inside $\Phi()$ in Equation 6.2 equal to zero (because the normal cdf evaluated at zero is equal to .5) and solving for x_i.

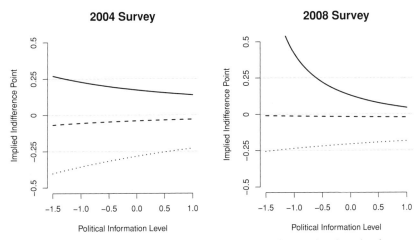

FIGURE 6.5. Implied indifference points by partisanship and political information level. Plots show estimated implied indifference points, calculated based on
coefficient estimates from Table 6.3 based on the formula in Equation 6.5, for
Democratic (solid lines), independent (dashed lines), and Republican (dotted lines)
respondents in the 2004 and 2008 surveys.

Figure 6.5 plots the estimated implied indifference points for Democratic, independent, and Republican voters in the 2004 and 2008 surveys
as a function of their political information levels. As with Figures 6.2
and 6.3, the most obvious feature of these plots is the convergence of
the behavior of Democratic (solid lines) and Republican (dotted lines)
voters toward those of independents (dashed lines) as information levels
increase. Independent voters in both 2004 and 2008 have implied indifference points that are estimated to be very close to the true midpoint
of zero between the Democratic and Republican candidates. In fact, the
implied indifference points of independents at all information levels are
indistinguishable from zero at the .05 significance level in 2008. Even in
the 2004 survey, while we can reject the hypothesis that independents
at most levels of political information have an implied indifference point
of zero, they are estimated to be fairly close. For example, independents
of average information levels in 2004 would have an estimated implied
indifference point of −.04. In other words, while the point at which these
voters are equally likely to choose Bush and Kerry does not fall precisely
at the midpoint of zero, as predicted by strictly unbiased spatial voting, it does fall quite close to this value. Even among some of the least
informed independents in 2004, their implied indifference point does not
stray nearly as far from zero as do those for the most informed partisans.

In other words, the least informed independents come closer to the spatial ideal of unbiased voting than do the most informed partisans, at least by this particular measure.

These implied indifference points also provide a powerful illustration of the magnitude of spatial bias exhibited by partisan voters. Less informed partisans show dramatic deviations from the predictions of unbiased spatial voting. In fact, the least informed partisans in both 2004 and 2008 must have their ideal point move to the opposite side of the opposing candidate's position before they have a 50 percent chance of voting for them. For example, in 2004, a Democratic voter at the fifth percentile of political information would have to have an ideal point of .31 – significantly more conservative than Bush's position of .25 – in order to be indifferent between the two candidates. Another way of looking at this is that such a partisan voter (as well as any other low-information partisan studied here) would be predicted to be more likely to vote for his or her own party's candidate even when his or her ideological position was identical to the position of the opposing party's candidate.

Another use of these implied indifference points is to provide a method of comparing the estimated effects of ideology and partisanship on the same scale, as was done in Chapter 5. The implied indifference points shown in Figure 6.5 represent the amount of ideological movement that would be required to have the same effect as the partisan bias for a given voter. For virtually all independents in both the 2004 and 2008 surveys, this quantity is quite close to zero, indicating that the effects of spatial bias are quite small relative to the impact of ideological proximity for these voters. For partisan voters, however, the story is quite different. For example, at average levels of political information in the 2004 survey, Democratic and Republican voters would have to have an ideological shift of .17 and .28 units, respectively, in order to offset the impact of their partisan biases. These represent huge moves in ideology. Furthermore, the situation is similar for partisans in the 2008 survey. Even at high levels of information, these quantities are quite large.

Discussion

The basic assumptions of spatial voting have been frequently criticized on the grounds that most ordinary voters do not think enough about politics or specific policy issues to have formed any sort of meaningful ideology themselves and also that they do not have enough information to form reasonable estimates of the ideological positions of candidates. The first of these two criticisms has been largely disproven by the findings presented in Chapter 3. Most citizens do possess meaningful ideologies that provide important structure to their political views. The second of these criticisms has been rebutted by evidence in Chapters 4 and 5 that voters, at least on average, have their vote choices strongly affected by their ideological proximity to the candidates in recent presidential elections, even after controlling for party identification.

This chapter asks a more nuanced question: are the voting decisions of all voters strongly affected by their ideological proximity to candidates, or does the logic of spatial voting apply only to the most informed voters? The analyses presented here reveal that while ideology does exert a strong influence on the choices of voters across virtually all information levels, the relative balance of ideology and partisanship varies systematically in relation to political knowledge. The decisions of the least informed voters show a relatively modest relationship with ideology and very strong effects of partisanship on the probability scale. As information levels rise, the effects of voters' ideological proximity to candidates increases, attenuating the effects of partisanship. Even among the most informed voters, however, significant differences remain between the behavior of Democrats, independents, and Republicans.

The decision rules used by independent voters are broadly consistent with the predictions of unbiased spatial voting, showing only a small amount of bias by spatial standards in 2004 and little or no bias in 2008. Furthermore, there is some evidence that the decisions of independent voters are more strongly influenced by spatial concerns than are the votes of partisans. Partisan voters appear to rely primarily on partisanship at low information levels, following the basic predictions of the Michigan school, but are increasingly influenced by spatial concerns as they obtain more information. Overall, these results reinforce the conclusions of the previous chapter that a hybrid model, incorporating both partisan and spatial influences, provides a realistic depiction of voter behavior. The findings of this chapter, however, add the important caveat that the degree of compromise between these two theories depends strongly on the information level of respondents, with less informed voters (and, in particular, less informed partisans) coming closer to the predictions of partisan theories of voting, whereas more informed voters have their decisions strongly influenced by spatial concerns.

These findings also raise important questions about why the effects of ideology are conditional on information. In particular, it would seem that some basic estimate of the ideological positions of candidates is a necessary prerequisite for the use of spatial decision rules. How, then, do voters with different levels of political information form these perceptions of the views held by candidates in a given election? In particular, do citizens at low information levels have the capacity to form any sort of meaningful impression of candidate positions? These questions, which are central not only to debates over spatial voting, but also to the functioning of democracy more generally, are addressed in the following chapter.

7

The Political Perceptions of Citizens

> If we are to understand what leads the voter to his decision at the polls we must know how he sees the things to which this decision relates.
>
> (Campbell, Converse, Miller, and Stokes 1960, 42)

Political scientists are quite fond of bemoaning the levels of political knowledge and political competence of the American public. In fact, this general strain of pessimism is among the most common reasons that many scholars are skeptical of the spatial approach as a useful framework within which to analyze the decisions of voters. Spatial models typically assume that voters base their decisions on their relative ideological proximity to the candidates in a given election, which would seemingly require that a reasonably accurate perception of the positions of each candidate is held by most voters. This chapter is principally concerned with the question of how well ordinary citizens understand the true ideological stances of the candidates in presidential elections. In other words, do voters possess the tools to cast their votes based on which candidate is closest to them?

The answers to these questions that are offered by the classic works in American political behavior (e.g., Campbell et al. 1960; Converse 1964; Kinder and Sears 1985; Zaller 1992) are not encouraging in terms of their suggestions about citizen attention, knowledge, or competence. How, then, can the findings of the previous chapters, which reveal an electorate that is able to cast reasonably accurate votes according to the spatial standard based on candidate positions, be reconciled with these earlier findings? This chapter examines citizen perceptions of candidate ideology using an extension of the survey and statistical methods employed in previous chapters. Specifically, the 2008 survey, which asks respondents for their own positions on specific policy proposals, but also includes items asking respondents what position they think Barack Obama and John McCain took on each of these issues, is analyzed in order to estimate the specific locations perceived for each candidate by each respondent.

The chapter begins by assessing the basic degree of voter knowledge of the specific issue positions of candidates in the 2008 presidential elections. It then describes a method for estimating respondents' perceptions of the ideological positions of Barack Obama and John McCain on the same scale as the candidates' actual ideological positions and those of voters. Next, it investigates the general characteristics of respondent perceptions, including their relative level of accuracy and their relationship with voter partisanship. Finally, models of spatial voting based on voter perceptions, rather than on candidates' true ideological positions, are presented and compared with the statistical models of spatial voting discussed in previous chapters.

Respondent Perceptions of Candidate Positions

Many of the activities of politicians are difficult for ordinary citizens to observe. For example, in the U.S. Congress, much important legislative activity, such as the drafting of bills, is conducted in private. Legislators do cast many roll call votes that are recorded and, if one were so inclined, that could readily be monitored. However, the sheer volume of these votes and the confusing details of most bills, amendments, and procedural motions make this type of monitoring unrewarding for most people who are not professional lobbyists. The situation is somewhat better in the case of candidates running for office and, in particular, for presidential candidates, largely because of the prominence of these campaigns. During the heat of a presidential race, the actions and statements of the major party candidates typically receive a great deal of attention in the news media and through other outlets. Even the most uninterested political observers are likely to hear, whether they like it or not, many details about the candidates. But how much specific information about issue positions taken by each candidate do members of the public actually possess?

This section analyzes data from the 2008 survey that ask survey respondents what position they think candidates Obama and McCain take on the same set of ten policy proposals that the respondents themselves were asked about. These data are informative about citizens' perceptions of the individual issue positions taken by Obama and McCain and also about the degree to which respondents can accurately assess the overall ideological positions of each of these candidates. Both of these things speak to the degree to which American voters are able to engage in the calculations necessary for some form of spatial voting.

Knowledge of Specific Candidate Positions

The most basic form of knowledge about candidate ideology is the specific positions that each candidate takes on notable and prominent political issues and proposals. If it is to be argued that ordinary voters have meaningful perceptions of the ideological positions of candidates in elections, it seems that these voters should display substantial knowledge of the actual stances taken by candidates on individual issues, particularly those that have been raised and discussed prominently during the campaign. This section examines the degree of knowledge that voters in the 2008 presidential election had about the specific issue stances of Obama and McCain.

Table 7.1 shows the actual positions taken by Obama and McCain on the ten policy statements included in the 2008 survey as well as the percentages of respondents who perceived each candidate to be for and against each statement and the percentage who gave "don't know" responses. Overall, respondents show a reasonably good understanding of the positions taken by the candidates. More than two-thirds of all responses across these questions correctly identified the position taken by the candidate in question. Furthermore, for all but one of these ten questions, more respondents chose the correct position for both candidates than chose the incorrect position. The lone exception is that more respondents thought that McCain opposed civil unions for homosexual couples than thought he would support them (47 versus 38 percent). This suggests that voters are likely to have a reasonable, although obviously not perfectly accurate, basis for understanding the positions of candidates in presidential elections.

It also seems as if respondents are doing more than simply placing Obama and McCain on the liberal and conservative sides of each issue according to their partisan stereotypes. In fact, 37 percent of responses placed both of these candidate on the same side of an issue. This is quite close to the percentage of actual agreement between Obama and McCain, who took the same stance on four of the ten surveyed policies.

Although these ten surveyed policy issues do not necessarily represent a random sample of all of the issues that were discussed during the 2008 presidential campaign, they do include many of the most prominently

TABLE 7.1. *Respondent Perceptions of Candidate Positions, 2008 Survey*

Policy Proposal	Candidate Positions		Respondent Guesses (For-Against-DK, %)	
	Obama	McCain	Obama	McCain
The United States should begin a phased withdrawal of troops from Iraq.	Yes	No	86-3-11	14-74-12
The definition of marriage should apply only to relationships between a man and a woman.	Yes	Yes	46-39-15	77-10-13
Younger workers should be allowed to invest some of their Social Security contributions in private investment accounts.	No	Yes	25-56-19	68-22-14
The Supreme Court's decision in *Roe v. Wade*, which legalized most forms of abortion, should be overturned.	No	Yes	16-69-14	64-22-14
A mandatory cap on carbon dioxide emissions by American companies should be imposed, with a credit trading system so that companies who pollute less can sell their credits to other companies.	Yes	Yes	73-6-21	43-32-24
A "windfall profits" tax should be imposed on large profits made by oil companies.	Yes	No	80-5-15	16-67-17
Tax cuts for those making over $250,000 should be reversed.	Yes	No	73-15-12	15-71-14
The federal government should require that all American children have health insurance.	Yes	No	86-3-11	25-59-17
Same-sex couples should be allowed to form civil unions that give them most of the same legal protections that married couples enjoy.	Yes	Yes	75-12-13	38-47-14
Up to $700 billion dollars should be spent to have the federal government purchase troubled assets from financial institutions in an attempt to remedy current economic troubles.	Yes	Yes	73-11-16	74-11-15

Table shows the positions taken by Obama and McCain and percentages of 2008 survey respondents perceiving that the candidates were for and against the policies as well as the percentage saying they did not know the candidate's position.

discussed issues. It is quite likely that voters have heard at least some information about the candidates' stances on many of these policies, and the data suggest that much of this information is likely to have been retained. While voter knowledge of the positions taken by Obama and McCain is far from perfect, many voters seem to have fairly accurate beliefs about the specific policy stances of the two candidates.

Perceptions of Candidate Ideology

A minimal criterion for the effective use of spatial voting may that voters have the ability to form some reasonably accurate perception of the ideological positions taken by the candidates in an election. While there may be some mechanisms by which voters can cast their ballots for the candidates closest to them without actually understanding the ideological locations of either candidate, the standard story of spatial voting involves citizens calculating the distances between their own ideal point and the positions of each candidate and choosing the one closest to them. A prominent objection to these theories, however, is that most voters have at most minimal knowledge about politics and, therefore, are unlikely to be capable of making these sorts of calculations.

Because the predictions of spatial voting models may be thought to relate to citizens' perceptions of the ideological locations of candidates, we should seek to obtain measures of these perceptions on the liberal–conservative scale. Furthermore, these measures would ideally be comparable with both respondents' ideological positions and the actual (true) ideological locations of the candidates. In Chapter 3, estimates of the ideological positions of both voters and candidates were obtained by applying ideal point estimation techniques to data that included the positions of both survey respondents and candidates on the same set of policies. By also including the data on respondent perceptions of candidate positions for these same issues, it is possible to obtain estimates of each respondent's perception of the ideological positions of Obama and McCain.

Scholars have tested various theories about citizen perception, including projection (Brody and Page 1972), likability (Brady and Sniderman 1985), and others, often by measuring perceptions using ordinal five- or seven-point ideology scales. As discussed in previous chapters, this approach has several potential problems. First, these scales are, in a fundamental way, undefined. For example, if one respondent perceives John McCain to be a five on a seven-point scale and another perceives him to be a six, there is no way of saying with much certainty which respondent actually thinks McCain is more conservative. Moreover, if two respondents state that Barack Obama is a two on this scale, it is quite possible that they think of this ideology scale in dramatically different ways, meaning that it is not clear how to compare these responses. Perhaps even more seriously, while it may be reasonable to compare a particular respondent's own stated ideological position to his or her perception of a given politician (i.e., whether he or she believes that his or her senator is more liberal or conservative than him- or herself), there is no objective way to compare a respondent's perceptions with the *actual* ideological positions taken by a particular politician. While several methods have been employed to attempt to estimate the true positions of politicians on these scales, such as assuming that the actual position of a given politician is equal to the average of all respondent perceptions, these methods represent quite strong assumptions. In particular, it seems quite undesirable to test theories about citizen perceptions, including those that may imply specific biases in individual or aggregate perceptions, by assuming that these perceptions are perfectly unbiased on average.

In order to overcome these obstacles and obtain objective estimates of citizen perceptions of the ideological positions of candidate and legislators that are comparable with both the citizens' own ideological positions and the true ideological positions of these politicians, the survey design and statistical estimation techniques employed in previous chapters are adapted to include measures of perceptions. In the 2008 survey, respondents are asked to state their own views on specific policy proposals on which we know the views of presidential candidates John McCain and Barack Obama. In previous chapters, these data were used to estimate the ideological positions of respondents alongside those of candidates. In addition to these questions, however, respondents also were asked to state what positions they thought that each of the two presidential candidates took on each of the policy proposals. By applying the ideal point framework discussed in Chapter 3, these data will allow for the estimation of the ideological positions of citizens and politicians as well as citizen perceptions about the ideological positions of candidates all on the same scale.

The data from the 2008 survey analyzed here can be thought of in three parts. The citizen positions data give the views (support or oppose) of each respondent on each of the ten surveyed policy proposals. Next, the candidate portion of the data contains the actual positions taken by Obama and McCain on each of these same policies. Finally, the candidate perceptions data give the perceptions of each citizen about the positions taken on each policy by both candidates.

To estimate the ideological positions of respondents and candidates, the same ideal point approach introduced in Chapter 3 is applied. It is assumed that each actor, whether a respondent or candidate, has some ideological position on a single liberal–conservative ideological dimension. It is assumed as before that the probability of each actor i supporting each policy j can be written as

$$P(y_{ij} = 1) = \Phi(\gamma_j x_i - \alpha_j), \qquad (7.1)$$

where x_i is respondent i's ideological position, γ_j and α_j are the policy proposal's discrimination and difficulty parameters, and Φ is the cumulative distribution function (cdf) for the standard normal distribution.

The key addition in this chapter's analyses is that it is assumed that each respondent holds perceptions about the ideologies of Obama and of McCain and that these perceptions can be represented by positions on the same ideological dimension on which the respondents and candidates hold their actual ideological positions. In other words, each respondent has a perception about the ideology of a given candidate and, when asked how he or she would guess that candidate would vote on a given policy, his or her answer is generated in accordance with the model in Equation 7.1 using the respondent's perception as x_i and the bill parameters γ_j and α_j for the policy in question. These assumptions allow for the estimation of pooled ideal point models of respondents, candidates, and respondents' perceptions of candidates all on the same scale, overcoming the fundamental issue of comparability that has hindered many past efforts to understand citizen perceptions.

This model is estimated on the data from the 2008 surveys introduced in Chapter 3. Each respondent is asked to state his or her own position on ten different policy statements, with the choices "agree," "disagree," and "not sure" (see Figure 3.2 and Table 3.2). In addition to this, we know the positions taken by Barack Obama and John McCain on these issues through their public statements during the 2008 presidential campaign. Finally, each respondent is asked, "Please tell us whether you think [Barack Obama or John McCain, asked separately for each policy] agrees or disagrees with the statements below." As in previous estimations, the model is identified by anchoring the positions of Obama and McCain at −.25 and .25, respectively.

Figure 7.1 shows the distribution of respondents' perceptions of Obama and McCain. On average, respondent perceptions of these candidates are fairly close to their true positions. For both candidates, however,

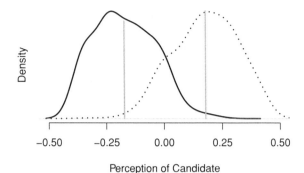

FIGURE 7.1. Estimated respondent perceptions of Obama and McCain. Density plots of estimated perceptions of Obama (solid line) and McCain (dotted line) among 2008 survey respondents. Gray vertical lines indicate average perceptions of each candidate. True ideological positions of Obama and McCain are −.25 and .25, respectively.

voters appear to perceive them as slightly more moderate (less ideologically extreme) than is actually the case. The mean perceptions for Obama and McCain are −.17 and .18, respectively, with a standard deviation of .13 in both cases. It seems, then, that voters in the 2008 election were in fact capable of forming reasonably accurate perceptions of both candidates' positions, albeit with a non-trivial amount of randomness.

Another important question is whether citizen perceptions of candidates are strongly related to partisanship. To investigate this possibility, Figure 7.2 presents a boxplot of respondent perceptions of Obama and McCain by respondent party identification. For both Obama and McCain, it appears that opposite-party respondents perceive the candidates to be slightly more extreme on average than do same-party and independent respondents. Independent and same-party respondents show relatively similar perceptions of the candidates. Overall, then, voters do show some partisan differences, albeit relatively small ones, in their perceptions of the ideological positions taken by candidates.

Perceived Ideological Distances from Candidates

In spatial voting theory, the key determinant of the vote is not simply a voter's perception of the ideological positions of each candidate, but rather how he or she perceives his or her relative ideological proximity to each candidate. Voters are assumed to choose (or at least to tend to choose) the candidate to whom they are ideologically closest.

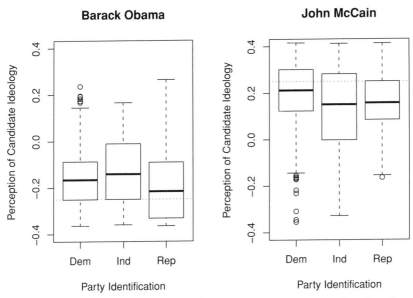

FIGURE 7.2. Perceptions of Obama and McCain by party identification. Boxplots of estimated respondent perceptions of Obama and McCain by respondent partisanship. Horizontal dotted lines show actual positions of Obama and McCain at −.25 and .25, respectively.

Beyond having some basic impression of the specific policy positions or even of the overall ideological positions of a candidate, it is crucial that voters be able to judge the ideological distances between themselves and the candidates. How accurately are voters able to make these judgments? Do there exist systematic biases in their perceptions of ideological proximity to candidates? This section addresses these questions using the estimated ideological positions and estimated perceptions shown in Figure 7.1.

The spatial models considered in Chapters 4, 5, and 6 assume that voters base their choices on the relative squared distances between their ideal points and each candidate in an election. Accordingly, an important question is whether voters are able to accurately estimate these distances. Figure 7.3 plots the actual squared ideological distances between respondents from the 2008 survey against their perceived squared distances from the candidates. While there are clear positive associations between these quantities for Obama and McCain, there also is considerable variation, with many respondents perceiving themselves as either significantly closer or significantly farther than they actually are from each candidate.

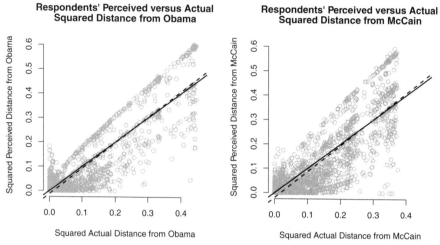

FIGURE 7.3. Perceived distance from candidates versus actual distance, 2008 survey. Scatterplots of respondents' perceived squared ideological distance from each candidate in 2008 election against actual squared ideological distance. Solid black line plots $y = x$. Dashed black line plots regression line of squared perceived distance on squared actual distance.

On average, however, respondents seem to perceive these ideological distances quite accurately. The dashed line in each of the two plots of Figure 7.3 shows regression fits predicting perceived squared distance, with actual distance and the solid lines represent accurate perceptions, that is, squared perceived distance equaling squared actual distance. For perceptions of both Obama and McCain, these lines are very close. It seems, then, that while there is considerable variation, voters in the 2008 election did not systematically perceive themselves as closer or farther than they were from either of the two presidential candidates.

Table 7.2 shows the regression estimates predicting respondents' perceived squared distances from candidates against their actual squared distances. Under accurate (unbiased) perceptions, the intercept and slope should be zero and one, respectively, indicating that on average, respondents' perceptions were correct. In fact, these estimates fall almost exactly at these values. While there exist statistically significant differences for each of the estimates, they are very close in substantive terms. It seems, then, that on average, respondents are able to accurately perceive their ideological proximity to each candidate. While, as Figure 7.3 shows, there is a good deal of variation in respondent perceptions of proximity to the candidates, respondents' actual distances from the candidates

TABLE 7.2. *Perceived Distance Regression Model Estimates, 2008 Survey*

	Obama	McCain
Intercept	−.01	−.02
	(.002)	(.003)
Actual Distance from Candidate	1.05	1.07
	(.01)	(.02)
r^2	.80	.70
N	2,000	2,000

Regression results predicting perceived squared distances from respondents to candidates using actual squared distance between respondents and candidates based on 2008 survey estimates.

predict a good deal of this variation. The r-squareds from these regressions for Obama and McCain are .80 and .70, respectively, indicating that actual distance can explain the vast majority of variation in perceived distance.

Partisan Biases and Perceptions

A key question related to the voters' judgments of the ideological proximity of candidates is whether these evaluations are systematically skewed by partisanship. In particular, the results from previous chapters demonstrate that, while voters on average seem to be engaging in relatively precise and largely unbiased spatial voting, breaking things down by party identification reveals that there exist significant biases for Democratic and Republican voters. While the vote choices of these partisans are still strongly affected by their ideological proximity to candidates, these voters also are much more likely to choose the candidate from their own party, even in many cases in which they are ideologically closer to the opposing candidate.

A natural question that stems from these findings is whether these observed spatial biases among partisans can be explained by perceptual biases in which these voters believe that candidates from their own political party are ideologically closer to themselves than is actually the case or in which they view candidates from the opposing party as being ideologically farther than they truly are. To put it differently, do partisan voters exhibit spatial biases because they are voting based on their perceived proximity to the candidates and because these perceptions tend to place their party's candidate at an advantage?

To investigate this hypothesis, we can first define a term called *net perceptual bias*. This is defined as

$$\text{Net Perceptual Bias}_i = \left[\hat{U}_i(R) - \hat{U}_i(D)\right] - [U_i(R) - U_i(D)]$$

$$= \left[-\left(x_i - \hat{c}_{i,R}\right)^2 - \left(x_i - \hat{c}_{i,D}\right)^2\right]$$

$$- \left[-\left(x_i - c_{i,R}\right)^2 - \left(x_i - c_{i,D}\right)^2\right], \quad (7.2)$$

where $U_i(R)$ and $U_i(D)$ are the (true) utilities received by respondent i for voting for the Democratic and Republican candidates, respectively, and $\hat{U}_i(R)$ and $\hat{U}_i(D)$ are the corresponding perceived utilities.[1] As before, c_D and c_R indicate the actual positions of the Democratic and Republican candidates, which are fixed at $-.25$ and $.25$, respectively, and $\hat{c}_{i,D}$ and $\hat{c}_{i,R}$ are respondent i's perceptions of the ideologies of the Democratic and Republican candidates, respectively. This quantity represents the difference between the perceived utility advantage a given respondent would receive from voting for the Republican candidate minus the actual utility advantage he or she would receive from doing so. In other words, this quantity represents the amount of spatial voting bias induced by a respondent's perceptions of proximity to the candidates above and beyond his or her actual proximities. Positive values indicate that the respondent perceives that voting for the Republican would be better for him or her in spatial terms than is actually the case, while negative values imply that the respondent believes that the Democratic candidate would be a more attractive choice than he actually is.

If perceptual biases were the central cause of the observed spatial biases in the choices of partisan voters, we should expect that the net perceptual bias should be positive for Republican identifiers and negative for Democratic identifiers. Presumably, because independents show little if any spatial voting bias, their net perceptual biases may be thought to be approximately zero. Figure 7.4 shows the distributions of net perceptual bias by respondent party identification. Surprisingly, these biases are roughly zero on average for Democrats, independents, and Republicans. In fact, we cannot come close to rejecting the hypothesis that the mean net perceptual bias for each of these three groups is zero.

---

[1] It should be noted that these utility functions, as written, omit the policy weight term a from the spatial voting models estimated previously. This omission, however, should not change the overall results reported, but only multiply them by some constant term.

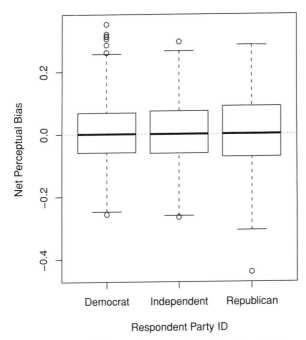

FIGURE 7.4. Net perceptual biases by party identification, 2008 survey. Boxplot of net perceptual bias, as defined in Equation 7.2, by respondent party identification.

These results suggest that perceptual biases are unlikely to be the central cause of the differences in spatial voting patterns between Democrats, independents, and Republicans. On average, voters from all three of these groups accurately perceive the relative amounts of spatial utility that would be offered by each candidate. Therefore, it appears that the voting biases exhibited by partisans are more basic, entering into these voters' decisions apart from policy considerations. Another way of examining this process is to re-estimate the vote choice models of previous chapters, substituting respondents' perceptions of the candidates' positions for the true positions of each candidate. If the partisan voting biases are reduced or disappear completely, this would suggest that perceptual biases are a central cause of these things. If, alternatively, strong differences between the voting behavior of Democratic and Republican voters remain, even for those with similar ideological positions, this would suggest that systematically skewed perception cannot be the primary explanation for the divergence in voting behavior between partisans.

The basic spatial voting framework employed here assumes that the utility that a voter receives from voting for a specific candidate is based on the squared distance between the voter's ideal point and the candidate's position. As shown in Chapter 4, assuming this model, along with independent normal errors to voters' utility functions, implies a probit regression model predicting vote choice. Substituting in voters' perceptions of candidate positions, we obtain a somewhat similar result. Voters are assumed to cast their ballots for the candidate who provides them with the most utility – in this case, utility that is based on the squared distance between the voter's own ideal point and his or her perception of the candidate's ideological position. This implies the equation

$$P(v_i = R) = P(\hat{U}_i(R) > \hat{U}_i(D))$$

$$= P(-a(x_i - \hat{c}_{iR})^2 + e_{iR} > -a(x_i - \hat{c}_D)^2 + e_{iD})$$

$$= \Phi(-a(x_i - \hat{c}_{iR})^2 + a(x_i - \hat{c}_{iD})^2), \qquad (7.3)$$

where the last line comes as a result of assuming that $e_{iD} - e_{iR} \sim N(0,1)$.

In order to assess the degree to which the decisions of partisans are biased, we can, as in Chapter 5, include a partisan bias term in this equation. It is straightforward to show that under this setup, the policy weight (a) and partisan bias ($\delta_{pty(i)}$) terms can be estimated using a probit regression predicting vote choice with respondents' perceived net proximity to the Republican candidate and their partisan affiliation. Formally, the model estimated is of the form

$$P(v_i = R) = \Phi\left(\beta_{dist}\left(-(x_i - \hat{c}_{iR})^2 + (x_i - \hat{c}_{iD})^2\right) + \beta_{pty(i)}\right), \qquad (7.4)$$

where β_{dist} estimates the effect of perceived net proximity to the Republican candidate and $\beta_{pty(i)}$ is a party-specific coefficient that estimates the bias of respondents of each partisan affiliation toward voting for the Republican.

The value $-(x_i - \hat{c}_{iR})^2 + (x_i - \hat{c}_{iD})^2$, which can be thought of as the net perceptual advantage for the Republican candidate, indicates how much more spatial utility respondent i would expect to receive from voting for the Republican candidate than for the Democratic candidate. When the voter perceives that the Republican candidate is ideologically closer to his or her own ideal point, this quantity will be positive, indicating that he or she will expect more utility from voting for the Republican than for the Democrat. If the respondent perceives the Democratic candidate as being closer, the quantity will be negative, implying that voting for the

TABLE 7.3. *Perceptions-Based Presidential Vote Choice Model with Party ID, 2008 Survey*

Variable	Parameter	Estimate (Standard Errors)
Perceived Net Proximity	β_{dist}	8.85 (.70)
Democratic Intercept	β_D	−.80 (.08)
Independent Intercept	β_I	.05 (.14)
Republican Intercept	β_R	1.19 (.09)
Log-likelihood		−329.7
N		1,715

Table reports probit regression results predicting reported vote for McCain (coded as 1) or Obama (coded as 0) in the 2008 survey. Perceived net distance is calculated as $-(x_i - \hat{c}_{iR})^2 + (x_i - \hat{c}_{iD})^2$ where x_i is respondent i's estimated ideal point and $\hat{c}_{iR}$ and $\hat{c}_{iD}$ are respondent i's estimated perceptions of the ideological positions of McCain and Obama, respectively.

Democrat offers more utility. When both candidates are perceived to be the same distance from the voter, this quantity will be zero.

Table 7.3 shows the estimated coefficients from this perceptions-based probit model of vote choice. The results are very similar to those presented in Chapter 5 (see Table 5.1) involving respondents' true (rather than perceived) proximities to the two candidates. In fact, the estimated partisan biases for Democratic, independent, and Republican voters, which are −.80, .05, and 1.19, respectively, here are nearly identical to the −.78, .09, and 1.17 estimated based on actual proximities. This suggests that the observed partisan bias (what has here been called $\delta_{pty(i)}$) from previous analyses is not simply due to voters relying on perceptions of candidate ideology that tend to be biased to make their party's candidate appear more favorable or the other party's candidate appear less attractive. Whether spatial proximity is measured in actual or perceived terms, partisan voters display strong and highly significant spatial biases that push them toward voting for the candidate of their political party, even in some cases in which they are actually ideologically closer, or perceive themselves to be closer, to the opposing party candidate.

The main difference for the perceptions-based model is that the effect of perceived distance seems to be larger than that estimated for actual

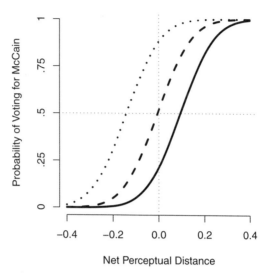

FIGURE 7.5. Predicted probability of voting for McCain by net perceptual distance and party identification, 2008 survey. Solid, dashed, and dotted curves plot the predicted probability of voting for McCain as a function of the net perceptual distance from the candidates for Democrats, independents, and Republicans, respectively. Estimates are based on 2008 survey analysis results presented in Table 7.3.

proximity in Chapter 5. This should not be surprising because, presumably, the main way that voters' true ideological proximities to candidates affects their vote choices is through their perceptions of how close the candidates in a given election are to their own positions. Directly modeling vote choice as a function of perceived ideological proximity, then, would be expected to produce stronger estimated effects.

Overall, the conclusions drawn from the perceptions-based spatial voting model are remarkably similar to those from the true ideological proximity model. Figure 7.5 plots the predicted probabilities of voting for McCain as a function of respondents' net perceptual distances from McCain relative to Obama. The solid, dashed, and dotted curves represent the predicted probabilities for Democrats, independents, and Republicans. There remain relatively large gaps between the vote probabilities of Democrats and Republicans. These relationships emphasize the independent effects that partisanship exerts on vote choice, wholly apart from ideological proximity.

In one sense, this finding may be thought to reinforce the standard Michigan school view of partisanship as an affective orientation. If voters' party identifications have a substantial effect on their vote choices even after accounting for their understandings of the relative ideological proximities of each candidate, it could be thought that partisanship may represent a more emotional, rather than calculating, quantity. Even in situations in which they are ideologically closer to the candidate of the opposing party and, even more, when they perceive themselves to be closer to that candidate, partisans are often more likely than not to vote for their own party's candidate.

Discussion

The findings presented here provide encouraging signs about the political competence of the American electorate. According to the spatial theory of voting, the core axioms of which have been empirically validated in the preceding chapters, the key requirement for casting a "correct" vote is that the voter be able to assess the relative ideological proximity of each candidate in an election to the voter's own ideal point. By this standard, the results presented in this chapter suggest an electorate that is relatively well equipped for the task of making such choices between candidates.

Although there is a relatively high amount of variance in the perceptions held by voters of the ideological positions of candidates, these perceptions appear quite sensible on average. Importantly, the approach taken here is fundamentally different from previous investigations of the political competence of citizens. For example, Campbell et al. (1960) posed open-ended questions to voters about what they liked and disliked about certain candidates. Here, by contrast, voters are asked what position they believe each candidate takes on specific political issues. These issue positions then reveal an underlying perception of the ideological positions of these candidates. In the 2008 election, voters on the whole held reasonably accurate perceptions of the positions of Obama and McCain. Although their perceptions saw each of these candidates as slightly more moderate than was actually the case, these evaluations indicate, at least at a basic level, a solid comprehension of the basic elements of electoral choice.

Moreover, respondents in the 2008 survey showed virtually no systematic bias in their perceptions of ideological proximity to candidates. In other words, the ideological distance that a voter perceived between him- or herself and either Obama or McCain tended to on average be equal to the true ideological distance between him- or herself and the candidate. Because spatial voting (alternately called proximity voting) posits that a voter's ideological distance from each candidate is the central determinant of vote choice, this finding paints an optimistic picture of the basic tools held by voters attempting to choose the candidate that is best for them.

Even when voter perceptions are examined separately by party identification, there surprisingly exists no consistent bias in the relative proximity perceived by voters to each candidate. These evaluations do not appear to be systematically skewed toward one candidate or the other based on the partisan affiliations of voters. These results are surprising, particularly given the large biases exhibited by partisans relative to the standard of unbiased spatial voting (see Chapter 5). Furthermore, when vote choice is modeled as a function of both voters' partisanship and their perceived distances from the candidates (as opposed to their actual distances from the candidates), this large partisan divergence remains. This suggests that the mechanism for partisan influence operates apart from that of spatial voting. To put it differently, voters of all partisan stripes have perceptions of their relative proximity to candidates that are on average correct. While independent voters tend to cast their ballots for the candidate whom they perceive to be ideologically closer to themselves (and who is, typically, actually closer), partisans often display a willingness to choose their party's candidate even in situations in which they believe him to be ideologically farther from their own views than is the candidate of the opposition party.

8

Conclusion

Spatial representations of politics, and of voting in elections more specifically, represent extremely powerful theoretical tools. The simple concept of a single-dimensional policy space forms the basis for a general framework that has the potential to explain the behavior of ordinary voters, candidates, and elected representatives, generating direct and testable predictions at each level. Perhaps more importantly, the basic spatial framework traces a clear and direct line from the views of individual voters to the policies implemented by democratic governments. Understanding the specific nature of the mechanisms connecting these two things is central to understanding and evaluating democratic governance in the American political system. Spatial theory provides arguably the clearest and most parsimonious way of explaining this connection. Individual voters, holding ideological positions on the liberal–conservative spectrum, cast their ballots for the candidate who locates himself closest to the voter's own position. Candidates, anticipating the behavior of voters, choose their positions with the aim of maximizing the number of votes they receive. Elected representatives, with an eye toward pleasing their constituents and keeping their jobs, tailor their voting to please the largest number of constituents possible.

The logic of spatial voting theory also has the potential to bridge what is a significant disconnect between approaches to the study of voting and institutional behavior, particularly in the U.S. Congress. For instance, a large number of theories and general frameworks for the study of Congress begin by assuming that each legislator holds some ideal point representing his or her most preferred policy outcome. These ideological positions are often taken as exogenous, dictating the preferences (and, by extension, the actions) of each member of Congress under a given set of rules. Most behavioral theories offer at most minimal guidance as to how the preferences and actions of citizens affect these legislator ideal points. Spatial theory, on the other hand, provides a direct link between the policy views of voters and the positions of elected officials. In fact, according to spatial theory, the central determinant of vote choice – voters' ideological positions – has a direct correspondence to the positions of the candidates who win elections.

But while most observers would agree that the spatial model offers explanations for a wide variety of political phenomena, two primary critiques have been levied against this approach. These critiques have focused primarily on the validity of spatial theory's predictions and on the realism of its assumptions. Some of the most common claims about the falsification of spatial theory, however, focus not on the spatial voting model itself, but on more elaborate extensions of it. For instance, the observation that Democratic candidates in American elections consistently take more liberal positions than do Republican candidates is often pointed to as disproving the predictions of spatial theory. In fact, the median voter theorem, which predicts that candidates should take identical positions at the median voter's position, relies on a list of many different assumptions above and beyond simple spatial voting. Its falsification, then, merely proves that at least one of these assumptions does not hold. In fact, some of the assumptions, such as full turnout or single-stage elections, are obviously false.

What the evidence presented in this book has shown is that simple spatial voting rules can predict the vast majority of vote choices by respondents in the 2004 and 2008 surveys analyzed here. The basic predictions of spatial voting, then, have stood up fairly well to empirical scrutiny, albeit with some important modifications. First, it has been demonstrated that partisanship plays an important role in spatial voting, as Adams et al. (2005) and others have proposed. While independent voters show little if any bias by spatial standards, partisans are powerfully drawn to their party's candidates above and beyond what simple ideological proximity would suggest. Second, political information plays a key role in spatial voting, with the decisions of more informed voters appearing to be based more on ideology and less on partisan concerns. Therefore, as voters become more informed, the gap between the behavior of Democrats, independents, and Republicans is reduced.

Even among the most informed voters, however, significant differences remain between the vote choices of partisans with similar ideological positions.

Although it has considerable normative appeal, spatial voting theory is, at a basic level, a positive theory. As such, spatial theory should be evaluated in terms of its ability to predict the choices of voters in elections. In fact, many positive theorists argue that the plausibility of a theory's assumptions is largely irrelevant for evaluating the usefulness of the theory itself (see, e.g., Friedman 1984). The predictive accuracy of spatial theory, whether in its simplest form or when expanded to include other determinants of the vote, has been evaluated extensively in this book. But in addition to predictive accuracy, political scientists also care deeply about testing the validity of the key assumptions of spatial theory. For example, it is an interesting and important question on its own whether the views of ordinary Americans can be represented as points on a single ideological dimension and, similarly, whether voters are capable of evaluating the ideological distances between themselves and the candidates in a given election. In both of these cases, the basic premises of spatial theory have largely been confirmed. As Chapter 3 shows, the policy views of citizens exhibit strong relationships across a variety of specific issues. These relationships, often referred to as ideological constraint, indicate that the policy positions of voters are far more than a collection of random, loosely held beliefs. In fact, a single ideological dimension is capable of explaining the vast majority of variation in the policy views of respondents. Furthermore, as Chapter 7 demonstrates, voters are capable of forming relatively accurate perceptions of the ideological positions of candidates as well as of legislators. These perceptions, although far from perfect, show that voters are able to judge the ideological distances between themselves and candidates in an unbiased fashion, even when separated by party identification.

Overall, then, the findings presented here have demonstrated the value of the spatial approach to politics, not just as an abstract theoretical construct, but also in explaining actual voter behavior in American elections. More broadly, these findings have shed important light on some of the central aspects of democratic governance. Do citizens possess meaningful opinions on important policy issues? Can electoral results be said to represent meaningful signals about the will of the people? While the answers presented here are not dispositive, I believe that they are, on balance, quite encouraging.

The Elephant in the Room: Endogeneity in Ideology, Partisanship, and Voting

Throughout most of this book, the vote choices of Americans in recent presidential elections have been modeled as a function of voters' ideological positions and party identifications. Vote choice, which has served as the dependent variable in these analyses, is assumed to have been determined by a voter's ideological proximity to the candidates in a given election as well as by the voter's partisanship. In reality, these factors are all interrelated. Voters' party identifications are influenced by their feelings toward candidates. If a voter realizes that choosing Obama in 2008 means that he or she has voted Democrat in the last three elections, he or she may be more likely to call him- or herself a Democrat. Ideological positions also are likely to be affected by one's vote choice. If someone likes Obama, he or she will, in many cases, be more likely to support policies advocated by the candidate. Furthermore, partisanship and ideology are related to each other. Liberal voters, for example, realizing that their views are more in line with those of the Democratic party, will be more likely to identify as Democrats. Conversely, those who identify with a political party may be more likely to adopt views consistent with those identifications (e.g., Brody and Page 1972).

In the study of voting and public opinion, endogeneity is a fact of life. Most of the important concepts in these areas have complicated reciprocal relationships. An important question, then, is not whether some y is caused by some x, or whether x is caused by y. Instead, researchers would ideally seek to understand *how much* of the causality runs in each direction. This is by no means a simple question, as evidenced by the many attempts to model these complex relationships using simultaneous equation models, which, more often than not, produced dramatically different results (e.g., Markus and Converse 1979; Page and Jones 1979). Taking a somewhat different approach, some scholars have sought to identify the causal effects of one particular factor on another through the use of survey experiments or instrumental variables. Kam (2005), for example, randomly varies the political party said to be supporting a given policy and demonstrates that these cues increase support among people who identify with that party and decrease support among opposite party identifiers. Gerber et al. (2010) employ a randomized mailing that they find affects the partisanship of voters, concluding that these changes in partisanship affect respondents' opinions of candidates. Tomz and Van Houweling (2008) randomly vary the policy positions and partisan affiliations of hypothetical candidates in order to examine the causes of vote choice. Ansolabehere and Jones (2010) employ a clever modeling approach in which legislators' true views are used as an instrument for constituent perceptions, identifying a clear causal effect of issue voting.

Ultimately, the goal of future work studying ideology and spatial voting should be not only to build on the findings presented here, but also to disentangle the (likely complex) causal relationships underlying the results of this work. Should the fact that vote choices correspond well to voters' ideological proximity to candidates be taken to indicate that votes represent powerful signals about the policy preferences of the electorate? Or does the observed congruence between these two quantities indicate that voters tend to rationalize their choices by adopting policy preferences they know to be advocated by their chosen candidate? While difficult to come by, the answers to these questions are of central importance to understanding voting and American politics in general.

Should Party Identification Be a Right Hand Side Variable?

Party identification is among the most analyzed variables in the field of political behavior. It is highly correlated with many quantities of interest to political scientists, most notably vote choice. For example, Figure 8.1 plots the percentage of Republican and Democratic identifiers from the ANES who reported voting for the Republican candidate in the last fifteen presidential elections. It is immediately clear that partisanship is strongly related to vote choice, being able to predict the choices of an extremely high percentage of partisan voters in virtually all recent presidential elections. There are, however, two dramatically different conclusions that can be drawn from these results and from other findings of a high degree of alignment between partisanship and vote choice about the relevance of party identification as an independent variable in models predicting vote choice.

The conclusion drawn by a majority of American political behavior scholars has been that partisanship represents a central variable in political thought generally as well as voter behavior more specifically and therefore should be included (controlled for) in virtually any statistical models analyzing vote choice or other political variables. For instance, the classic and still widely cited studies of the Michigan school (e.g., Campbell et al. 1960; Converse 1964) emphasize that partisanship serves as the predominant factor determining vote choice for the vast majority of citizens. Because party identification has been clearly demonstrated as

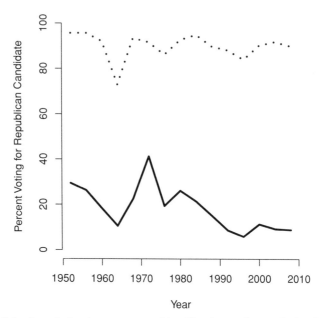

FIGURE 8.1. Association between party identification and vote choice. Percent of Democratic (solid line) and Republican identifiers (dotted line) from ANES who reported voting for the Republican presidential candidate in each presidential election.

such a powerful predictor of vote choice, it is argued, any statistical (or, for that matter, theoretical) model that fails to consider partisanship has the strong potential for generating misleading results. This is particularly true given the fact that party identification has been shown to be correlated with many other variables typically studied as predictors of vote choice. Because of this, the omitted variable bias produced by failing to include party identification in a regression specification may render the estimated coefficients on many of the included variables useless.

A far less conventional, but in my view still important, conclusion that can be drawn from results such as those shown in Figure 8.1 is that perhaps party identification should *not* be used as a predictor in statistical models analyzing vote choice in American elections. To see why, we can begin by taking a step back and thinking about the reasons that studying vote choice is so important. To be sure, vote choice is important in and of itself. Voting represents the primary mechanism by which citizens in a democracy influence their government. The results of voting, both direct and indirect, constrain the government and make rule by the people possible. But vote choice also is of central interest to political scientists because of what it represents. We want to know what makes people decide to cast their ballots for one candidate instead of another. In this sense, we may care less about the actual vote itself than about the feelings and attitudes it represents: "Why does a person come to favor Obama over McCain?" On this note, it is unclear whether partisanship can serve as a right hand side variable that adds to our understanding or whether it is just as likely to obscure it.

Considering a different, but analogous example, imagine that you have been hired by Ford Motor Company to analyze what makes pickup truck buyers choose a Ford instead of a Chevrolet. They have paid you a significant consulting fee and asked you to come back to them with some new findings that will help them better understand their market and what determines the choices of potential truck buyers. Imagine further that after many hours toiling away, conducting surveys of potential truck buyers and analyzing the results, you return to your clients triumphantly, announcing that you have found the answer they were looking for. "I've found a single variable that on its own can explain the vast majority of the variation in truck buying behavior," you exclaim, bringing the Ford representatives to the edge of their seats. "If you ask people whether they consider themselves a 'Ford man' or a 'Chevy man,' their answers predict their ultimate truck buying decisions in an extremely high percentage of cases." How useful would these clients find this information? Would it be likely to tell them something that had not yet occurred to them?

Similarly, would television executives marvel at the finding that people's feelings toward a television show – whether they feel a kinship with or an interest in its characters – predict whether they watch it? Would a publisher be fascinated by the finding that people who believe a given author to be smart or to have intriguing ideas are more likely to purchase books written by him or her in the future? The problem with such findings, and what I argue is a potential problem that should at least be considered for studies involving party identification, is that the predictor is very closely related to the dependent variable. In fact, it could be argued that partisanship is so intertwined with vote choice that using it as a predictor can reduce the amount of understanding that is added by a given analysis.

In the last four presidential elections, roughly 90 percent of partisan voters (including those who identify as independents, but, upon further prodding, admit to leaning toward one party or the other) have cast their ballots for the nominee of their political party. While this renders partisanship an impressive predictor of vote choice, it begs the question of whether voting scholars should focus on which variables can explain the relatively small amount of variance leftover in vote choice after controlling for party identification or whether they should instead be interested in explaining the entirety of vote choice, employing regression specifications that omit partisanship.

One argument would state that it seems ridiculous to intentionally omit a predictor that not only is known to have a strong relationship with a given dependent variable, but also is correlated with many of the other predictors that are likely to be included in the model. On the other hand, however, it is important to assess whether the independent variables included in a given model are conceptually similar to the dependent variable. For instance, it would seem silly to include as a predictor of vote choice respondents' answers to a survey question asking which candidate they most preferred to vote for. At least in a formal sense, the candidate a respondent prefers to vote for is a different thing than the candidate a respondent actually does vote for – it is possible for someone to cast a ballot for one candidate but prefer another.[1] But we would clearly expect there to be an extremely high degree of agreement between these two variables, to the point that a regression predicting actual vote choice with candidate preference would be unlikely to be useful. Clearly in such a regression, the coefficient on candidate preference would be extremely large in magnitude. But given the inclusion of this candidate preference variable, the coefficients on other predictors would change significantly in meaning. Instead of being what we would typically think of as the effects of some X on vote choice, they would now be interpreted as the effects of some X on vote choice after controlling for candidate preference. To put it differently, these other predictors would essentially be used to explain which people failed to cast their ballots for their most preferred candidate – a potentially interesting question, but much narrower than investigating the general determinants of vote choice.

In fact, many scholars of European political behavior essentially regard party identification as synonymous with vote choice. This issue presents itself most strongly in electoral systems under which voters cast their ballots for political parties rather than for specific candidates running

---

[1] There is some literature on this subject, including work on "balancing" in which voters intentionally cast their ballots for congressional and presidential candidates from opposing parties in the hopes of obtaining the moderate policy outcomes likely to result from divided government (e.g., Lacy and Paolino 1998). This, however, is a somewhat different situation from the examples discussed here.

under a party label (see Adams et al. 2005, 248–50 for a discussion of this issue). Although this concern may be somewhat weaker in American politics, particularly at the presidential level, because candidates have a relatively high degree of independence and tend to cultivate strong individual images during campaigns, this issue still remains at least somewhat applicable.

Another reason why it may be appropriate to place less emphasis on partisanship as a central determinant of vote choice is that, as discussed in Chapter 5, it appears quite likely that the effects of partisanship have been overestimated as a result of error in measures of voter ideology. Furthermore, to the extent that partisanship is driven by policy agreement with candidates of each party, the overall effects of ideology may be underestimated when party is included because the indirect effects of ideology on the vote that operate through partisanship will not be included in the estimated ideology coefficient. A somewhat related point is made by Achen (1992), who argues that the effects of party identification will be overestimated if partisanship is measured during the campaign rather than before it. This is because partisanship will be affected by information specific to the current campaign, including feelings toward the competing candidates. Overall, then, there also exist practical, in addition to more conceptual, concerns with including partisanship as a predictor of vote choice.

Clearly, the decision to include or exclude party identification from regression models predicting vote choice is a fundamentally subjective one, depending largely on the preferences and aims of individual researchers. The ideal approach would be to formulate a full model of the causal relationships between all relevant variables: vote choice, party identification, ideology, and so forth. But while this would be preferable to the standard approach of assuming that one variable, here vote choice, is predicted (going further, perhaps caused) by a given set of variables, it also brings with it many additional complications. Most notably, the requirements for studies identifying such complicated causal relationships are typically beyond the reach of the data and modeling approaches available in political behavior. While some previous studies have taken this approach, most have been forced to rely on heroic assumptions or narrow their focus to specific situations (often, survey experiments involving hypothetical elections) in order to estimate these models. Scholars are then left with a somewhat uncomfortable choice between, on the one hand, omitting a predictor known to be highly correlated with the dependent variable and, on the other hand, including a right hand side variable that is at best conceptually related to the dependent variable and at worst largely synonymous with it.

Implications for Citizen Competence

The spatial voting model paints voters as calculating utility maximizers who systematically evaluate the ideological distances between themselves and each candidate in a given election, casting their vote for the candidate who takes a position closest to their own. This picture, at least in terms of its implications for voter competence, is quite a flattering one. First, spatial voting suggests that voters hold policy views that are structured by an underlying unidimensional ideology. Next, it is assumed that voters understand the positions taken by candidates on this ideological dimension. Finally, citizens are assumed to make their voting decisions based on coldly rational maximization of utility.

The findings presented here have largely confirmed the first of these two assumptions, but have suggested the need for important revisions to spatial theory to accurately depict the vote choices of ordinary Americans in presidential elections. Chapter 3 demonstrated that the views of citizens on specific policies can be explained quite well with a single ideological dimension. In fact, adding further ideological dimensions adds little explanatory power. On the one hand, the relatively strong degree of constraint found between people's views across different policy issues could be thought to suggest that these positions are well thought out and possibly a part of some larger, coherent political philosophy. Clearly, this conclusion is likely to be too strong for the vast majority of voters. But at the least, the discovery of ideological constraint among issue positions would seem to refute claims that the vast majority of citizens do not hold any sort of meaningful policy views, giving essentially random answers to most questions about political choices.

Chapters 4 through 6 demonstrate that the choices of voters in recent presidential elections are powerfully affected by the voters' ideological positions. In fact, these decisions are largely consistent with the predictions of unbiased spatial voting if the party identification of voters is ignored. Even within partisan groupings, citizens' vote choices depend strongly on their ideological proximity to each candidate. This would seem to suggest that voters must have some way of understanding, or at least estimating, the ideological positions taken by candidates. Chapter 7 goes further to investigate the actual perceptions that voters hold about the ideological positions of candidates. It is shown that citizen perceptions of the ideological distances between themselves and candidates are essentially unbiased both at the aggregate level and, somewhat surprisingly, within each partisan grouping.

Finally, the vote choices of citizens are strongly consistent with the spatial voting model, at least at a baseline level. While the spatial voting model is not necessarily a normative ideal, it does have important parallels with some theories of representation. In particular, while some level of representation may be possible without ideological or spatial voting (see, for example, theories of retrospective voting by Key [1966], Fiorina [1981], and others), the empirical validation of the basic concept of spatial voting suggests that ordinary citizens are capable of both forming coherent ideological beliefs and evaluating the congruence between these beliefs and the platforms put forth by candidates. This account stands in sharp contrast to previous work emphasizing the paucity of ideological thought and the general lack of political competence in the American electorate.

Discussion

The spatial theory of voting, introduced decades ago, offers a powerful, direct, and parsimonious account of how voters make decisions in elections. Even more than this, spatial theory offers a general framework that has the potential to explain behavior across all levels of the political system, from ordinary voters to elected officials and ultimately to implemented policies. While the logic of spatial politics has taken a firm foothold in the study of institutions such as Congress and the courts, the spatial study of the behavior of voters has typically fallen out of the mainstream of the political behavior subfield. The early work by Downs (1957), Enelow and Hinich (1984), and others explored the theoretical consequences of various assumptions of spatial voting, and a robust theoretical literature exists in this area. Furthermore, more recent work such as Adams et al. (2005) has incorporated the partisan effects of the Michigan school of voting behavior along with the influence of spatial concerns in order to test theories of candidate competition. What this book has done is focused on ideological proximity as an explanation for the choices of American voters. Through a novel measurement approach allowing for the estimation of voter and candidate ideology on the same scale, this book has provided the most direct evidence to date on the use of spatial voting in actual elections.

In political science, it is rare that simple, formalized theory can clearly explain important phenomena. The findings presented here demonstrate that the spatial voting model, a direct and extremely parsimonious theory, can powerfully predict the electoral choices of a wide range of American voters. This finding should highlight the utility of spatial voting as well as shore up the foundations of a wide range of other political science theories that assume the use of some sort of spatial voting.

Survey Question Wordings

This appendix presents full question wordings from primary surveys analyzed in this book, which are referred to as the 2004 and 2008 surveys.

2004 Survey Question Wording

Generally speaking, do you usually think of yourself as a Republican, a Democrat, or an Independent? [follow up on strong Republican/Democrat or independent leaning Republican/Democrat/no lean]

How did you vote in the 2004 election?
  I voted for George Bush.
  I voted for John Kerry.
  I voted for someone else (please specify):_____.
  I was not able to vote.

As you know, your Representatives and Senators in Washington vote on issues that affect our country. On the following pages, we will ask you about some actual proposals before the U.S. Senate. We will give you a brief description of each proposal. Please tell us whether you would support each proposal and how you think your Senators would vote when these issues come up. If you aren't sure how one or both of your Senators would vote, please try to guess how they would vote when faced with this proposal based upon what you know about them.

[For each Senate proposal question, respondents were asked, "How would you vote on this measure?," with response options: "I support this measure and would vote 'yes,'" "I oppose this measure and would vote 'no,'" and "Don't know." They also were asked "Please tell us how you think your Senators will vote on this measure," with response options "Probably for," "Maybe for," "Maybe against," "Probably against," and "Not sure" for each of their senators.]

S 397: Protection of Lawful Commerce in Arms Act

- Prevents people from suing gun manufacturers and dealers for the misuse of their products, including when crimes are committed with guns they make or sell.
- The bill would still allow lawsuits for product defects and malfunctions.
- Requires safety locks for all guns sold or transferred.
- Increases penalties for possession or use of "armor piercing" ammunition when committing a crime.

S 1307: Central American Free Trade Agreement

- Promotes free trade between the U.S. and Central American countries.
- Reduces tariffs, duties, and other fees and taxes on imports and exports between the U.S. and Central American countries for things such as textiles and agricultural goods.

S AMDT 826 to HR 6: Greenhouse Gas Reduction and Credit Trading System

- Would require that industries reduce their production of greenhouse gases to year 2000 levels within five years.
- Would establish a credit trading system that would allow companies who are unable to reduce emissions to this level to buy credits from other companies who reduce their pollution to farther below the limit.

S AMDT 44 to S 256: Minimum Wage Increase

- Would raise the minimum wage to $5.85 immediately, then to $6.55 after one year, and to $7.25 in two years.
- The minimum wage before this bill was proposed was $5.15.

HR 1997: Unborn Victims of Violence Act

- Makes it an additional crime to harm or kill a fetus while committing a violent crime against a pregnant woman.
- Does not require that the attacker knew the woman was pregnant.
- Does not apply to abortions.

S AMDT 3183 to S 2400: Hate Crimes Amendment

- Would classify crimes motivated by a victim's race, color, religion, sexual orientation, disability, or national origin as "hate crimes" to be prosecuted in federal (not state) courts.
- Authorizes $5 million per year over the next two years for the Justice Department to assist state and local authorities in investigating and prosecuting hate crimes.

S AMDT 1085 to HR 2419: Remove Funding for "Bunker Buster" Warhead

- The "bunker buster" is a small nuclear warhead designed to destroy fortified underground positions by breaking through rock or concrete to a certain depth before exploding.
- This amendment would stop the use of federal funds for the development of the proposed "bunker buster" nuclear warhead.
- The money would instead be used to pay down the national debt.

S AMDT 367 to HR 1268: Remove Funding for Guantanamo Bay Detention Center

- Eliminates $36 million in funding which was planned to build a new permanent prison facility at Guantanamo Bay, Cuba, to house detainees from the war on terrorism.

S AMDT 1626 to S 397: Child Safety Locks Amendment

- Requires gun manufacturers and sellers to include child safety locks on all firearms sold or transferred.

S 256: Bankruptcy Abuse Prevention and Consumer Protection Act

- In Chapter 7 bankruptcy, a debtor sells off most of his or her property and pays as much of his debts as he can and the rest of his debts are erased. In Chapter 13 bankruptcy, debtors work out a payment plan to pay off all or most of their debts.
- This bill would force debtors into Chapter 13 bankruptcy in which they must pay off their debts (rather than have them erased) if they are able to do so while still earning above their state's median income.
- Places child support and alimony payments into the category of non-dischargeable debts, which must still be repaid under all forms of bankruptcy.
- Allows some special treatment for active-duty military members, veterans, and those with serious medical conditions.

- Requires debtors to pay for and attend credit counseling before filing for bankruptcy.
- Requires that monthly credit card statements include warnings and explanations about interest rates and fees.
- Caps home equity protection at $125,000 if debtor purchased the home within 40 months of filing for bankruptcy.

S 5: Class Action Fairness Act

- Class action lawsuits are brought in the name of a group of people who all claim to have been affected similarly by a product, procedure, or other act. These lawsuits try to get companies who allegedly caused this harm to pay the group that was affected.
- This bill requires that all class action settlement proposals include estimates of lawyers' fees if payment for the court's ruling are in the form of coupons.
- Requires that all members of the affected class be notified about settlement proposals.
- Sends to federal (not state) court all civil action in which the case involves more than $5 million, concerns a plaintiff of one state and a defendant of another, or involves a foreign state or its citizens.
- Grants judges expanded powers to determine if class action settlements are fair, reasonable, and adequate.

S AMDT 2807 to S CON RES 95: Reverse Tax Cuts on High Incomes

- Rolls back tax cuts for those whose income is above $1 million per year.
- Uses the funds raised for increases in homeland security spending and for paying down the national debt.

S AMDT 168 to S CON RES 18: Prohibit Drilling in ANWR

- Would keep the Arctic National Wildlife Refuge in Alaska closed to oil drilling.

S AMDT 1615 to S 397: Broaden Definition of Armor Piercing Ammunition

- Would classify any handgun ammunition that is capable of penetrating body armor as "armor piercing."
- Would ban all such "armor piercing" handgun ammunition as well as rifle ammunition that is marketed or designed specially for armor piercing.

S J RES 40: Federal Marriage Amendment

- Amends the Constitution of the United States to include a definition of marriage being only between a man and a woman.
- Prevents individual states from recognizing marital status or legal benefits from any other unions except those between a man and a woman.

S AMDT 2799 to S CON RES 95: Cigarette Tax Increase

- Increases taxes on cigarettes to $1 (the tax was previously 39 cents).
- Uses the funds raised by these taxes (estimated at $30.5 billion) to pay for increased spending on health programs such as medical research, disease control, wellness, tobacco addiction counseling, and preventative health efforts including substance abuse and mental health services.

S AMDT 3107 to S 1637: Overtime Pay Regulations

- The Department of Labor has proposed regulations that would eliminate overtime pay for anyone making over $100,000 per year or anyone making between $23,660 and $100,000 per year who works as an administrator or in a professional "white collar" job.
- This amendment would get rid of these regulations.

S AMDT 3379 to S 2400: Raise Tax Rate on Highest Income Bracket

- Raises the tax rate on all income above $326,450 per year from 35% to 36%.
- Uses the funds raised to pay for the security and stabilization of Iraq.

HR 4250: Jumpstart Our Business Strength Act

- Will reduce the corporate tax rate on domestic manufacturers and small corporations from 35% to 32% and provide about $145 billion in tax reductions to U.S. corporations over the next 10 years.
- Allows individual taxpayers who pay no state income tax to deduct their state sales tax on their federal tax returns.
- Would repeal certain tax regulations on foreign imports. The World Trade Organization had ruled these taxes in violation of their regulations, so repealing them will stop the WTO from penalizing U.S. exports.
- Allows private collection agencies to track down citizens who have not fully paid their taxes.

- Eliminates certain tax shelters and tax avoidance practices for businesses. This is expected to bring in about $63 billion in new tax revenue over the next 10 years.
- Ends federal price supports for tobacco farmers and allots $10 billion to tobacco farmers as compensation.
- Allows the Food and Drug Administration to regulate tobacco products.

S 2061: Healthy Mothers and Healthy Babies Access to Care Act

- Places a limit of $250,00 on noneconomic (pain and suffering) damages in lawsuits against obstetricians, gynecologists, and nurse midwives for medical malpractice.
- Allows people to sue these types of doctors for malpractice only within three years of the date of the appearance of injury or one year after the claimant discovers the injury.
- Allows punitive damages (meant to punish the accused) only in cases where doctors intentionally or knowingly harmed patients.
- When punitive damages are allowed, they are limited to two times the economic damages or $250,000 – whichever is greater.
- Limits the liability of manufacturers, distributors, and providers of gynecological products that have been approved by the Food and Drug Administration.
- Allows payments of certain medical malpractice verdicts to be paid in installments over time (rather than all at once).

S AMDT 2937 to HR 4: Child Care Funding for Welfare Recipients

- Provides an additional $6 billion to states over the next 5 years for child care for welfare recipients.
- This is paid for by renewing customs fees that would have expired.

S AMDT 3158 to S 2400: Military Base Closing Delays

- This measure would delay for two years the planned closing of several military bases in the U.S.
- Would also limit some of the planned closings of overseas military bases.

S AMDT 3584 to HR 4567: Stopping Privatization of Federal Jobs

- Would stop the government from contracting out 1,100 jobs in the Homeland Security Department's Citizenship and Immigration

Services bureau to private companies and would keep these jobs within the federal government.

HR 1308: Working Families Tax Relief Act

- Would extend the $1,000 per child tax credit through 2009.
- Would reduce taxes by extending the upper limit adjustment for the 10% tax bracket through 2010. This means that married couples would pay a 10% tax rate on their first $14,000 of yearly income. Without this extension, only the first $12,000 would be taxed at 10% and the rest at a higher rate.
- Would extend tax breaks for married couples (the elimination of the so-called "marriage penalty") through 2008.
- Would extend the existing income tax exemption from the alternative minimum tax for couples with incomes below $58,000.
- Extends the Research and Development tax credit, which allows businesses to deduct 20% of qualified research expenses, through 2010.

S AMDT 1026 to HR 2161: Prohibiting Roads in Tongass National Forest

- Would prohibit federal funds from being used to plan or build new roads for the purpose of logging in the Tongass National Forest in Alaska.

S AMDT 902 to HR 6: Fuel Economy Standards

- Would require that passenger cars made before 2008 average 25 miles per gallon.
- This requirement would be gradually increased to 40 miles per gallon by the year 2016.
- Nonpassenger (or commercial) vehicles would have to average 16 miles per gallon before 2008, and this standard would gradually increase to 27.5 miles per gallon.

HR 3199: USA Patriot Act Improvement and Reauthorization Act of 2005

- The USA Patriot Act gives the federal government expanded powers of surveillance, investigation, and prosecution against suspected terrorists, their associates, and those suspected of financing terrorism.
- This bill would extend two of the Patriot Act's provisions for four more years. These provisions involve allowing the government to use roving wiretaps to listen in on phone conversations and other communications

and permitting secret warrants for books, records, and other items from businesses, hospitals, and organizations such as libraries.

- The bill would permanently extend most of the other provisions in the Patriot Act allowing the government to have broader powers of investigation over its citizens and others living within its borders.

S AMDT 278 to S 600: Family Planning Aid Policy

- Under current U.S. policy, government money cannot be given to family planning organizations in other countries if these organizations perform or promote abortions, even if the U.S. money is not specifically used for this purpose.
- This vote would reverse this policy and allow U.S. funds to go to family planning organizations in other countries whether or not they promote or perform abortions.

S J RES 20: Disapproval of Mercury Emissions Rule

- This vote would replace the current credit-trading system for mercury emissions from power plants with a policy of strict limits on the amount of mercury that power plants can release into the atmosphere.

S AMDT 1977 to HR 2863: Banning Torture by U.S. Military Interrogators

- Would prohibit "cruel, inhuman or degrading treatment or punishment" against anyone in the custody of the U.S. military.
- Limits interrogation techniques to those authorized in the U.S. Army Field Manual on Intelligence Interrogation.

S AMDT 1645 to S 397: Increase Criminal Penalties for Armor Piercing Ammunition

- Would increase penalties for the use or possession of armor piercing ammunition while committing a crime.
- Would direct the Attorney General to conduct a study regarding such armor piercing ammunition and report back to Congress.

Have federal income tax rates increased or decreased since 2000?

Increased
Stayed the same
Decreased
Don't know

Has the federal budget surplus increased or decreased since 2000?

Increased
Stayed the same
Decreased
Don't know

Who provides most of the money to run public schools in this country?

Federal government
State and local governments
About equal
Don't know

When people are charged with a crime such as burglary, driving while intoxicated, or murder, what type of law are they usually charged with violating?

Federal law
State law
Don't know

Who favors raising the minimum wage?

Democrats
Republicans
Both
Neither
Don't know

Who favors developing a national missile defense shield?

Democrats
Republicans
Both
Neither
Don't know

Who favors putting fewer government restrictions on businesses?

Liberals
Conservatives
Both
Neither
Don't know

Who currently controls the U.S. House of Representatives?

> Democrats
> Republicans
> Don't know

Who currently controls the U.S. Senate?

> Democrats
> Republicans
> Don't know

Most people view themselves, as well as elected officials, as either liberals, conservatives, or somewhere in between. Thee following scale goes from 1, which represents an extremely liberal person, to 7, which represents an extremely conservative person. Where would you place the following people? ["Yourself," "George W. Bush," each of respondent's senators]

2008 Survey Question Wording

Generally speaking, do you usually think of yourself as a Republican, a Democrat, or an Independent? [follow up on strong Republican/Democrat or independent leaning Republican/Democrat/no lean]

Thinking about politics these days, how would you describe your own political viewpoint?

> Very liberal
> Liberal
> Moderate
> Conservative
> Very Conservative
> Not sure

If the election for president were held today, for whom would you vote?

> Barack Obama
> John McCain
> Someone else
> Not sure
> Will not vote

Did you vote in a presidential primary or caucus earlier this year?

Democratic
Republican
Did not vote
Not sure

Would you say Barack Obama is . . .

Very liberal
Somewhat liberal
Moderate
Somewhat conservative
Very conservative
Not sure

Would you say John McCain is . . .

Very liberal
Somewhat liberal
Moderate
Somewhat conservative
Very conservative
Not sure

[Introductory prompt] As you know, elected officials and candidates must make important decisions across many policy areas. For example:

[Three randomly chosen examples of positions held by Obama and McCain]

Now, we'd like to ask you about some of these sorts of issues.

Please tell us whether *you personally* agree or disagree with each of the statements below: [For each policy statement, options "Agree," "Disagree," and "Not sure" shown. Question order is randomized independently across respondents.]

The definition of marriage should apply only to relationships between a man and a woman.

A "windfall profits" tax should be imposed on large profits made by oil companies.

The Supreme Court's decision in *Roe v. Wade*, which legalized most forms of abortion, should be overturned.

Same-sex couples should be allowed to form civil unions that give them most of the same legal protections that married couples enjoy.

Up to $700 billion dollars should be spent to have the federal government purchase troubled assets from financial institutions in an attempt to remedy current economic troubles.

A mandatory cap on carbon dioxide emissions by American companies should be imposed, with a credit trading system so that companies who pollute less can sell their credits to other companies.

Tax cuts for those making over $250,000 should be reversed.

The United States should begin a phased withdrawal of troops from Iraq.

The federal government should require that all American children have health insurance.

Younger workers should be allowed to invest some of their Social Security contributions in private investment accounts.

[Note: Respondents were also asked, "Please tell us whether you think [Barack Obama or John McCain, presented in random order] agrees with each of the statements below," with the same set of ten policy statements shown for each candidate, each with answer options "Probably agrees," "Maybe agrees," "Maybe disagrees," "Probably disagrees," "Not sure."]

Do you happen to know what job or political office is currently held by Dick Cheney?

Speaker of the House
Senate Majority Leader
Vice President
Supreme Court Justice
Not sure

Whose responsibility is it to determine if a law is constitutional or not?

President
Congress
Supreme Court
Not sure

How much of a majority is required for the U.S. Senate and House to override a presidential veto?

One half
Two-thirds

Three-fourths
Nine-tenths
Not sure

Do you happen to know which political party currently has the most members in the House of Representatives?

Democratic
Republican
Not sure

Would you say that one of the political parties is more conservative than the other at the national level? Which party is more conservative?

Democratic
Republican
Not sure

Survey Sample Characteristics

This appendix presents tabulations of various demographic, political, and other characteristics from the primary surveys analyzed in this book (referred to as the 2004 and 2008 surveys). All tabulations from these surveys are of raw (unweighted) survey data, which are compared with tabulations from other surveys and sources. Breakdowns of demographic characteristics in the population of voters in the 2004 and 2008 general elections are taken from the U.S. Census Current Population Survey's (CPS) "Voting and Registration in the Election of November 2004"[1] and "Voting and Registration in the Election of 2008"[2] tables using only respondents in the "reported voted" category. Political information comparisons are made with the Pew Research Center for the People and the Press report titled "What Americans Know: 1989–2007"[3] and the American National Election Studies (ANES) Time Series Studies for 2004 and 2008.[4]

As discussed in the main text of the book, the 2004 survey was not designed to be nationally representative, having fewer minorities and generally being more educated and politically informed. The survey was drawn from the Polimetrix PollingPoint panel, but was not extensively matched or stratified for representativeness. Furthermore, the 2004 survey's sampling design was such that it included at least 100 respondents from each state, which caused smaller states to be significantly overrepresented. Accordingly, results from the 2004 survey should be interpreted

[1] http://www.census.gov/population/www/socdemo/voting/cps2004.html.
[2] http://www.census.gov/population/www/socdemo/voting/cps2008.html.
[3] http://people-press.org/reports/pdf/319.pdf.
[4] http://www.electionstudies.org/.

with some caution, particularly with regard to making generalizations to the population of all American voters.

Distributions of demographic and political factors from the 2008 survey, by contrast, correspond quite closely with those of the American electorate more generally. This survey was drawn from the YouGov/ Polimetrix PollingPoint panel using a sample matching technique (Rivers 2006). A random sample stratified by age, gender, race, education, and region was selected from the 2005–2007 Census Bureau's American Community Survey.[5] Voter registration, turnout, religion, news interest, minor party identification, and non-placement on an ideology scale were imputed from the 2004 Current Population Survey Registration and Voting Supplement[6] and the Pew Religion in American Life Survey.[7] Matching respondents were then selected from the PollingPoint panel, which is an opt-in Internet panel.

Respondents in the 2008 survey also showed comparable levels of political information to respondents from other surveys. For example, percentages of respondents correctly recognizing which party controlled the House of Representatives or which party is generally more conservative were quite close to proportions from other national surveys, particularly when focusing only on voters, which the surveys used here are intended to do (see Tables B.7 and B.8). A notable exception is that respondents to the 2008 ANES showed significantly lower levels of knowledge of House party control (58.1 percent among all respondents and 61.0 percent among reported voters). It should be noted, however, that the ANES asks this question in the post-election wave of the survey. Furthermore, they ask whether respondents know which party had more members in the House *before the last election*. While the 2008 election did not produce a shift in House party control (which would, presumably, increase the likelihood of respondents being confused by it), it still seems likely that this question is somewhat more challenging and perhaps more confusing than simply asking before an election which party currently controls the House.

Overall, more skeptical or conservative readers may think of results from the 2004 survey as being more tentative and speculative, while those from the 2008 survey serve to confirm these earlier findings with highly representative data. Comfortingly, virtually all of the book's main conclusions are supported by both surveys.

---

[5] http://www.census.gov/acs/.

[6] http://www.census.gov/hhes/www/socdemo/voting/index.html.

[7] http://religions.pewforum.org/.

TABLE B.1. *Gender*

	2004 Survey	2004 CPS	2008 Survey	2008 CPS
Male	.52	.47	.50	.46
	(3,077)	(58,455)	(996)	(60,729)
Female	.48	.53	.50	.54
	(2,790)	(67,281)	(1,004)	(70,415)

TABLE B.2. *Race*

	2004 Survey	2004 CPS	2008 Survey	2008 CPS
White	.85	.79	.72	.76
	(5,001)	(99,567)	(1,430)	(100,071)
Black	.03	.11	.12	.12
	(195)	(14,016)	(236)	(16,181)
Hispanic	.02	.06	.12	.07
	(110)	(7,587)	(247)	(9,734)
Other	.10	.04	.04	.02
	(561)	(4,593)	(87)	(5,226)

TABLE B.3. *Survey Sample Education Distributions*

	2004 Survey	2004 CPS	2008 Survey	2008 CPS
Less than High School	.01	.08	.05	.07
	(87)	(10,132)	(102)	(9,046)
High School Graduate	.13	.29	.38	.27
	(751)	(35,894)	(761)	(35,866)
Some College/Assoc. Degree	.50	.31	.31	.32
	(2,902)	(38,922)	(621)	(41,477)
Bachelor's Degree	.22	.21	.15	.22
	(1,308)	(26,579)	(300)	(29,330)
Advanced Degree	.14	.11	.11	.12
	(811)	(14,210)	(216)	(15,425)

TABLE B.4. *Survey Sample Age Distributions*

	2004 Survey	2004 CPS	2008 Survey	2008 CPS
18–24	.06	.08	.08	.09
	(350)	(11,639)	(161)	(12,515)
25–44	.33	.29	.34	.32
	(1,902)	(42,845)	(687)	(42,366)
45–64	.47	.31	.46	.39
	(2,753)	(47,327)	(916)	(50,743)
65–74	.12	.21	.10	.11
	(671)	(13,010)	(189)	(14,176)
75 and over	.03	.11	.02	.09
	(177)	(10,915)	(47)	(11,344)

TABLE B.5. *2004 Survey Sample Income Distributions*

	2004 Survey	2004 CPS
Less than $30,000	.15	.16
	(905)	(15,352)
$30,000–$49,999	.21	.18
	(1,254)	(17,610)
$50,000–$69,999	.20	.21
	(1,173)	(20,559)
$70,000–$99,999	.20	.14
	(1,187)	(13,434)
$100,000–$149,999	.13	.12
	(731)	(11,600)
$150,000 or more	.06	.07
	(377)	(7,137)
No answer	.04	.12
	(244)	(11,711)

TABLE B.6. *2008 Survey Sample Income Distributions*

	2008 Survey	2008 CPS
Less than $10,000	.03	.02
	(67)	(2,166)
$10,000–$14,999	.04	.02
	(82)	(2,248)
$15,000–$19,999	.04	.02
	(80)	(2,251)
$20,000–$24,999	.05	.07
	(97)	(6,606)
$25,000–$29,999	.06	–
	(120)	
$30,000–39,999	.11	.09
	(215)	(8,793)
$40,000–$49,999	.10	.07
	(198)	(7,307)
$50,000–$59,999	.09	.20
	(177)	(19,743)
$60,000–$69,999	.07	–
	(137)	
$70,000–$79,999	.08	.14
	(155)	(13,846)
$80,000–$99,999	.09	–
	(175)	
$100,000–$119,999	.05	.14
	(107)	(13,739)
$120,000–$149,999	.04	–
	(83)	
$150,000 or more	.05	.10
	(106)	(10,269)
No answer	.10	.13
	(199)	(13,286)

Note: CPS income categories differ somewhat from those used in the book's survey. Therefore, cell counts have been collapsed to roughly correspond to those used here. CPS categories are <$10,000, $10,000–$14,999, $15,000–$19,999, $20,000–$29,999, $30,000–$39,999, $40,000–$49,999, $50,000–$74,999, $75,000–$99,999, $100,000–$149,999, $150,000 and over, and Not reported.

TABLE B.7. *Survey Sample Political Information Distributions: Knowledge of House Party Control*

	2004 Survey	2004 Pew Study	2008 Survey	2007 Pew Study
Democrats	.03	.08	.76	.76
	(144)	(240)	(1,529)	(1,141)
Republicans	.94	.56	.09	.10
	(5,532)	(1,680)	(181)	(150)
Not sure/Skipped	.03	.36	.15	.14
	(195)	(1,080)	(290)	(211)

Note: Cell counts not available for 2004 and 2008 Pew studies, approximated based on survey's sample size of 3,000 and 1,502, respectively.

TABLE B.8. *Survey Sample Political Information Distributions: Which Party Is More Conservative?*

		2008 ANES	
	2008 Survey	All	Voters
Democrats	.06	.17	.13
	(108)	(344)	(217)
Republicans	.80	.67	.74
	(1,563)	(1,394)	(1,200)
Neither	–	.12	.10
		(246)	(160)
Not sure	.15	.05	.02
	(298)	(94)	(40)

Note: ANES measures are weighted. This question was not asked in the 2004 survey. In the 2008 survey, there was no "Neither" option, which, by removing an incorrect answer, might be expected to slightly increase the proportion of all other responses, including correct ones.

TABLE B.9. *Survey Sample Presidential Vote Distributions*

	2004 Survey	2004 Election	2008 Survey	2008 Election
Democrat	.49	.48	.51	.53
	(2,776)	(59,028,439)	(942)	(69,499,428)
Republican	.49	.52	.43	.46
	(2,792)	(62,040,610)	(797)	(59,950,323)
Other Party	.02	.10	.05	.01
	(138)	(1,224,499)	(96)	(2,013,371)
Not sure/Will not vote/Skipped	–	–	–	–
	(132)		(165)	

Note: Survey proportions omit "not sure" and "will not vote" responses for comparability.
Source: Dave Leip's Atlas of U.S. Presidential Elections (http://uselectionatlas.org).

Simplified Analyses of Ideology and Spatial Voting

In this appendix, simplified models of vote choice are presented based on additive ideology scales, partisanship, and additive political information scales in contrast to the more sophisticated analyses involving latent traits model estimates for ideology and political information. While more sophisticated models confer important advantages, including the ability to obtain meaningful measures of uncertainty and to perform direct statistical tests of specific hypotheses, they also rely on assumptions whose validity can be questioned. Therefore, it is useful to attempt to replicate these analyses using simpler measures. The results presented here demonstrate that the central findings of the book are not driven by the specific statistical models employed, but that the same conclusions also are reached when using more basic measures and models.

This appendix introduces a simpler method of estimating the ideological positions of voters and candidates based on the percentage of surveyed issues on which each respondent or candidate took a conservative position. These liberal–conservative issues are coded based on common understandings of the ideological direction of each proposal. Furthermore, these ideological directions were in agreement with the signs of the discrimination parameters estimated in more sophisticated models (see Tables 3.1 and 3.2) in all but two cases. First, S. Amdt. 3107 to S. 1637, which dealt with altering overtime pay regulations, was coded here as a liberal proposal despite having a positive (albeit very small in magnitude) discrimination parameter estimate. Second, the "bailout bill" included in the 2008 survey, which, despite being estimated to have a negative discrimination parameter, does not have as natural of a liberal or conservative slant, was omitted from these analyses.

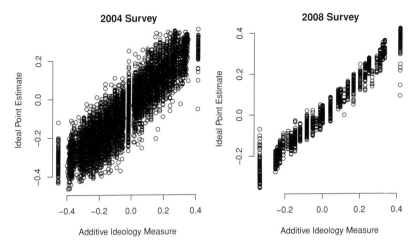

FIGURE C.1. Comparison of simple additive ideology measure with ideal point estimates

For easier comparison to the analyses presented in the main text, these new ideology measures are rescaled so that the Democratic and Republican candidates in each election have scores of $-1/4$ and $1/4$, respectively, in ideal point estimates in the main text. This linear transformation does not change any of the information in the scale and is equivalent to measuring a temperature in degrees Celsius instead of Fahrenheit (or a distance in inches instead of centimeters) – for each score, a certain number is simply subtracted and the difference is then divided by another number. Because the candidates are now at the same position on this new ideology measure and the original ideal point measure, the coefficients in these new models can be compared more easily with those presented in the main text.

At the outset, it is comforting to note that these new ideology measures are correlated very highly with the ideal point measures used in the main analyses. Figure C.1 shows a scatterplot of the two ideology measures against each other for survey respondents in the 2004 and 2008 surveys. The correlations between these measures are .89 and .97 for the 2004 and 2008 surveys, respectively. It should not be surprising that the 2004 survey estimates are somewhat noisier. Each respondent to the 2004 survey was shown only a random subset of the full set of policy proposals, which would be expected to increase the variance of the simple additive ideology measure. This issue also applies to the estimated ideal points of Kerry and Bush, who took positions on only seventeen and fifteen, respectively, of the issues analyzed. Therefore, the precise location of their

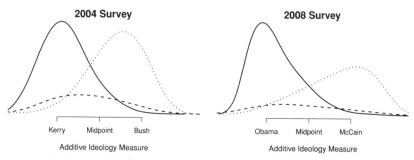

FIGURE C.2. Density of simple additive ideal point estimates. Plots show density of estimated ideology, using simple additive method, for respondents in the 2004 and 2008 surveys separated by party identification, with solid, dotted, and dashed lines indicating Democratic, independent, and Republican respondents, respectively. Candidate positions are shown on the horizontal axis.

ideological positions and of the midpoint between them will be estimated with a nontrivial amount of error. The ideal point approach to measuring ideology, by contrast, is likely to reduce this variation because it is based on a full model, which, among other things, estimates and accounts for the differences in the ideological characteristics of each proposal shown to respondents. On the whole, though, these measures are quite similar to the ideal point measures used in the main text of the book. Furthermore, as shown in Figure C.2, the shapes of the distributions of respondent ideology based on the simple additive measures are nearly identical to those based on ideal point models (see Figure 3.6).

Presidential Vote Choice Model Replications with Additive Measures

In addition to showing that the simple additive ideology measures are highly correlated with the more advanced ideal point estimates, another relevant question is whether the conclusions drawn from the probit regression models of presidential vote choice also hold when using these more basic ideology estimates. Table C.1 shows the estimated coefficients from models predicting 2004 and 2008 presidential vote with the simple additive ideology measures. In both cases, we see similar conclusions to those drawn from the models presented in the main text involving ideal point estimates of ideology. For both elections, there is estimated to be a slight spatial bias toward the Republican candidate (positive and statistically significant estimates for the intercept term) and a very large estimated effect for ideology on vote choice. Recall that these estimates are directly

TABLE C.1. *Spatial Utility Model Parameter Estimates, Simple Additive Ideology Measure*

Coefficient	Vote Model Parameter	2004 Estimates (Standard Errors)	2008 Estimates (Standard Errors)
Intercept	δ	.38 (.02)	.16 (.05)
Ideology	a	7.12 (.16)	6.57 (.26)
	Log-likelihood	−1,984.2	−534.1
	N	5,567	1,711

comparable with those in Table 4.1 because in both cases, the scales are identified such that the Democratic and Republican candidates are located at $-1/4$ and $1/4$, respectively. The estimated effects of ideology are somewhat smaller using the simple additive measures, particularly in 2004, although this is to be expected given the larger variability discussed in the previous paragraph, which presumably leads to attenuation of the estimated coefficient.

Table C.2 presents replications of the models from Table 5.1, which include separate intercepts for Democratic-, independent-, and Republican-identifying respondents. These estimates are overall quite similar to those presented in the main text. Partisans exhibit strong spatial biases toward the candidate of their party, whereas independent voters

TABLE C.2. *Spatial Utility Model Parameter Estimates from Varying Intercept Model, Simple Additive Ideology Measure*

Coefficient	Utility Model Parameter	2004 Estimates (Standard Errors)	2008 Estimates (Standard Errors)
Democrat Intercept	δ_{Dem}	−1.32 (.06)	−77 (.08)
Independent Intercept	δ_{Ind}	.09 (.06)	.13 (.14)
Republican Intercept	δ_{Rep}	1.83 (.06)	1.19 (.09)
Ideology	a	4.89 (.24)	4.64 (.32)
	Log-likelihood	−807.4	−326.9
	N	5,411	1,690

TABLE C.3. *Estimated Spatial Utility Model Parameters from Varying Intercept, Varying Slope Model, Simple Additive Ideology Measure*

Coefficient	Utility Model Parameter	2004 Survey			2008 Survey		
		Dem	Ind	Rep	Dem	Ind	Rep
Intercept	$\delta_{pty(i)}$	−1.38	.15	1.81	−.79	.14	1.20
		(.07)	(.06)	(.06)	(.08)	(.14)	(.09)
Ideology	$a_{pty(i)}$	3.98	5.97	4.50	4.40	4.81	4.89
		(.42)	(.41)	(.42)	(.46)	(.75)	(.56)
	Log-likelihood	−259.4	−276.5	−265.1	−188.4	−55.8	−118.5
	N	2,325	644	2,441	861	125	703

are largely unbiased. Ideology is estimated to have substantively large and highly statistically significant effects on vote choice, albeit again with somewhat smaller effects than those estimated based on ideal point measures of ideology. We also see similar conclusions when the effects of ideology are estimated separately, as shown in Table C.3.

Finally, Table C.4 shows the results of probit models of presidential vote choice based on simplified additive measures of not only ideology, but also respondents' political information levels. These information measures, in contrast to the latent-traits estimates employed in the main text, are calculated simply by summing up the number of political information

TABLE C.4. *Spatial Model with Information Coefficient Estimates, Simple Additive Ideology and Information Measures*

	2004 Survey			2008 Survey		
	Dem	Ind	Rep	Dem	Ind	Rep
Intercept	−1.38	.09	1.79	−.71	.14	1.18
	(.07)	(.07)	(.06)	(.09)	(.16)	(.09)
Ideology	4.18	6.51	4.92	4.58	5.07	4.71
	(.47)	(.46)	(.45)	(.52)	(.84)	(.61)
Information	−.06	−.09	−.14	.31	.09	.12
	(.06)	(.06)	(.07)	(.10)	(.12)	(.11)
Ideology × Information	1.18	1.63	.73	2.34	1.37	.51
	(.43)	(.39)	(.42)	(.49)	(.67)	(.85)
Log-likelihood	−251.6	−259.7	−256.5	−176.9	−53.6	−117.9
N	2,325	644	2,441	861	125	703

questions that each respondent in the 2004 or 2008 survey answered correctly. For each of these surveys, the measures are then standardized by subtracting off the mean and dividing by the standard deviation. This produces simple political information measures that have the same scale as those used in the main text. The results from these new models are again quite similar to those based on the more advanced latent traits measures of ideology and information. The only meaningful differences are the slightly smaller effects estimated for ideology and information, which, because of the rougher measures used for each, are to be expected.

Nonparametric Models of Presidential Vote Choice

In addition to the statistical models used to measure ideology and political information, the choice of model used to predict presidential vote choice necessarily involves adding a set of specific assumptions. In general, the probit regression models used in the main text of the book are common and well accepted in the social sciences and in the statistical community more generally, having a long history of use in modeling binary dependent variables. These models do, however, imply (at least in the specifications used here) that the relationship between ideology and the probability of casting a Republican vote for president is monotonic and, even more specifically, that it follows the shape of the normal cumulative distribution function, which is a specific type of *s*-shaped curve. In order to verify these assumptions, this section presents the results of several nonparametric LOESS regression fits. LOESS regression is a very flexible method for estimating the relationship between variables without making strong assumptions about the specific shape of the relationship. The focus of this section is on verifying that the relevant characteristics of the relationships between ideology and vote choice that were estimated in the main text still remain when estimated not only when using simpler measures for ideology, but also when using these more flexible regression methods.

Figure C.3 shows the estimated relationships between ideology and vote choice, which are extremely similar to those seen in Figure 5.2. In both the 2004 and 2008 elections, voters are estimated to have their vote choices strongly affected by their ideological positions, with more conservative voters being much more likely to cast their ballots for the Republican candidate. Furthermore, we see that just as predicted by the probit models in the main text, the 2004 vote probability curve passes slightly above .5 for voters at the actual midpoint of zero between the two candidates, whereas in 2008, the curve crosses quite close to the point predicted by unbiased spatial voting.

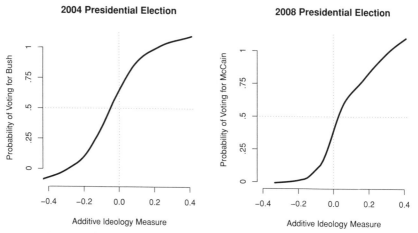

FIGURE C.3. Predicted vote probabilities, simple additive ideology measure. Plots show LOESS curves of presidential vote choice (coded 1 for Republican candidates and 0 for Democratic candidates) as a function of simple additive ideology measures.

The relationships estimated by separate LOESS fits for Democrats, independents, and Republicans also are broadly similar to those from the probit model fits of Figure 5.3. Both show that while voters of all partisan stripes are affected by ideology, partisans also are strongly biased

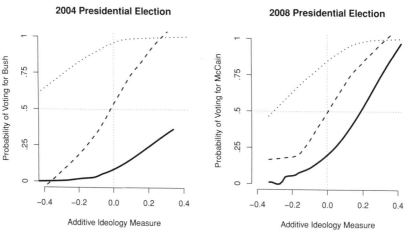

FIGURE C.4. Predicted vote probabilities by party identification, simple additive ideology measure. Plots show LOESS curves of presidential vote choice (coded 1 for Republican candidates and 0 for Democratic candidates) estimated as a function of simple additive ideology measures. LOESS curves are estimated separately for each party identification group.

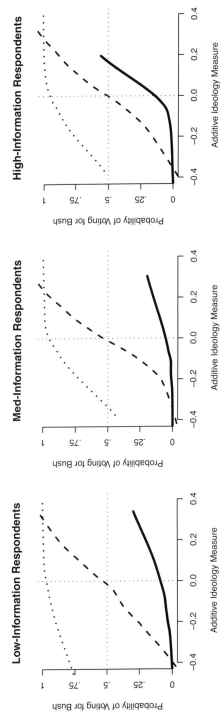

FIGURE C.5. Predicted vote probabilities by party identification and information level, simple additive ideology measure, 2004 survey. Plots show LOESS curves of presidential vote choice (coded 1 for Bush and 0 for Kerry) estimated as a function of simple additive ideology measures. LOESS curves are estimated separately by party identification and information level.

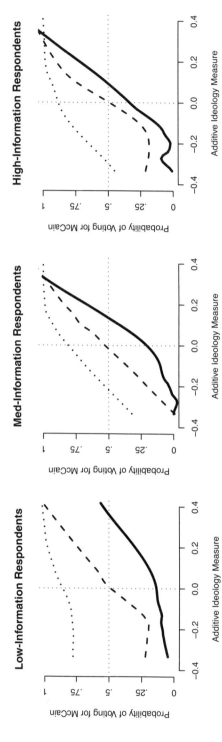

FIGURE C.6. Predicted vote probabilities by party identification and information level, simple additive ideology measure, 2008 survey. Plots show LOESS curves of presidential vote choice (coded 1 for McCain and 0 for Obama) estimated as a function of simple additive ideology measures. LOESS curves are estimated separately by party identification and information level.

toward their party's candidate. Independents in both 2004 and 2008 are estimated to have predicted vote curves that pass almost exactly through the point (0, .5), which indicates perfectly unbiased spatial voting. The chief difference between these LOESS estimates and the probit estimates in the main text are that the nonparametric fits show slightly flatter relationships between ideology and vote choice, particularly in the 2004 election. As discussed previously, however, this is to be expected given the somewhat noisier estimates that are produced by the simple additive measures.

Figure C.4 shows LOESS fits of vote choice as a function of ideology and partisanship. Again, these results are substantively similar to those presented in the main text (see Figure 5.2). All respondents show higher probabilities of voting for the Republican candidate as they become more conservative, but large gaps remain between partisans of different types. Independent voters are predicted to be close to unbiased spatial voters.

Finally, Figures C.5 and C.6 show LOESS fits of presidential vote choice as a function of ideology, separated by both partisanship and political information level. Again, these results are quite similar to the probit model predictions from Figures 6.2 and 6.3. Low-information voters show larger partisan gaps than medium- or high-information voters, with all voters being affected by ideology and independents exhibiting little or no spatial bias. These nonparametric fits are slightly more noisy because of the larger number of categories, which results in smaller numbers of observations per LOESS fit.

Discussion

Overall, these simplified analyses serve to reinforce the conclusions drawn from the more complicated (and, I would argue, more appropriate, measures) used in the main text. They demonstrate the best of both words for the substantive findings found here. Both simple models, which rely on fewer assumptions, but may not use the data as effectively as possible, and more sophisticated models, which allow for more principled estimates, but also involve stronger assumptions, produce the same conclusions. The central findings presented in this book are therefore clearly not driven by obscure statistical assumptions or scaling techniques, but instead are broadly suggested by the data, even when analyzed using multiple methods.

APPENDIX D

American National Election Studies Analyses

This appendix presents the results of analyses of ideology and spatial voting using the 2004 and 2008 American National Election Studies (ANES) Time Series Studies. Because the ANES is the most commonly used data source in American political behavior research, readers may be curious whether the results in the main text of this book can be "replicated" by analyzing the ANES. As discussed in the main text (see Chapter 3 in particular), the measures used in the ANES are not ideally suited to an investigation of spatial voting. Accordingly, to "replicate" the book's main analyses using ANES data necessarily entails strong (I would argue heroic) assumptions. This exercise is still likely to be useful, however, both because it highlights the benefits of the main measurement approaches used in the book in contrast to the standard approach in the field and also because of the centrality of the ANES to American political research.

The main ANES measure of ideology is a simple ordered seven-point scale on which respondents are asked to place themselves from "extremely liberal" to "extremely conservative." For better or worse, these items have provided the most commonly used measures of the ideological positions of survey respondents in both the ANES and other political surveys. The ANES also asks respondents to place presidential candidates on this same scale. The most common method for attempting to compare the positions of candidates and voters on such self-placement scales is to assume that the means of respondent placements of each candidate are accurate. In other words, scholars often assume that respondents are perfectly unbiased in their assessments of candidate ideology. This assumption, while dubious for reasons that I argue in the main text, is employed in this appendix as a way of investigating how the answers yielded by traditional approaches to

214

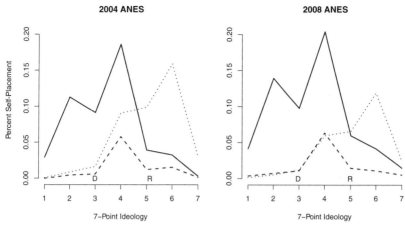

FIGURE D.1. Distributions of self-placed seven-point scale ideology, 2004 and 2008 ANES. Plots show the proportion of Democratic, independent, and Republican respondents in the 2004 and 2008 ANES who placed themselves at each point (1–7) on the ideological scale. Solid, dotted, and dashed lines indicate Democratic, independent, and Republican respondent distributions, respectively. Average respondent perceptions of Democratic and Republican presidential candidates are shown as "D" and "R," respectively, in each plot.

the measurement of respondent and candidate ideology would compare to those produced in the book.

Figure D.1 shows the distribution of self-placed seven-point ideology among respondents to the 2004 and 2008 ANES surveys. These distributions, while much lumpier because of the discrete nature of the ANES ideology scales, generally have somewhat similar characteristics to those presented in the main text (see Figure 3.6). The main difference is the higher proportion of self-identified moderates, particularly among Democratic identifiers, in the ANES results. This should not be unexpected, however, given the well-known bias observed in symbolic identification with the terms "liberal" and "conservative" (see, e.g., Stimson 1975) as well as the connotations of the term "moderate." In particular, this discrepancy highlights the conceptual difference between the standard ANES measure, which is essentially about ideological self-identification, and the primary measure of ideology used in the main text, which is a measure of policy ideology.

Table D.1 presents estimates of a probit model predicting presidential vote (coded as 0 for Democratic and 1 for Republican) as a function of respondents' self-placed ideologies. In both the 2004 and 2008 ANES,

TABLE D.1. *Estimated Spatial Utility Model Parameters, ANES Data*

Coefficient	2004 Estimates (Standard Errors)	2008 Estimates (Standard Errors)
Intercept	−2.42	−2.37
	(.17)	(.13)
Self-Placed Ideology	.57	.48
	(.04)	(.03)
Log-likelihood	−1178.3	−962.4
N	852	1,447

Probit regression results predicting presidential vote choice (coded 0 for Democratic candidate and 1 for Republican candidate) with self-placed seven-point ideology.

strong and highly significant positive effects are estimated for ideology indicating that more conservative respondents are much more likely to vote for the Republican candidate for president. It should be noted here and elsewhere in this appendix that the scale of the ideology measures used here is significantly different from those used in the main text. Therefore, predicted probability figures are the easiest way to understand the specific forms of the relationships between self-placed ideology and vote probability.

As Figure D.2 shows, the predicted vote probabilities based on the results in Table D.1 correspond somewhat closely, although not exactly, to the predictions of unbiased spatial voting. Both curves are clearly increasing, and the curve for the 2004 ANES crosses .5 almost exactly at the estimated midpoint between the candidates' positions. The 2008 curve, by contrast, suggests some bias toward the Democratic candidate, with voters having to place their ideology at a 5, almost exactly at the average placement of John McCain's ideology, in order to be equally likely to choose either candidate. These results are somewhat skewed toward the Democratic candidate as compared with those in the main text (Figure 4.6). This is not unexpected given the fact that some ANES respondents may be reluctant to call themselves "liberals" even if their policy views suggest they clearly are.

Table D.2 presents estimates of the coefficients from probit models predicting vote choice, now including separate intercepts for each partisan grouping. These results are somewhat similar to those in the main text (see Figure 5.2), but, as Figure D.3 shows, with Democrats and Republicans being strongly biased toward their party's candidate. Perhaps more

TABLE D.2. *Estimated Spatial Utility Model Parameters Varying Intercept Model, ANES Data*

Coefficient	2004 Estimates (Standard Errors)	2008 Estimates (Standard Errors)
Democrat Intercept	−2.17 (.21)	−2.13 (.15)
Independent Intercept	−1.07 (.29)	−1.27 (.19)
Republican Intercept	.23 (.26)	.09 (.18)
Self-Placed Ideology	.26 (.05)	.20 (.03)
Log-likelihood	−588.5	−994.7
N	850	1,436

Cells show estimated probit coefficients with standard deviations underneath in parentheses from models predicting presidential vote with self-placed seven-point ideology and separate intercepts by respondent partisanship.

notably, although independent voters in the 2004 ANES are estimated to have little if any spatial bias, respondents to the 2008 ANES are skewed toward the Democratic candidate when compared with the baseline of unbiased spatial voting.

Table D.3 and Figure D.4 show the results of estimated probit coefficients from vote choice models estimated separately by partisanship in both the 2004 and 2008 ANES. Although Democratic and Republican respondents in both studies show strong effects for ideology on vote

TABLE D.3. *Estimated Spatial Utility Model Parameters Varying Intercept, Varying Slope Model, ANES Data*

Coefficient	2004 Estimates			2008 Estimates		
	Dem	Ind	Rep	Dem	Ind	Rep
Intercept	−2.12 (.26)	.24 (.78)	−.20 (.40)	−2.02 (.18)	−.51 (.42)	−.52 (.30)
Self-Placed Ideology	.24 (.07)	−.04 (.17)	.35 (.08)	.17 (.04)	.02 (.10)	.32 (.06)
Log-likelihood	−141.8	−30.5	−98.6	−236.4	−65.3	−203.1
N	409	44	396	815	103	517

Cells show estimated coefficients, with corresponding spatial utility model parameters from separate probit models for Democrat, independent, and Republican voters, predicting vote choice with self-placed seven-point ideology.

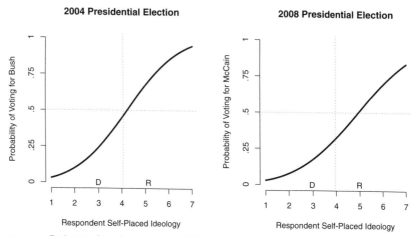

FIGURE D.2. Predicted vote probabilities, ANES data. Plots show the predicted probabilities of voting for the Republican candidate as a function of respondent ideal point based on the probit model coefficient estimates shown in Table D.1. Vertical dotted lines are plotted at the midpoint between estimated candidate positions, and horizontal dotted lines are at .5.

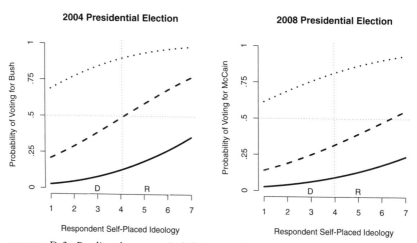

FIGURE D.3. Predicted vote probabilities, varying intercept model, ANES data. Curves show the predicted probabilities of voting for the Republican candidate in the 2004 and 2008 election as a function of a voter's self-placed seven-point ideologies for Democrats (solid lines), independents (dashed lines), and Republicans (dotted lines). Probabilities are calculated based on the estimates presented in Table D.2.

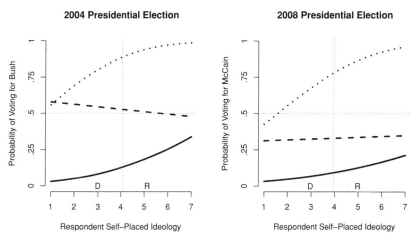

FIGURE D.4. Predicted vote probabilities, varying intercept and slope model, ANES data. Curves show the predicted probabilities of voting for the Republican candidate in the 2004 and 2008 elections as a function of a voter's ideological position for Democrats (solid lines), independents (dashed lines), and Republicans (dotted lines). Probabilities are calculated based on the estimates presented in Table D.3 separated by respondent party identification.

choice, independent voters show little influence from ideology. This stands in sharp contrast to the results presented in the main text (Table 5.5) in which independents were actually estimated to to be influenced more strongly by ideology than partisans. There are several possible reasons for these discrepancies. First, the ANES studies contain a relatively small number of independent respondents who stated a presidential vote intention as well as placed themselves on the seven-point ideological scale. It is possible that with only 44 and 103 such independents in the 2004 and 2008 ANES, respectively, there are simply not enough data to reliably estimate the effects of ideology within this subset of respondents. It should be pointed out, however, that the 2008 survey analyzed in the book had only 130 respondents and was able to estimate a large and highly statistically significant effect for ideology on the vote choices of independents. It is also possible that the nature of the seven-point scale is such that it provides less (or less detailed) information about respondent ideology. Finally, it is possible that independent voters are simply less likely describe themselves in ideological terms. Figure D.1 shows that the majority of independents in both ANES studies categorize themselves as moderates. This leaves little variation within this subgroup and is likely to contribute to these null findings.

TABLE D.4. *Estimated Spatial Utility Model Parameters from Party and Information Spatial Model, ANES Data*

	2004 ANES		
	Dem	Ind	Rep
Intercept	−2.20	−.46	−.23
	(.30)	(1.03)	(.42)
Self-Placed Ideology	.26	.11	.35
	(.07)	(.23)	(.09)
Political Information	−.91	−.88	−.28
	(.31)	(.83)	(.41)
Self-Placed Ideology × Political Information	.18	.20	.06
	(.08)	(.18)	(.09)
N	409	44	396
Log Likelihood	−128.7	−29.8	−89.1

Cells show estimated coefficients, with corresponding with standard deviations underneath in parentheses, for probit model predicting presidential vote (coded 0 for Democratic candidate and 1 for Republican candidate) with respondent self-placed seven-point ideology, political information level, and an interaction between the two. Analyses of the 2008 ANES data are not included because open-ended political information items have not been coded at this time.

Finally, Table D.4 shows the results of probit models for Democratic, independent, and Republican respondents to the 2004 ANES predicting vote choice with self-placed ideology, political information level, and an interaction between the two. Political information level is estimated using the same latent traits estimation technique used in the main text (see Equation 6.1) based on ANES respondents' answers to questions about whether income taxes have increased, decreased, or stayed about the same during George W. Bush's time as president; whether the difference in incomes between rich and poor is larger, smaller, or about the same as it was twenty years ago; which political party controls the House of Representatives; and name recognition items for Tony Blair, Dick Cheney, Dennis Hastert, and William Rehnquist. The 2008 ANES is not included in these analyses because the survey's open-ended political information items had still not been coded at the time of writing.

The results are somewhat similar to those from the main text (Table 6.3 and Figure 6.2), but show weaker evidence for an interactive effect for ideology and information. The interaction term is only statistically significant for Democratic respondents. Although the size of the estimated interaction term is actually largest for independents, its standard error is

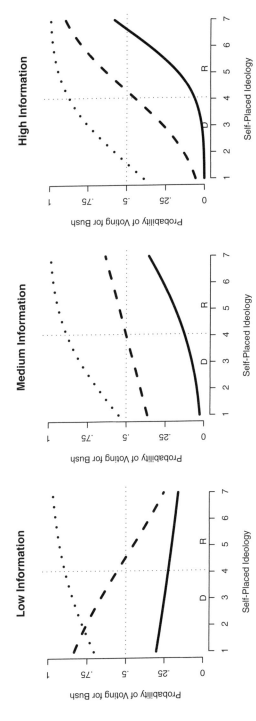

FIGURE D.5. Predicted vote probabilities from partisan spatial model, 2004 ANES data. Curves show the predicted probabilities of voting for the Republican candidate in the 2004 election as a function of a voter's ideological position for Democrats (solid lines), independents (dashed lines), and Republicans (dotted lines) at low, medium, and high information levels defined as the .05 quantile, mean, and .95 quantiles, respectively, of political information for the sample. Probabilities are calculated based on the estimates presented in Table D.4.

221

nearly as large as the coefficient itself, suggesting that it is unclear whether ideology actually has a stronger effect on vote choice for more informed independents and Republicans. As in the previous analyses, it is likely that the smaller sample sizes, particularly for independents, as well as the granularity of the data both contribute to the null findings here.

Figure D.5 plots predicted probability curves for low-, medium-, and high-information voters based on the model's estimates. The overall behavior of these curves is somewhat similar to those in the main text, although the results for low-information voters are somewhat surprising. The effects of ideology are actually estimated to be negative for these respondents, but it should again be noted that the interaction terms that produce these relationships are not themselves statistically significant.

Overall, the results of these analyses of ANES data demonstrate that while some of the findings presented in the main text also are supported by analyzing more traditional surveys, many are not. Furthermore, these analyses highlight the limitations of traditional ideology measurement as well as the basic differences in their meaning. While the results of an analysis of ideology and spatial voting based on ANES data reach some of the same conclusions as do the approaches used in the main text, they are limited in what they can demonstrate and, even more seriously, they rely on strong, often unreasonable, assumptions in order to reach these conclusions.

Bibliography

Alan I. Abramowitz and Kyle L. Saunders. Ideological realignment in the U.S. electorate. *Journal of Politics*, 69:634–52, 1998.

Christopher H. Achen. Mass political attitudes and the survey response. *The American Political Science Review*, 69(4):1218–31, 1975.

Christopher H. Achen. Toward theories of data: The state of political methodology. In Ada W. Finifter, editor, *Political Science: The State of the Discipline*, 69–93. Washington, DC: American Political Science Association, 1983.

Christopher H. Achen. Social psychology, demographic variables, and linear regression: breaking the iron triangle in voting research. *Political Behavior*, 14(3):195–211, 1992.

James F. Adams. Multicandidate spatial competition with probabilistic voting. *Public Choice*, 100:103–22, 1999.

James F. Adams. A theory of spatial competition with biased voters: party policies viewed temporally and comparatively. *British Journal of Political Science*, 31: 121–58, 2001.

James F. Adams and Samuel Merrill III. Voter turnout and candidate strategies in American elections. *The Journal of Politics*, 65(1):161–89, 2008.

James F. Adams, Samuel Merrill III, and Bernard Grofman. *A Unified Theory of Party Competition*. New York: Cambridge University Press, 2005.

John H. Aldrich. A Downsian spatial model with party activism. *American Political Science Review*, 7:974–90, 1983.

John H. Aldrich and Richard D. McKelvey. A method of scaling with applications to the 1968 and 1972 presidential elections. *The American Political Science Review*, 71(1):111–30, 1977.

Michael R. Alvarez and Jonathan Nagler. Economics, issues and the Perot candidacy: voter choice in the 1992 presidential election. *American Journal of Political Science*, 39:714–44, 1995.

Stephen Ansolabehere and Philip E. Jones. Constituents' responses to congressional roll-call voting. *American Journal of Political Science*, 54(3):583–97, 2010.

Stephen Ansolabehere and James M. Snyder. Valence politics and equilibrium in spatial elections models. *Public Choice*, 103:327–36, 2000.

Stephen Ansolabehere, Jonathan Rodden, and James M. Snider. Issue preferences and measurement error. MIT Working Paper, 2006.

Stephen Ansolabehere, Jonathan Rodden, and James M. Snyder. The strength of issues: using multiple measures to gauge preference stability, ideological constraint, and issue voting. *American Political Science Review*, 102:215–32, 2008.

Peter H. Aranson and Peter C. Ordeshook. Spatial strategies for sequential elections. In Richard Nieme and Herbert Weisberg, editors, *Probability Models of Collective Decision Making*, 298–331. Columbus, OH: Merrill, 1972.

Joeseph Bafumi and Ian Shapiro. A new partisasn voter. *Journal of Politics*, 71(1):1–24, 2009.

Bernard R. Berelson, Paul F. Lazarsfeld, and William McPhee. *Voting: A Study of Opinion Formation in a Presidential Campaign*. Chicago: University of Chicago Press, 1954.

Duncan Black. On the rationale of group decision-making. *The Journal of Political Economy*, 56:23, 1948.

Robert G. Boatright. Who are the spatial voting violators? *Electoral Studies*, 27 (1):116–25, 2008.

Henry E. Brady and Paul M. Sniderman. Attitude attribution: a group basis for political reasoning. *The American Political Science Review*, 79(4):1061–78, 1985.

Richard A. Brody and Benjamin I. Page. Comment: the assessment of policy voting. *American Political Science Review*, 66(2):450–8, 1972.

Melvin J. Hinich, Lawrence Cahoon, and Peter C. Ordeshook. A statistical multidimensional scaling method based on the spatial theory of voting. In Peter C. Wang, editor, *Graphical Representations of Multivariate Data*, 243–78. Orlando: Academic Press, 1978.

Angus Campbell, Warren E. Converse, Phillip E. Miller, and Donald E. Stokes. *The American Voter*. Chicago: University of Chicago Press, 1960.

Albert Cantril and Susan D. Cantril. *Reading Mixed Signals: Ambivalence in Public Opinion about Government*. Washington, DC: Woodrow Wilson Press, 1999.

David Chapman. Models of the working of a two-party electoral system – i. *Public Choice*, 3:19–37, 1967.

David Chapman. Models of the working of a two-party electoral system – ii. *Public Choice*, 5:19–37, 1968.

Joshua Clinton, Simon Jackman, and Douglas Rivers. The statistical analysis of roll call data: a unified approach. *American Political Science Review*, 98: 355–70, 2004a.

Joshua Clinton, Simon Jackman, and Douglas Rivers. 'The most liberal senator'?: Analyzing and interpreting congressional roll calls. *PS: Political Science and Politics*, 37:805–11, 2004b.

James S. Coleman. The positions of political parties in elections. In Richard Nieme and Herbert Weisberg, editors, *Spatial Strategies for Sequential Elections*, 332–57. Columbus, OH: Merrill, 1972.

Pamela J. Conover, Virginia Gray, and Steven Coombs. Single-issue voting: elite-mass linkages. *Political Behavior*, 4(4):309–31, 1982.

Philip E. Converse. The nature of belief systems in mass publics. In Richard Nieme and Herbert Weisberg, editors, *Ideology and Discontent*, 322–57. New York: Free Press, 1964.

Philip E. Converse and Gregory A. Markus. Plus ca change...: the new CPS election study panel. *American Political Science Review*, 73:32–49, 1979.

Peter Coughlin. *Probabilistic Voting Theory*. New York: Cambridge University Press, 1992.

Michael X. Delli Carpini and Scott Keeter. Measuring political knowledge: putting first things first. *American Journal of Political Science*, 37(4):1179–206, 1993.

Anthony Downs. *An Economic Theory of Democracy*. New York: HarperCollins, 1957.

Bradley Efron. Bootstrap methods: another look at the jackknife. *The Annals of Statistics*, 7(1):1–26, 1979.

Christopher Ellis and James A. Stimson. Pathways to ideology in American politics: the operational-symbolic "paradox" revisited. Unpublished Manuscript, 2007.

James Enelow and Melvin J. Hinich. *The Spatial Theory of Voting: An Introduction*. New York: Cambridge University Press, 1984.

Robert S. Erikson. The SRC panel data and mass political attitudes. *British Journal of Political Science*, 9(01):89–114, 2009.

Robert S. Erikson and David Romero. Candidate equilibrium and the behavioral model of the voter. *American Political Science Review*, 84:1103–26, 1990.

Robert S. Erikson, Gerald C. Wright, and John P. McIver. *Statehouse Democracy: Public Opinion and Policy in the American States*. New York: Cambridge University Press, 1993.

Scott Feld and Bernard Grofman. Voter loyalty, incumbency advantage, and the benefit of the doubt. *Journal of Theoretical Politics*, 3:115–37, 1991.

Morris P. Fiorina. *Retrospective Voting in American National Elections*. New Haven: Yale University Press, 1981.

Lloyd A. Free and Hadley Cantril. *The Political Beliefs of American: A Study of Public Opinion*. New Brunswick, NJ: Rutgers University Press, 1967.

Milton Friedman. The methodology of positive economics. In Daniel M. Hausman, editor, *The Philosophy of Economics: An Anthology*, 180–213. New York: Cambridge University Press, 1984.

Alan S. Gerber, Gregory A. Huber, and Ebonya Washington. Party affiliation, parisanship and political beliefs: a field experiment. *American Political Science Review*, 104(4):720–45, 2010.

Paul Goren. Political expertise and issue voting in presidential elections. *Political Research Quarterly*, 50(2):387–412, 1997.

Donald Green and Ian Shapiro. *Pathologies of Rational Choice Theory: A Critique of Applications in Political Science*. New Haven, CT: Yale University Press, 1994.

Bernard Grofman, William Koetzle, and Anthony J. McGann. Congressional leadership 1965–96: A new look at the extremism versus centrality debate. *Legislative Studies Quarterly*, 27(1):87–105, 2002.

Bernard Grofman. Downs and two-party convergence. *Annual Review of Political Science*, 7:25–46, 2004.

Timothy Groseclose. A model of candidate location when one candidate has a valence advantage. *American Journal of Political Science*, 45:862–86, 2001.

James J. Heckman and James M. Snyder. Linear probability models of the demand for attributes with an empirical application to estimating the preferences of legislators. *RAND Journal of Economics*, 28:142–89, 1997.

Seth Hill, James Lo, Lynn Vavreck, and John Zaller. The opt-in Internet panel: survey mode, sampling methodology and the implications for political research. Unpublished Manuscript, 2007.

Melvin J. Hinich. Equilibrium in spatial voting: the median voter result is an artifact. *Journal of Economic Theory*, 16(2):208–19, 1977.

Melvin J. Hinich and Michael Munger. *Ideology and the Theory of Political Choice*. Ann Arbor: University of Michigan Press, 1994.

Harold Hotelling. Stability in competition. *The Economic Journal*, XXXIX: 41–57, 1929.

Patricia A. Hurley and Kim Q. Hill. The prospects for issue-voting in contemporary congressional elections. *American Politics Research*, 8(4):425, 1980.

Simon Jackman. *pscl: Political Science Computational Laboratory (R library)*, 2009.

William G. Jacoby. Ideological identification and issue attitudes. *American Journal of Political Science*, 1:178–205, 1991.

William G. Jacoby. The structure of ideological thinking in the American electorate. *American Journal of Political Science*, 39(2):314–35, 1995.

Stephen A. Jessee. Spatial voting in the 2004 presidential election. *American Political Science Review*, 103(1):59–81, 2009.

Stephen A. Jessee. Partisan bias, political information and spatial voting in the 2008 presidential election. *Journal of Politics*, 72(2):327–40, 2010a.

Stephen A. Jessee. Voter ideology and candidate positioning in the 2008 presidential election. *American Politics Research*, 38(2):195, 2010b.

Stephen A. Jessee. "Hidden knowledge," personality and political information. Unpublished Manuscript, 2011.

Stephen A. Jessee and Douglas Rivers. Voter perceptions of legislator positions. Stanford University Working Paper, 2008.

Cindy D. Kam. Who toes the party line?: cues, values and individual differences. *Political Behavior*, 27:163–82, 2005.

V.O. Key, Jr. *The Responsible Electorate: Rationality in Presidential Voting, 1936–60*. Cambridge: Cambridge University Press, 1966.

Donald R. Kinder and David O. Sears. Prejudice and politics: symbolic racism versus racial threats to the good life. *Journal of Personality and Social Psychology*, 40(3):414–31, 1981.

Donald R. Kinder and David O. Sears. Public opinion and political action. In G. Lindzey and E. Aronson, editors, *The Handbook of Social Psychology, Volume II*, 659–741. New York: Random House, 3rd edition, 1985.

Kathleen Knight. Ideology in the 1980 election: ideological sophistication does matter. *Journal of Politics*, 47:828–53, 1985.

Gerald H. Kramer. Political science: the science of politics. In Herbert F. Weisberg, editor, *Political Science as Science*, 11–23. Washington, DC: American Political Science Association, 1986.

Dean Lacy and Philip Paolino. Downsian voting and the separation of powers. *American Journal of Political Science*, 42(4):1180–99, 1998.

Richard R. Lau and David P. Redlawsk. Voting correctly. *American Political Science Review*, 91:585–98, 1997.

Richard R. Lau and David P. Redlawsk. Advantages and disadvantages of cognitive heuristics in political decision making. *American Journal of Political Science*, 45(4):951–71, 2001.

Paul F. Lazarsfeld, Bernard Berelson, and H. Gaudet. *The People's Choice*. New York: Columbia University Press, 1944.

Teresa E. Levitin and Warren E. Miller. Ideological interpretations of presidential elections. *American Political Science Review*, 73:751–71, 1979.

Tse-min Lin, James M. Enelow, and Han Dorussen. Equilibrium in multiparty probabilistic spatial voting. *Public Choice*, 98:59–82, 1999.

Arthur Lupia. Shortcuts versus encyclopedias: information and voting behavior in California insurance reform elections. *The American Political Science Review*, 88(1):63–76, 1994.

Arthur Lupia and Mathew D. McCubbins. *The Democratic Dilemma: Can Citizens Learn What They Need to Know?* New York: Cambridge University Press, 1998.

Robert C. Luskin. Measuring political sophistication. *American Journal of Political Science*, 31(4):856–99, 1987.

Stuart Elaine Macdonald and George Rabinowitz. Solving the paradox of nonconvergence: valence, position, and direction in democratic politics. *Electoral Studies*, 17:281–300, 1998.

Neil M. Malhotra and John A. Krosnick. The effect of survey mode and sampling on inferences about political attitudes and behavior: comparing the 2000 and 2004 ANES to Internet surveys with nonprobability samples. *Political Analysis*, 15(3):286, 2007.

Gregory A. Markus and Philip E. Converse. A dynamic simultaneous equation model of electoral choice. *American Political Science Review*, 73:1055–70, 1979.

Monika L. McDermott. Voting cues in low-information elections: candidate gender as a social information variable in contemporary united states elections. *American Journal of Political Science*, 41(1):270–83, 1997.

Gary Miller and Normal Schofield. Activists and partisan realignment in the United States. *American Political Science Review*, 97:245–60, 2003.

Jeffrey J. Mondak. Reconsidering the measurement of political knowledge. *Political Analysis*, 8(1):57, 1999.

Jeffrey J. Mondak. Developing valid knowledge scales. *American Journal of Political Science*, 45(1):224–38, 2001.

Norman H. Nie and Kristi Andersen. Mass belief systems revisited: political change and attitude structure. *Journal of Politics*, 36(3):540–91, 1974.

Norman H. Nie, Sidney Verba, and John R. Petrocik. *The Changing American Voter*. Cambridge: Harvard University Press, 1979.

Benjamin I. Page and Calvin C. Jones. Reciprocal effects of policy preferences, party loyalties and the vote. *American Political Science Review*, 73:1071–89, 1979.

Keith T. Poole and Howard Rosenthal. A spatial model for legislative roll call analysis. *American Journal of Political Science*, 29(2):357–84, 1985.

Samuel L. Popkin. *The Reasoning Voter*. Chicago: University of Chicago Press, 1991.

George Rabinowitz and Stuart E. Macdonald. A directional theory of issue voting. *The American Political Science Review*, 1:93–121, 1989.

Wendy M. Rahn, John H. Aldrich, Eugene Borgida, and John L. Sullivan. A social-cognitive model of candidate appraisal. In John A. Ferejohn and James H. Kuklinski, editors, *Information and Democratic Processes*, 136–159. Urbana and Chicago: University of Chicago Press, 1990.

George Rasch. *Probabilistic Model for Some Intelligence and Attainment Tests*. Copenhagen: Danmarks Paedogogische Institut, 1960.

George Rasch. An item analysis which takes individual differences into account. *British Journal of Mathematical and Statistical Psychology*, 2:45–57, 1966.

Douglas Rivers. Sample matching: representative sampling from Internet panels. Polimetrix White Paper, 2006.

John Roemer. *Political Competition: Theory and Applications*. Cambridge: Harvard University Press, 2001.

David Sanders, Harold D. Clarke, Marrianne C. Stewart, and Paul Whiteley. Does mode matter for modeling political choice?: evidence from the 2005 British election study. *Political Analysis*, 15(3):257, 2007.

Norman Schofield. Existence of a general political equilibrium. Unpublished Manuscript, 2002.

Norman Schofield. Valence competition in the spatial stochastic model. *Journal of Theoretical Politics*, 15:371–84, 2003.

Norman Schofield. Equilibrium in the spatial "valence" model of politics. *Journal of Theoretical Politics*, 16:447–81, 2004.

Norman Schofield, Andrew Martin, and Kevin Quinn. Multiparty electoral competition in the Netherlands and Germany: a model based on multinomial probit. *Public Choice*, 97:257–93, 1998.

Norman Schofield, Andrew Martin, Kevin Quinn, and Andrew Whitford. Equilibrium in the spatial "valence" model of politics. *Journal of Theoretical Politics*, 16:447–81, 2004.

Paul M. Sniderman and Edward G. Carmines. *Reaching beyond Race*. Cambridge: Harvard University Press, 1997.

Paul M. Sniderman, Richard A. Brody, and Philip E. Tetlock. *Reasoning and Choice: Explorations in Political Psychology*. Cambridge University Press, 1991.

James A. Stimson. Belief systems: constraint, complexity, and the 1972 election. *American Journal of Political Science*, 19(3):393–417, 1975.

Donald E. Stokes. Spatial models of party competition. *American Political Science Review*, 57:368–77, 1963.

Walter J. Stone and Elizabeth N. Simas. Candidate valence and ideological positions in U.S. house elections. *American Journal of Political Science*, 54(2): 371–88, 2010.

Patrick Sturgis, Nick Allum, and Patten Smith. An experiment on the measurement of political knowledge in surveys. *Public Opinion Quarterly*, 85(1): 90–102, 2008.

Michael Tomz and Robert P. Van Houweling. Positioning and voter choice. *American Political Science Review*, 102(2):303–18, 2008.

Shawn Treier and D. Sunshine Hillygus. The nature of political ideology in the contemporary electorate. *Public Opinion Quarterly*, 73(4):679, 2009.

Herbert F. Weisberg and Jerrod G. Rusk. Dimensions of candidate evaluation. *The American Political Science Review*, 64(4):1167–85, 1970.

John Zaller. *The Nature and Origins of Mass Opinion*. New York: Cambridge University Press, 1992.

Index

Abortion, 5, 16, 36, 45, 186, 192, 195
Abramowitz, A. I., 25, 223
Achen, C. H., 27, 46, 223
Adams, J. F., 34, 61, 72, 105, 106, 223
Aldrich, J. H., 35, 61, 132, 223, 228
Alito, S., 39n2
Allum, N., 134n2, 229
Alvarez, M. R., 34, 49, 72, 223
American Community Survey, 199
American National Election Studies (ANES), 19, 30, 44
  age distribution, 199, 201t
  history of, 19–20
  ideology and, 19–22, 25, 26t, 214, 215, 219–222. *See also* ideology
  liberal-conservative values, 25, 27. *See also* liberal-conservative scale
  "neither" option, 135n4
  other surveys and, 134–135, 135n4, 198, 214, 215, 222. *See also specific surveys*
  partisanship and, 177, 178f, 217. *See also* party identification
  questions on, 19–22, 25, 29, 96, 134–135
  response rates, 27, 44, 96
  self-placement and, 33. *See also* self-placement

  seven-point scale, 19–22, 25, 29, 96
  spatial models and, 214–215, 216t, 217t. *See also* spatial theory
  Time Series Studies, 198, 214
  voter information, 134–135. *See also* information, political
  See also specific topics
American Voter, The (Campbell, et al.), 4, 47, 103
Andersen, K., 25, 27, 227
Ansolabehere, S., 28, 34, 48, 76, 88, 114, 125n5, 132, 177, 223, 224
Aranson, P. H., 61, 224

Bafumi, J., 27, 46, 224
bailout bill, 204
balancing, voting and, 180n1
bankruptcy, 187–188
Bayesian methods, xii, 50
belief systems. *See* ideology
Berelson, B. R., 4, 224, 227
bias, 75–91, 165–172. *See also specific topics*
Black, D., 6n3, 8, 224
Blair, T., 220
Boatright, R. G., 96, 224
Borgida, E., 132, 228
Brady, H. E., 34, 224
British Election Study, 44
Brody, R. A., 131, 176, 224, 228

Bush, G. W., 220
  bias toward, 97, 97f, 101, 120–121,
    141
  conservatives and, 57, 96
  ideological position, 52–54, 57, 57f,
    59, 97, 112, 205
  indifference points for, 90–91,
    151–152
  Kerry and, 53–54, 57, 59
  party identification and, 85–86, 86f,
    111, 129, 210
  political information and, 142, 144
  survey questions and, 185, 194
  valence and, 114

Cahoon, L., 35, 224
Campbell, A., 4, 14, 24, 46, 103, 105,
    132, 155, 177, 224
candidates, U.S.
  convergence of, 9, 33, 58, 59
  divergence of, 58, 60–63, 149
  Downsian model and, 58, 64
  Green-Shapiro model, 9, 58
  ideological positions and, 3, 7, 13,
    34, 38, 60–61, 159–165
  knowledge and, 36, 72, 76, 114,
    157. See also information,
    political
  liberal-conservative, 59. See also
    liberal-conservative scale
  multicandidate elections, 72
  perceptions and, 34, 156–165, 158t
  presidential. See presidential
    elections; specific candidates
  spatial theory and, 9, 33–34, 38.
    See also spatial theory
Cantril, A., 16, 30, 224
Cantril, S. D., 16, 30, 224
Carmines, E. G., 32, 228, xii
causality. See deterministic models
Census Bureau. See U.S. Census
    Bureau
Chapman, D., 105, 224
Cheney, D., 134, 134n3, 196, 220
child care, 40, 42, 54, 93, 158t, 187,
    190, 196
civil liberties, 36

Clarke, H. D., 44, 228
class actions, 188
Clinton, J., 50, 51, 51n7, 224
Clinton model, 51, 51n7
Coleman, J. S., 61, 224
Columbia school, 4
competence, of electorates, 155–172.
    See also information, political
Conover, P. J., 4, 225
conservatives, 17, 30
  Bush and, 96. See also Bush, G. W.
  discrimination parameters and, 51
  ideological positions. See ideology
  liberals and, 17. See also
    liberal-conservative scale
  partisanship and. See party
    identification
  Republicans and, 9, 56, 79, 197,
    203, 203t
  See also specific persons, topics
constraints, in models, 16, 17, 182
  ideology and, 27, 44–48, 175
  individuals and, 18
  issue beliefs and, 33
  logical, 18
  mechanisms of, 17
  policy views and, 175
convergence, 9, 33, 58–59
Converse model, 7, 15–18, 24–28,
    32
Converse, P. E., 4, 14, 15, 16, 24, 28,
    32, 46, 64, 103, 105, 132, 155,
    176, 177, 224, 225, 227
Coombs, S., 4, 225
Cooperative Congressional Election
    Study (2006), 44
core values, 19
correlation matrices, 46, 47f
Coughlin, P., 72, 225

decision making, 50
defense spending, 36, 187
Delli Carpini, M. X., 32, 135, 225
democratic ideal, 1
Democrats, 57, 104, 108f, 127
  biases for, 165
  House party control, 135

ideal points and, 55, 60t
ideological positions and, 124, 221,
221f. *See also* ideology
information and, 142, 151. *See also*
information, political; *specific
topics*
liberals and, 56, 144, 174, 197. *See
also* liberal-conservative scale
moderates and, 215
Obama and, 144
partisanship and, 12, 13, 107, 128f,
149. *See also* party identification
probit models for, 220
Republicans and, 218, 218f. *See
also* party identification
spatial models and, 147
U.S. elections and, 9, 39n2. *See also
specific candidates*
See also specific candidates, topics
demographics
GBS and, 198
online samples and, 44
scaling and, 20
survey data and, 59, 198–205
uncertainty and, 61, 61n12
U.S. Census and, 43, 44
See also specific factors
deterministic models
central properties of, 71
ideological proximity and, 94,
177
instrumental variables and, 176
issue voting and, 177
party identification and, 105
reciprocality in, 176
spatial models and, 67–71
utility and, 73, 74
difficulty parameters, 40t, 42t, 137
discrimination and. *See*
discrimination parameters
ideal points and, 53, 53n9
liberal-conservative scale and, 161
policy positions and, 51–52, 54.
See also specific issues
Rasch method and, 134
dimensionality
factor analysis and, 48

ideological space and, 27, 47f, 56
liberal-conservative scale. *See*
liberal-conservative scale
multidimensional models, 27
scree plots and, 46, 47f
directional voting theory, 77–78
discrimination parameters, 53n9
bailout bill and, 204
difficulty and. *See* difficulty
parameters
ideal point and, 51, 53, 53n9, 161
identification and, 53, 53n9
ideology and, 54–55
information and, 134
liberal-conservative scale and,
51–52, 204
policies and, 51, 54–55, 161. *See
also specific issues*
Rasch method and, 134
divergence, 58, 60–63, 149
Dorussen, H., 34, 72, 227
Downs, A., 6, 8, 58, 60–67, 183,
225

education, 50, 96, 200t
Effron, B., 90, 225
electorate, U.S.
competence of, 46, 131, 134. *See
also* information, political
composition of, 43. *See also*
demographics
ideology and. *See* ideology
liberal-conservative values. *See*
liberal-conservative scale
Michigan school and, 103. *See also*
Michigan school
partisanship. *See* party identification
policy views of, 37, 38–44. *See also*
policy models
spatial theory and. *See* spatial
theory
See also specific topics, parameters
Ellis, C., 16, 30, 225
Elmira, New York study, 4
endogeneity, policy and, 176
Enelow, J. M., 6, 34, 66, 72, 183,
225, 227